BETTER TRAFFIC AND REVENUE FORECASTING

Cover Photo Credit: Luis Willumsen and Puerto Rico Highways and Transportation Authority
Cover Design by Guillermo Vallejo

Luis Willumsen © 2014

All rights reserved. No part of this book may be reproduced or transmitted in any form or by any means without the written permission of the author. This text makes reference to trademarks for editorial purposes only; the author makes no claims on their use. Nothing contained in this text is intended to press judgement on or affect the validity of the legal status of any term or word as trademark, service mark or other property mark.

The right of Luis Willumsen to be identified as the author of this work has been asserted in accordance to the Copyright, Designs and Patents Act 1988.

DISCLAIMER

This book contains the views of the author on how to improve traffic and revenue forecasts for transport concessions. It is not intended to be a comprehensive guide to this professional activity or an alternative to any professional advice or standard. The author accepts no liability or responsibility for any loss or damage caused by following the ideas in this book and recommends that you use it in conjunction with other advice and standards applicable to each case.

ISBN – 13: 978-0-9928433-0-4

Better Traffic and Revenue Forecasting

Luis Willumsen

 Maida Vale Press

TABLE OF CONTENTS

Preface

PART I CONTEXT

1. Introduction — 1
1.1 Organisation of the text — 1
1.2 Models — 1
1.3 Modelling and forecasting — 5
1.4 Aggregation — 8
1.5 Risk and uncertainty — 9
1.6 Repeatability, precision, accuracy, error — 9
1.7 The uncertain future — 12
1.8 Errors and forecastability — 14

2. Involvement of the Private sector — 15
2.1 Motivation — 15
2.2 Simplified view of the process — 17
2.3 Risks cost money — 23
2.4 The future is not what it used to be — 28
2.5 Optimism bias — 29
2.6 Forecasting error — 31
2.7 Summary — 32

Part II Analysis — 33

3. The classic transport model — 35
3.1 Introduction — 35
3.2 Behavioural responses — 36
3.3 Levels of aggregation — 37
3.4 Trips, tours, purposes — 38
3.5 Generalised costs — 39
3.6 Zones — 40
3.7 Networks — 41
3.8 The classic four stage model — 46
3.9 Induced demand — 48
3.10 Calibration and validation — 49

4. Surveys to establish the base year — 51
4.1 The Base Year — 51
4.2 Understanding the context — 51
4.3 Data collation — 53
4.4 Time series — 54
4.5 Modelled periods — 54
4.6 Sampling — 55
4.7 Surveys — 57
4.8 Traffic counts — 63
4.9 Road and service surveys — 64
4.10 Quality — 64
4.11 Analysis — 65
4.12 Trip matrix building — 65
4.13 Calibration and Validation — 67
4.14 Accuracy of trip matrices — 72

5. Willingness to pay — 77
5.1 Values of Time — 77
5.2 Stated Preference — 79
5.3 WTP and income — 82
5.4 Travel time reliability — 83
5.5 Freight — 85
5.6 Meta analysis of VTTS — 86

6. Trip Generation and Attraction — 91
6.1 Trip end models — 91
6.2 Trip generation models — 92
6.3 GDP growth, trip generation and accessibility effects — 93
6.4 Trip attraction — 93
6.5 Vehicle ownership — 94

7. Destination choice — 99
7.1 Trip Matrices and their growth — 99
7.2 Modelling destination choice — 99
7.3 Gravity models — 100
7.4 Observed and synthetic matrices — 101
7.5 Incremental modelling — 101
7.6 Sense checks — 103

8. Mode choice — 105
8.1 General concepts — 105
8.2 Modelling mode choice — 107

8.3	Discrete choice modelling	107
8.4	Logit models	108
8.5	Limitations	111
8.6	Nested Logit	112
8.7	Other choice models	113
8.8	Sub-mode choice	114
8.9	Sense checks	114

9. Time of travel choice — 117

9.1	Background	117
9.2	Macro and Micro Departure Time Choice	117
9.3	Micro Departure Time Choice	118
9.4	Macro time choice	118
9.5	Simplified approaches	119
9.6	Sense checks	119

10. Assignment — 121

10.1	Principles	121
10.2	Modelling vehicle route choice and assignment	122
10.3	Equilibrium assignment	123
10.4	Limitations of conventional assignment	125
10.5	Dynamic Traffic Assignment	127
10.6	Stochastic effects	129
10.7	Travel time reliability	129
10.8	Modelling tolls	131
10.9	Public Transport Assignment	132
10.10	Within public transport mode choice	135
10.11	Sense checks	136

11. Induced Demand — 139

11.1	Background	139
11.2	Methods for estimation	140
11.3	Benchmarking induced traffic	141

Part III Practice — 143

12. Uncertainty, Risk and Forecasting — 145

12.1	Introduction	145
12.2	Urban and Interurban projects	146
12.3	Identifying uncertainty and risk	147
12.4	Steps	150
12.5	Procuring Authority studies	151
12.6	Bid support model	155

13. Pricing — 157
- 13.1 The complexities of pricing — 157
- 13.2 Optimal pricing — 160
- 13.3 Price and revenues — 161
- 13.4 Inflation and tax — 162
- 13.5 Pricing different users — 164
- 13.6 Transitional period — 165
- 13.7 Annualisation factors — 168
- 13.8 Price Elasticities and sentiment — 169

14. Toll roads — 173
- 14.1 Modelling simple toll roads — 173
- 14.2 Tolled roads on a network — 179
- 14.3 Means of payment and delays — 180
- 14.4 Tolling structures — 181
- 14.5 Time of day tolling — 184
- 14.6 Means of payment and market share — 186
- 14.7 Leakage — 187
- 14.8 Frequent users — 189
- 14.9 Sense checks — 189
- 14.10 Future uncertainties — 190

15. Managed Lanes — 193
- 15.1 The concept — 193
- 15.2 Dynamic tolling with Managed Lanes — 193
- 15.3 The design and specification of Managed Lanes — 196
- 15.4 Projecting revenues on Managed Lanes — 197
- 15.5 Pricing and revenue optimisation in Managed Lanes — 198
- 15.6 Imperfect information — 201
- 15.7 Sense checks — 202

16. Congestion charges — 203
- 16.1 Demand management — 203
- 16.2 User charges and road pricing — 204
- 16.3 Congestion charging in practice — 205
- 16.4 Lessons learnt from existing systems — 206
- 16.5 Modelling Congestion Charge Schemes — 208

Contents

17. Public transport Concessions — **209**
17.1 Rail and public transport concessions — 209
17.2 Public transport modelling — 209
17.3 Access — 211
17.4 Mode choice — 212
17.5 Competing modes — 213
17.6 Fare systems — 213
17.7 Crowding — 214
17.8 Sense checks — 215

18. The future — **217**
18.1 Introduction — 217
18.2 Future uncertainties — 217
18.3 Population and land uses — 219
18.4 Changes in supply — 220
18.5 Growth drivers — 221
18.6 GDP and demand growth — 222
18.7 Sensitivity analysis — 226
18.8 Future scenarios — 227
18.9 Model review — 228
18.10 An audit checklist — 229
18.11 Uncertainty envelope — 232

19. Risk analysis — **233**
19.1 Handling Risk — 233
19.2 Stochastic Risk Analysis — 233
19.3 Forecast de-construction — 237
19.4 Mitigation — 239

20. Finalising demand and revenue forecasts — **241**
20.1 Introduction — 241
20.2 Project rationale — 242
20.3 Providing confidence in the results — 243
20.4 Unmodelled influences on traffic and revenue — 245
20.5 Interpretation of results — 246
20.6 Disclaimers and reliance letters — 247

21. The makings of a good forecast — **249**
21.1 Desirable traits in the young analyst — 249
21.2 The T&R Advisor — 251
21.3 The process — 252
21.4 Coda — 253

Dedication

To Adriana, Juana, Alex and Georgina

PREFACE

This book is the result of many years of practice in the production of patronage and revenue projections for a number of private sector projects. Most of these studies were undertaken for consortia bidding for concessions; others were done for financial institutions to make sure their credit risk analysis was reasonably sound. In a few occasions I worked for national governments wishing to improve traffic and revenue forecasting tools or preparing a scheme to take it to the market. Sometimes I worked on my own, mostly as a peer reviewer or technical auditor of revenue projections supported by a model; most of the time I led a team, or at least made some major contribution to a group of professionals, tackling a complex forecasting problem.

I have contributed to traffic and revenue projections for over 40 toll roads, bridges and tunnels in Europe, the Americas, Asia and Australia. A number of these have been Open Road Tolling concessions that introduce a variety of new issues additional to cash only roads. A few have been fully dynamic tolls, HOT or Managed Lanes; these again are more complex to model but offer a raft of advantages over conventional toll roads. I have also managed, among others, patronage and revenue forecasts for a number of public transport projects: Rail, Metro, LRT and BRT systems in the UK, France, Spain, UK, Portugal, South Africa, India, Colombia, Chile, Mexico and Venezuela.

I have also reviewed a number of traffic and revenue projections produced by others. This has not always been a happy exercise; sometimes I discovered limitations in their work, perhaps driven by meagre budgets and short timescales. A number of these limitations are deftly identified in Robert Bain's book[1]. Robert and I worked together on a small number of toll road projects, mostly in Puerto Rico. We believe there is much scope to improve forecasting theory and practice and I have tried to convey my own experience and ideas in this text.

The profession has significantly improved the approach and techniques used in the last 10 years or so. These views correspond to my thinking at the time of writing; as better evidence comes my way I am likely to improve my approach and provide better advice, perhaps in a subsequent edition of this text.

I hope that this book will be of interest to professionals and consultants working for clients such as:

---

[1] Bain, Robert (2009) Toll Road Traffic & Revenue Forecasts: an interpreter's guide. ISBN 978-0-9561527-1-8

Better Traffic and Revenue Forecasting

- Governments preparing projects to take to the market;
- Financial institutions judging the credit worthiness of a particular scheme and selecting the most appropriate debt instruments;
- Consortia bidding for transport concessions or seeking to extract maximum value from an existing one;
- The investment community considering allocating funds to a transport concession; and
- Local Authorities planning projects where patronage and revenue are critical, for example a new BRT system or a Congestion Charging scheme.

It may also be of interest to post graduate students seeking to understand better issues of risk and the requirements and potential pitfalls of forecasting for private sector concessions in transport. This task is quite different from developing models to support transport plans.

The book should not be considered as a complete manual for undertaking Traffic and Revenue Projections for transport concessions. It assumes good knowledge of the underlying techniques and terminology; plus some years of experience in applying them before producing revenue projections that may cost millions if not properly developed and may risk the company you work for.

The technical aspects of transport modelling and forecasting are based on our book with Prof. Ortúzar *Modelling Transport*[2] in particular its 2011 edition. I follow here a more intuitive approach and refer the reader to *Modelling Transport* for greater depth in the theory behind each model; for example MT 183 (Modelling Transport 4th Ed. Page 183) for singly and doubly constrained Gravity Models.

Most of the private sector forecasting work I have done was undertaken between 1989 and 2009 while I was a Director at Steer Davies Gleave, an excellent international consultancy. Important projects that influenced my development during this period include forecasting for five urban Open Road Tolling concessions in Santiago, Chile (now in successful operation for many years), Western Sydney Orbital (now M7) in Australia, PR66 in Puerto Rico, FARAC I in Mexico, Panamericana Norte in Argentina, and the Western Freeway Sea Link in India. I also led a useful project to improve traffic and revenue forecasting methodologies for the Mexican Government, the

---

[2] Ortúzar, J. de D. and L. Willumsen (2011) Modelling Transport. Fourth Edition. John Wiley & Sons, Chichester, UK.

Preface

resulting text is available (in Spanish) at the SCT website[3]. For the special case of public transport and rail projects key experiences were the design of the Transmilenio BRT in Bogotá, bidding for transport concessions in Santiago, the extensions of the Delhi Metro to the Airport and metro concessions in Mumbai, the Leslys (Fast tram to the Airport) project in Lyon, the Caracas Metro extension to Los Teques and preparation of forecasts for High Speed Rail in Portugal.

In all these projects my understanding and approach benefited from working and discussing issues with intelligent and generous professionals. Charles Russell, another director at Steer Davies Gleave, has provided some of the most insightful ideas on modelling and forecasting, several of which are included in this text. Enrique Lillo is one of the best transport modellers I know and he taught me several of the key and subtle issues of extracting reliable results from models. Gloria Hutt is a very intelligent and dedicated professional that influenced my understanding and treatment of real issues hidden behind Terms of Reference and the conventional approaches preferred by financial institutions. I had great pleasure working with them as with many others that will forgive me for not listing them for fear of an involuntary omission.

Since late 2009 I have been working on my own. This has provided me with new experiences and ideas as I have the opportunity to work with other consultancies and tackle new challenges. It was particularly interesting for me to dip my toes into Managed Lanes forecasting including the most appropriate algorithms to implement good ideas on optimal tolling. It has also given some new independence to express my views without worrying if they may create problems for another project in the same company.

Several of the examples discussed in this text are based on real cases undertaken between 1989 and 2014. The exact location and nature of the project have been omitted to maintain the confidentiality of the assignment.

Shareholders and lenders have recently sued consultants providing traffic and revenue forecasts. I do not know whether this is a trend or an isolated couple of cases. I am sure that at least part of the problem is the result of commoditising traffic and revenue forecasts: converting a difficult problem into a standardise technique that can be undertaken by any consultant following conventional practices. In this case, the consultant with the cheapest price gets appointed and adopts as many

---

[3] Secretaria de Comunicaciones y Transportes, México (2006) Modelación de demanda para carreteras de cuota. Accessible at:
http://uac.sct.gob.mx/index.php?id=526. visited 12 December 2013.

shortcuts as necessary to meet the budget. This is a high-risk approach to deliver one of the most critical numbers in the success of a transport concession.

The next ten years in transport are going to be very different from the last 10 (nothing new in this) presenting new challenges, taking advantage of new data sources and a fresh understanding of human behaviour stemming not from Economic theory but from Behavioural Economics and Social Psychology. Inevitably, this book will have a short shelf life. I hope to be able to update it, by whatever means are current at the time, as necessary.

The book is far from perfect. It has benefitted from comments and suggestions from several friends who read an early draft. I am particularly grateful for the contributions and insights of Ray Bacquaie, Richard Di Bona, Serbjeet Kohli, Yaron Hollander, Germán Lleras, Enrique Lillo, Alex Lima, Alejandro Niño, Charles Russell, Ricardo Sanchez, Miguel Seisdedos and Mark Wardman. However, any failings in this text, and there is plenty of scope for improvement, are my own responsibility. I would be grateful for any comments, identified mistakes and suggestions that readers may provide. I have set up a website: www.bettertandr.com to receive comments and deliver updates.

I should also thank my wife, Adriana, who took me to the most inaccessible place in Corfu to produce the first draft; her support and encouragement have been invaluable.

This is a fairly personal book and therefore it has at least a couple of quirks. The eagle-eyed reader will note that the Traffic and Revenue Advisor and other agents change gender in different pages of the text; this is intentional. Moreover, I always wanted to write a book with an "interesting" quotation opening each chapter. It is a bit contrived but I hope that the reader may at least smile at some of them.

I do not expect anybody to read this book from cover to cover. For this reason, there is some degree of repetition around concepts I consider important; I apologise a little bit for this. Of course, readers familiar with the material in certain sections should feel free and confident to skip them as appropriate.

Part I Context

PART I CONTEXT

This section provides some context to the rest of the text. The introduction discusses some key elements in modelling and forecasting that gain particular importance in the case of traffic and revenue projections. The second chapter outlines the role of the private sector in transport concessions. It provides a simplified version of the tendering process, from scheme preparation to third stage finance, as this is necessary to understand where and how traffic and revenue projections play such a key role. This Part is of general interest although financial and procurement professionals will find Chapter 2 perhaps a bit simplistic. It is only there to provide context to the task for producing Traffic and Revenue projections.

Introduction

> "I always avoid prophesying beforehand because it is much better to prophesy after the event has already taken place."
> **Winston Churchill**

1. INTRODUCTION

1.1 Organisation of the text

This text is organised in three parts. The first one covers the general context of producing Traffic and Revenue (T&R) projections. As they are normally based on the use of models there is an initial discussion on their role. This is followed by a brief introduction to projects involving private finance, the different stakeholders and their perspective. This section concludes with comments on the issues surrounding forecasting under uncertainty.

The second part deals with the tools for analysis and modelling. It covers key issues like behavioural responses to prices and congestion, willingness to pay and the main components of the most commonly used models: trip generation, distribution, mode and time of travel choice, and assignment.

Part III deals with the practice of preparing and delivering T&R projections for toll roads and public transport schemes. It treats issues like sensitivity tests and risk analysis. As the name suggests, the emphasis is on the practical application of some of the models discussed in Part II. This part concludes with some comments on what makes a good T&R practitioner.

1.2 Models

We regularly use models to understand and solve problems. These may be mental models, an estimation of how satisfied we would be in the future with a choice we make today. Some models are analytical in nature and they play a key role in finding good solutions to complex problems, as illustrated in Figure 1.

FIGURE 1 RELATIONSHIP BETWEEN PROBLEMS AND MODELS

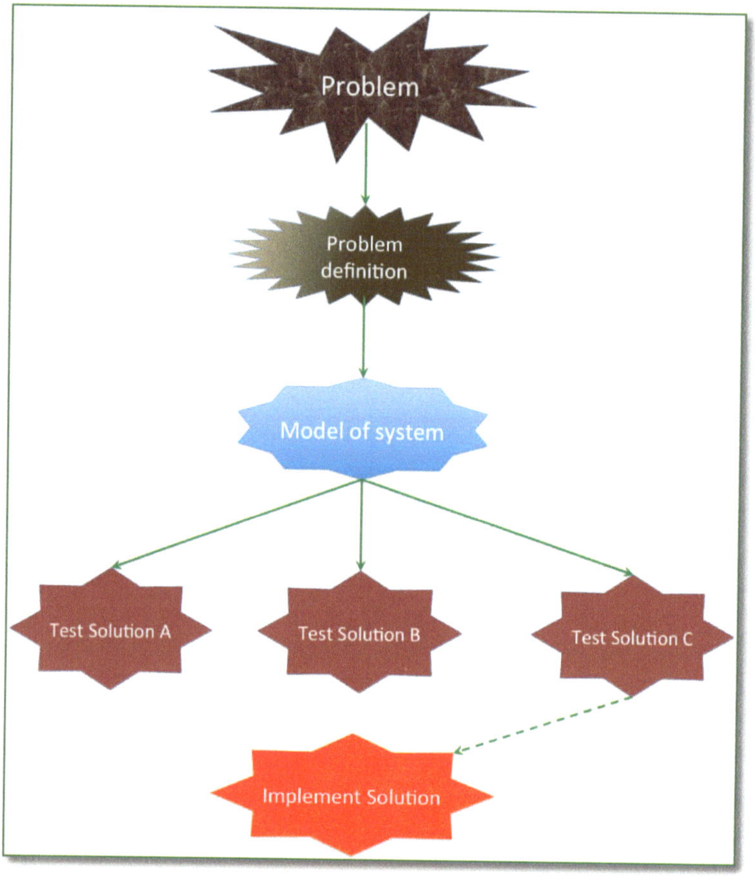

A Real Problem (a dissatisfaction with current or future state of affairs) leads to a definition of the same by decision makers. This definition is a description of the mismatch between aspirations and performance together with a narrative of its implications and possible courses of action. As part of this definition the real problem becomes more constrained and loses some detail. Problem definition is a powerful political tool.

As it is not possible to run experiments in the transport field (it would be too expensive in resources and political terms) a Model is developed to represents the system of interest. The model is, of course, a simplification of reality focussed on the defined problem. The model is then used to test alternative solutions so that the best one can be identified and implemented.

Introduction

Indeed, transport models depicting the details of large areas and networks can simulate multiple interactions impossible to track and follow by our human brains. A good model should augment human powers to assess complex systems. Transport problems are particularly difficult non-linear systems with plenty of opportunities for unforeseen consequences and unwanted side effects.

Models are certainly used in this form when dealing with transport planning or traffic engineering issues and the objective is to find the best solution for a given set of current or assumed future conditions. The results from the model can then be used to demonstrate that the "best solution" produces a Benefit to Cost ratio greater than 1 (or such a test) and passes a Multi-Criteria Analysis where other qualitative indicators are used.

Our case is different. The issue at hand is to determine the most likely patronage and revenue stream over time for a future transport concession. The "best solution" is not enough; a stream of numbers representing future revenues for the proposed concession is required. This problem is seen in slightly different light at different stages in the concession process as discussed later on in this section.

A model is only realistic from a particular perspective or point of view: their value is limited to a range of problems under specific conditions. The appropriateness of a model depends on the context where it will be used. The ability to choose and adapt models for particular problems is one of the important elements in the forecaster's tool-kit.

One must distinguish early on the differences between short and long-term forecasting; in the case of transport concessions the latter may extend to 30, 50 or even 100 years. In the case of short term forecasting many assumptions about the regularity of events and travel preferences may be valid. In the case of long-term forecasting, these assumptions are unlikely to remain valid; moreover, many of the key inputs to any forecast: GDP, population, income, technology, are much less predictable. Only a range of forecasts can be produced under these conditions. The choice of models and approach must be different for these two timescales.

There are, of course, different types of models, appropriate to different circumstances. The simplest ones are probably *trend extrapolations*; the future is likely to be similar to the recent past. These models can be simple using linear regression (MT 144-151) or more complex ones incorporating elements of seasonal variations including *time series analysis*.

A second group is that of *econometric models;* these are more general in that they do not require a particular functional form (linear or quadratic, for example); examples of these are the so-called Direct Demand models (MT 220-221).

A third group of models is based on theories of *travel behaviour*. These require assumptions about how people, or groups of people, make travel choices; having interpreted these theories as mathematical equations it is necessary to find the parameters in these models that fit the data best. Some of these models are aggregate, in the sense that they are based on the behaviour of group of people assigned, in practice, to zones. Others are called disaggregate in that they refer to representative individuals that may or may not be allocated to specific zones.

There is also a distinction to be made about what is the basic **action** of interest. Most classic models use the *trip* as the main unit of analysis. This is defined as a movement from an origin to a destination that may or may not involve stages and different modes of travel, for example walk, wait and ride stages in a rail trip. A more realistic approach is to focus on *tours*, that is linked set of trips normally starting and ending at home. An example of a simple tour would be a trip to work linked to the return home trip. The advantage of focussing on tours is that, for example, the choice of mode for the return trips must be linked to that of the journey to work; you are unlikely to return by car if you went by bus.

Recent years have seen an increased interest in viewing travel as a consequence of linking *activities* separated by space and time. *Activity Based Modelling* is gaining some currency, mostly in the US, as an advanced modelling technique that may be used in practice although its value in forecasting mode is yet to be established.

It is fair to say that all these approaches rely on an *Activity Regularity Assumption*: activities, tours and trips are reasonably regular and repetitive and constitute the universe from which to sample behaviour; it is therefore possible to combine observations on different days to obtain a "representative activity pattern". This is a necessary but demanding assumption. First, the choices people make about activities, location and allocation of time are quite complex with subtle interactions. It is very likely that who undertakes what activity and when is actually negotiated at home, even if some are reasonably regular: dad plays golf and mum does Pilates; both work but increasingly not to a fixed schedule; both shop but who buys the food depends on activities by other members of the family. Moreover, these choices and interactions change over time and will change even more in the future thanks to technology, Internet and remote working. Finally, **the data we rely on is poor**: it is usually a small sample, and cross section only, collected over a few months, a noisy snapshot of what happens on an "average" day or week.

Introduction

Moreover, user preferences or tastes, as cast onto the parameters of the estimated models, are assumed to remain constant: the 40 years old of today will be replaced in 10 years time by new 40 years old with the same tastes and preferences, even if their histories, experiences and options may be different. A key exception to this is willingness to pay to save time; this is usually allowed to grow in association with income.

Each model component, or sub-model, is underpinned by its own assumptions and theories about human behaviour and these are important in interpreting results. Each model requires a certain amount of quality data to estimate its parameters: model estimation or calibration.

A good calibration is not enough to justify the use of a model; its results must be explainable. If the model produces results that defy logic and interpretation it should not be used. Human intuition and logic must be superior to even the best model using the most advanced software.

1.3 Modelling and forecasting

Modelling and forecasting are related but different activities. **Modelling** attempts to build and apply appropriate tools that are sensitive to the choices of interest and respond logically to changes in key policy instruments: investment in capacities, prices, vehicle restrictions. It is important therefore that the model produces consistent results for all expected interventions, policies and projects, such that they can be ranked fairly, even if the correspondence to reality is imperfect, as it is bound to be.

Forecasting is an attempt to envision and quantify future conditions. It normally involves estimating future travel demand and the resulting flows on all modes and all costs over time. In many cases, including private sector projects, these projections must be associated to revenue forecasts that investors and lenders will use to estimate risks and potential rewards (upsides) to decide their involvement.

Forecasting is usually based on formal models, but they alone cannot provide the full picture; it is necessary to incorporate other analyses and assumptions.

As the future is unlikely to be just an extrapolation of the past any formal model will have to reflect this fact. In general, good advice on complex future issues cannot be based solely on modelling, however excellent. Models require interpretation and this, in turn, is based on experience and the intelligent consideration of other factors and assumptions, in particular about possible futures and the limitations of any modelling approach. This deeper understanding of the drivers behind future outcomes must be communicated through a coherent narrative.

Interpretation requires good judgement and this is only acquired with experience and a thorough understanding of the theories underpinning models and their limitations. Practically all transport-modelling approaches rely on the assumption that travellers belong to the species *homo economicus.* This artificial construct is capable of comparing alternatives and always chooses the one that maximises his own utility. He is rational, has consistent tastes and preferences that do not change over time and almost invariably has full and perfect information about all alternatives.

Ever since the financial crisis of 2007-2008 the world has come to realise that *homo economicus* was still born. Behavioural Economics and Social Psychology have thoroughly demonstrated that homo sapiens is more complex and occasionally rational, see for example the work of Ariely[4] and Kahneman[5]. McFadden, one of the key originators of Random Utility Theory underpinning some of the most useful transport models, has recognised that much for some time[6].

There are several relevant departures from the perfectly rational human being that influence our interpretation of model results based on *homo economicus*. In my view the most important are:

    a. There is a difference between the **"experiencing self"** and the **"remembering self"**. The first one experiences the congested and free flowing elements of a journey but the second may only remember the salient frustration of 5 minutes queueing at a stand still. Decisions on future travel are made by the remembering self. This may also explain why we are poor at estimating travel times and distances.

    b. **We overvalue what we "own"**; we may not be willing to contribute € 500 to plant trees in our street but once they are there we ask for much more in compensation for their removal. A consequence of this is our **loss aversion**. We are more averse to a loss than keen to the equivalent gain.

    c. **We care more about changes** from the status quo than absolute values; we compare ourselves to our past and peers/neighbours rather than assess our objective level of welfare.

---

[4] Ariely, D. (2009) "Predictably Irrational". Harper Collins, London

[5] Kahneman, D. (2013) "Thinking Fast and Slow". Farrar, Straus and Giroux. New York.

[6] McFadden, D. (2013) "The New Science of Pleasure". National Bureau of Economic Research Working Paper No. 18687

Introduction

d. **We may not react to small changes.** We tolerate small increases in travel time but react quickly to the introduction of a congestion charge. The concept of "search costs" helps to explain this: if a small improvement is expected relative to the "cost" (effort, time, hassle) of searching for the better choice then it is probably not worthwhile to seek to improve. Related to this is the reality that travel decisions are always made under conditions of *imperfect and asymmetric knowledge*. Note that marketing and good customer information may play a role in reducing this search cost.
e. There are **lags in our responses** to changes in levels of service. We cannot change jobs or residence quickly but we can take advantage of a new metro line for our shopping trips almost straight away.
f. We have a **diminishing sensitivity to changes in utility**. The value of a €100 gain when we have €1,000 in our bank account is greater than the same amount when we have € 10,000 in savings. Saving 5 minutes in a 30-minute trip is worth more than in a 3-hour journey.
g. We **cannot rationally cope with too many alternatives**; we only consider a few route options, not all possible ones, and use heuristics when choices are too complex.
h. We seem to have **two modes of thinking**. Most of the time we use intuition and inertia to make fast decisions (**System 1** thinking in Kahnemann's terms); whenever we face a significant new problem or change we engage a more rational and reflective mode (**System 2**). A small increase in fuel prices does not change our commuter journey; but the introduction of an equivalent parking charge at work (to promote car pooling) makes us think afresh.
i. Our behaviour is influenced directly by what other people do or say they do, not just indirectly through supply, demand and price relationships.
j. Cultural preconceptions and self-image matter. "Winners drive their cars, losers use public transport" and/or "I am not going to pay for something that is my right: the freedom of the road" may evolve with time into more rational and sensitive attitudes. Linked to this is the conception of public transport in some places as an inferior mode where a reduction in price does not lead to an increase in demand.

These issues influence how we perceive time and how we value prices as will be discussed in subsequent sections. We will come back to this miss-match between *homo economicus* and *homo sapiens* when discussing completing Traffic and Revenue forecasts.

1.4 Aggregation

The question of aggregation is central to demand modelling. We need to decide:

- How many population types (or segments/strata) do we need to distinguish in order to achieve a good representation and understanding of travel choices in a particular context? Is it enough to have car owners and non-car owners or should we distinguish a larger number of representative individuals?
- How many details and characteristics do we need to include to fairly represent travelling?
- Are average speeds enough or should we actually describe a speed profile and freedom to overtake to capture the "cost" of driving on a road? Do we need to include travel time reliability when modelling mode choice to the airport?
- Space is crucial in transport; at what level of detail do we need to code the origin and destination of travellers to model their trip making behaviour? Are zones enough or do we need individual addresses?
- Time plays also a key role and can be aggregated at different levels: whole day, peak period, critical hour or 15 minute time slices to capture some of the dynamics of congestion.

The distinction between aggregate and disaggregate models is not as clear-cut as it may appear at first glance. A fully disaggregate model (activity based or not) must use a set of representative individuals based, in turn, on the sample of household or other surveys. This sample is generally small, some 2-3% of the households.

We often mix levels of aggregation. Representative individuals may be allocated to zones to calculate changes in travel costs under future conditions; travel costs between zones will be different than between actual addresses. Zones may contain different representative groups, for example households with different number of members, ages and vehicles. These may perform a limited set of tours and trips, again based on the limited set of observations available. Different approaches have advantages and disadvantages and the Traffic and Revenue analyst must choose the best approach given constraints of time and monetary budgets.

Introduction

1.5 Risk and uncertainty

In this book we use the Knightian concepts of risk and uncertainty[7]. Uncertainty is the lack of complete certainty, that is, the existence of more than one possibility some of which may be completely unknown; uncertainty is unquantifiable. Risk is a quantifiable uncertainty, at least in probabilistic terms.

There is **uncertainty** about the eventual impact of distance and computer assisted learning on formal education, and therefore on the journey to school, by 2030. In the UK the **risk** of accident per passenger kilometre is 9 times higher on a car than on a bus.

Uncertainty reflects our failure to ascertain a present or future event with certainty. It is a reflection of our lack of knowledge and it is, in principle, impossible to quantify. For example, it is uncertain whether we will eventually abandon the idea of owning a private car and decide to rent them by the hour as and when needed. Such a change would affect car usage and traffic and may or may not strengthen demand for public forms of transportation. However, the probability and timing of such a change is, at present, practically impossible to estimate; but we can make a subjective judgment setting some likely bounds to that shift.

In producing Traffic and Revenue forecasts we need to deal with both uncertainty and risk. In general terms we try to obtain reasonable estimates of uncertainty to convert them into quantifiable risks. Note that with this terminology, a risk is not only associated to a negative outcome, it may also be a positive one. However, it sounds unusual to say that there is a 20% risk that a new competing road will not be built and therefore the revenue stream of this toll road will not be negatively affected. In Traffic and Revenue terminology we usually refer to positive risks as potential or probabilistic upsides, and negative risks as downsides.

1.6 Repeatability, precision, accuracy, error

There is a useful distinction between precision and accuracy, sometimes confused in practice. The **repeatability** of a measurement instrument (say a particular type of survey) is the degree to which repeated measurements under unchanged conditions show the same results. For example, in my experience the repeatability of Stated Preference surveys requires extreme care in sample selection, the delivery of the survey instrument and the subsequent analysis of the data.

---

[7] Knight, F.H. (1921) "Risk, uncertainty and profit". In Hart, Schaffner, and Marx Prize Essays, no. 31. Boston and New York: Houghton Mifflin.

Better Traffic and Revenue Forecasting

Precision is the measurement resolution; the level of detail the instrument is capable of resolving; in normal speech, the number of significant figures in a measurement. We could say that a model based on more and smaller zones would be more precise, in particular during the assignment stage.

The **accuracy** of this measurement tool is the degree of closeness of measurements of a quantity to that quantity's actual (true) value. The calibration process tries to ensure that the model is as accurate as possible. However, here we are more interested in the **forecasting accuracy** of a model, that is fidelity to a future set of conditions that we do not yet know whether they will actually materialise. Forecasting accuracy can only be established *ex post*.

Model error is the difference between the actual true value of an attribute and the value the model would state it is. This is illustrated in Figure 2 where a true value of 9 is estimated, after repeated measurements, as 14 with an error, or inaccuracy, of 5. The precision of the instrument in this case is not high but the error seems to be systematic rather than random.

Note that Figure 2 presents a well-behaved probability function with short and "thin tails". Many authors have argued that the real world is much more likely to present "fat tails" where large departures from the mean are more likely than a Normal distribution would suggest, an idea popularised by Taleb's[8] "black swans".

---

[8] Taleb, N (2007)) "The Black Swan". Random House, New York.

Introduction

FIGURE 2 ACCURACY AND PRECISION DEFINED

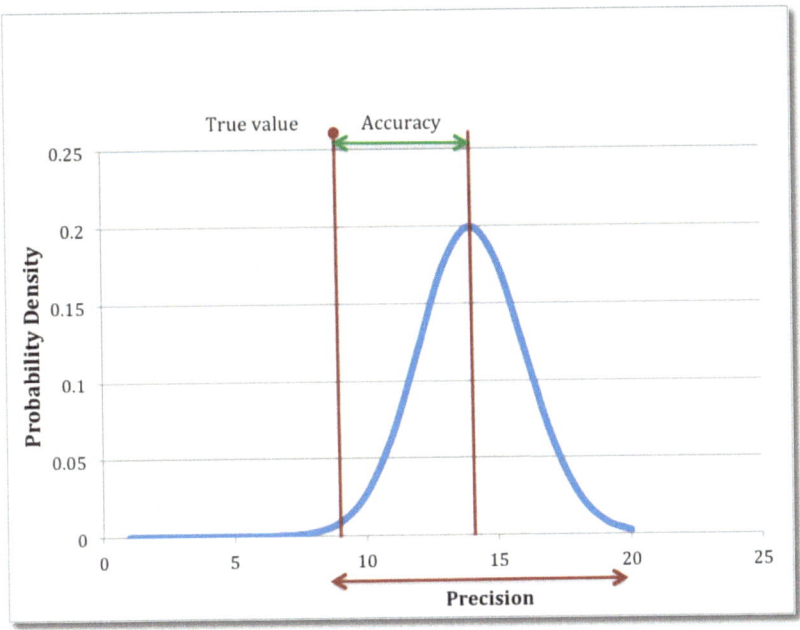

Even with the best calibration effort for a base year the model will not be able to eliminate errors between observed and modelled traffic counts. There are many reasons for this, among them the Activity Regularity Assumption. We know from experience that repeated measurements of traffic on a link at the same time on equivalent days will produce flows with a day-to-day variation around 10 to 13%. The variations at the level of the trip matrices that generate these flows will be even greater.

It is risky to pursue precision when we should be aiming for accuracy. A model may offer four alternative combinations of accuracy and precision, as illustrated in Figure 3:

FIGURE 3 PRECISION AND ACCURACY IN FORECASTING

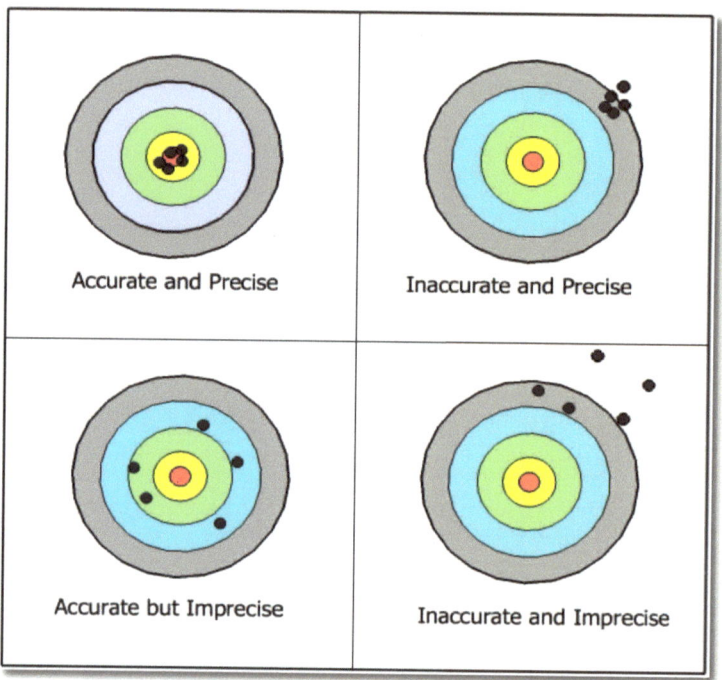

As shown, we would certainly prefer to be accurate and precise but we must recognise that in forecasting this is impossible. In that case, accuracy at the cost of some imprecision would be preferable to inaccuracy. **Note that when accepting we can only be accurate but imprecise it is not that useful to have only one shot at the target.**

Bias refers to the tendency of measures to systematically shift in one direction from the true value; these shifts are often called **systematic errors**. In contrast, **random errors** are produced by the statistical fluctuations observed when measuring a quantity. These result in a spread of observed measurements about a centre value. If the application of the same tool (forecasting approach and model) to different cases produces inaccuracies in the same direction we have identified a bias.

1.7 The uncertain future

Any talk about precision and accuracy in forecasting is somewhat misleading. Figure 3 is appropriate to discuss how well a model or a measurement tool can estimate an existing real value. But the future has not yet happened and it depends on a number of factors that we cannot control nor guess correctly how they will materialise.

Introduction

We cannot eliminate future uncertainty. Mathematicians and engineers, because of our education, tend to fall into the Laplacian illusion: *"Given perfect knowledge of present conditions and perfect knowledge of the laws that govern the universe we ought to be able to make perfect predictions"*. Sadly, this is not true, even in the (almost) pure physico-chemical domain of weather forecasting. We have only a very partial knowledge of present conditions driven by influences and behavioural traits we do not fully understand, and probably never will. We certainly do not have sufficient knowledge of the laws of the universe and according to Deutsch[9] we will never completely achieve this aim, although we should keep trying and improving our understanding.

A common mistake is to assume that because a model is more detailed and precise it will also be more accurate and reliable. This view is associated to a natural trend to develop more disaggregated and complex models, what some call a "model extravaganza".

We ignore the risks that are hardest to measure, even when they pose the greatest threats to our wellbeing. We make approximations and assumptions about the world that are much cruder than we realise.

Under these conditions, it is more realistic to think of our projections as estimating "how safe are our bets". How safe is it to lend half a billion dollars to an urban toll road project at x% interest if capacities on free roads start increasing after 2025 due to the presence of self driving vehicles? In cases like this the success of the bet is the timely financial return on a loan. The question is a bit more complex when it is a matter of equity investment; now there is also the potential of a bigger reward beyond the satisfaction of loan conditions: "if congestion forces the introduction of parking restraint is really implemented then public transport revenues will increase above our conservative assumptions".

In any case, any investment implies a level of risk and uncertainty. So the risks and rewards of transport concessions are judged against other alternative investments with their own potential downsides.

Answering these questions requires good analytical techniques, several shots at the target, risk analysis and professional judgement.

---

[9] Deutsch, D. (2011) "The beginning of infinity: explanations that transform the world". Allen Lane.

1.8 Errors and forecastability

We are dealing with a difficult problem, that of forecasting future outcomes of decisions we make today. In that context it is also useful to distinguish between projections and forecasts.

In this book a *projection* is a conditional ("if, then") statement about the future. Projections are estimates of future conditions that may exist (the "then") as a result of adopting a set of assumptions (the "if"). For example, "<u>If</u> current economic trends continue and no other competing roads are built <u>then</u> traffic and revenue will continue to increase at a similar rate. This is not predicting that it *will* happen, only stating what is likely to happen *if* our assumptions remain valid.

A *forecast* is a judgmental statement of what the professional believes to be the most likely future. Unlike analysts who only state what would happen if a set assumptions are satisfied (a projection), forecasters accept the responsibility of evaluating the "ifs" and selecting those that are most likely to occur. This is, of course, a more risky position to take, but it may be the one that is required or at least requested in a particular case.

This book does not advocate the production of forecasts in all cases. In many situations, decision makers would be able to accept conditional projections. They will also consider the opportunities they have to adapt the project to changing conditions or to influence them through policies and regulations.

Basing decisions and recommendations on projections prepared by others, without understanding their conditional nature or determining whether the assumptions underlying the projections are reasonable, is a recipe for disaster.

Even worse, analysts may prepare projections that they suspect will be accepted as forecasts without investigating the assumptions supporting their estimations. Transparency and ethics in producing and reporting projections and forecasts are paramount. Modellers should improve their communication skills to convey more clearly their assumptions and what is a fair interpretation of results.

Involvement of the private sector

"Economists have allowed themselves to walk into a trap where we say we can forecast, but no serious economist thinks we can. You don't expect dentists to be able to forecast how many teeth you'll have when you're 80. You expect them to give good advice and fix problems."
Tim Harford

2. INVOLVEMENT OF THE PRIVATE SECTOR

2.1 Motivation

The private sector has been involved in the development and operation of transport infrastructure for a long time. It was responsible for the development of early tolled roads or turnpikes. The Turnpike Trusts, originally set up in 1706 in the UK, led to serious outbreaks of rioting in which toll-gates were destroyed - largely because the population objected to paying tolls to travel on roads which had previously been free. Nevertheless, the Turnpike Trusts were a success, and the money raised was used to finance the building of new and better roads; between 1750 and 1800, the average journey from London to Edinburgh was reduced from twelve to four days.

The private sector was also a main driver behind the construction and operation of canals, railways and early tram and metro systems. It was only in the twentieth century that public funding for transport infrastructure became the norm. At the same time the public sector became significantly involved in running railways, ports, airports and public transport systems. This includes the development of transport infrastructure using some private capital secured with government or sovereign guarantees.

From the mid 1980's onwards there has been a resurgence of the involvement of the private sector in the provision and running of transport infrastructure and services. Despite early objections, toll road concessions have been a very active form of investment in new roads in developed and developing countries. There are well-developed networks of toll roads in France, Spain, Italy, Australia, the US and Canada. Some emerging countries have also adopted the tolling of roads as means of providing badly needed good quality infrastructure. China, Mexico, Brazil, Argentina and Chile have developed extensive systems of toll roads whilst countries like South Africa, India, Colombia and the Philippines are developing their own.

The private sector involvement is not restricted to toll roads. It is important also in the provision of port facilities, major tunnel and water crossings, railways, metro systems, airports and so on. In most of these projects, the private sector is involved through concessions awarded by local or central government. Some of these are ideas generated by private entrepreneurs; in most cases the Government has studied a project and prepared it for bidding in a market auction.

There are several motivations for this more recent enthusiasm for private sector involvement. Fiscal pressures on most governments have resulted in constraints on funding large infrastructure project, regardless of how much they may be needed. This has created an incentive to obtain private sector involvement and finance, even if more expensive than sovereign debt.

It is necessary to consider, however, that obtaining government funds for investment or to pay back loans is not pain free. The Marginal Cost of Public Funds (MCPF) reflects the cost incurred by society in raising additional revenues (taxes) to finance government spending. This reflects both the cost of raising taxes (and some are cheaper to collect than others) and the loss in welfare resulting from this collection[10]. Depending on the country and the type of tax considered this MCPF might range from values around 1 to even 1.5[11]. The latter would reflect a condition where increasing taxation by 1% would incur in a 1.5% loss in welfare. In this view, recovering the cost of a transport investment from those who benefit the most is a very sensible policy, regardless of who actually builds and operates the new facility.

Another reason is the desire to avoid the large and frequent budget and time overrun on large projects[12]. It has been shown that the involvement of private sector finance results in a tighter scrutiny of investment opportunities and a closer control on costs and time schedules. In essence, involving the private sector finance in large transport projects shifts risk from the taxpayer to capital markets. Provided, of course, that the Government is not forced to rescue a failed concession at a later stage.

Private investors are believed to be better than governments (and ideally better incentivised) at operating infrastructure assets with excellence. This should be not only apparent at the design and construction phases; many useful innovations happen at the operational level: electronic toll collection, roadside services, etc.

---

[10] Barrios, S. Pycroft, J and Saveyn, B. (2013) The marginal cost of public funds in the EU: the case of labour versus green taxes. European Union Taxation Papers. Working Paper N.35.

[11] Values below 1 are possible if the tax corrects a market distortion.

[12] Flyvbjerg, B., Skamris Holm, M.K. and Buhl, S.L. (2005) How (in)accurate are demand forecasts in public works projects? *Journal of the American Planning Association* **71**, 131-146.

Involvement of the private sector

Finally, there is the desire to tap onto the creativity and entrepreneurial skills of the private sector to device better solutions more in line with their experience with projects of that nature elsewhere in the world. International competitions are often encouraged to achieve that goal and to reduce the opportunities for collusion among a restricted set of local construction companies.

In this book we use the concepts of transport concession to encompass the wide variety of procurement models that are used in practice. These may include Franchising, BOT (Build Operate Transfer), PPP (Public Private Partnership) and a wide combination of the features in them. A key element, for this text, is the full or partial allocation of revenue risk and we focus on this item throughout.

2.2 Simplified view of the process

The process of preparing a project to take it to the market, organising bids for it, awarding a contract for the concession and operating, maintaining and finally transferring the facility back to the Government, is quite complex. Many agents, stakeholders, professionals and advisors play key roles in the process of developing a transport project from conception to successful implementation by the private sector. We simplify these here into four main participants:

- **Procurer**, usually the Government either directly or more likely through a Procuring Authority; it identifies a project, develops it and takes it to the marketplace. The role of the Procuring Authority is to deliver a project that is financeable and, most important, protects the welfare of its citizens from conception to the final transfer of the assets to the community. Treasury departments will also have an interest in the process and risks involved as it may commit, or end up committing, significant resources in future years thus restricting freedom to allocate tax revenues to other objectives.

- **Bidders or sponsors**, often consortia of infrastructure developers, construction companies, equipment suppliers, operators and their advisors, who prepare offers for a concession to build, operate and eventually transfer the asset back to the Government. Normally, they will constitute a Special Purpose Vehicle (SPV) or Project Company to undertake these tasks. In some PPP contracts the Government will retain an equity stake in the project and may be considered a sponsor.

- **Financial institutions**, often a combination of banks or capital investors, which would either invest in the concession or lend money under different forms of debt to the concessionaire. Pension and other funds may buy bonds issued to finance concessions.

- **Contractors**. The main performance obligations of the Project Company to construct and operate the project will usually be delivered through Engineering Procurement and Construction (EPC) and Operations and Maintenance (O&M) contracts respectively.

We recognise the role of other agents like insurance companies, monoline insurers, rating agencies and infrastructure funds that may take some degree of risk and/or influence the outcome of the transaction. For example, an SPV may mitigate revenue performance "tail risk" through insurance against low frequency/high impact events (e.g. earthquakes, major flooding or accidents); in particular, probable maximum loses policies are standard in the industry and most governments require them protecting up to one year worth of revenue.

For Public Transport concessions there may be a Feedstock Provider and perhaps even an Offtaker. In the first case, a party will be contractually obligated to provide feedstock (fuel or electricity) to the project at an agreed price in return for payment. In the second case a party will be contractually obligated to 'offtake' (purchase) some or all of the product or service produced by the project, for example students' passes.

Figure 4 provides a simplification of the process and the role and concerns of the three main agents: Banks and financial institutions, bidders and Procuring Authority. We look at each stage in turn.

Project preparation. The Procuring Authority attempts to define a concession that will provide significant benefits to its population and will offer an attractive role for the private sector. In doing this, the Procuring Authority will identify and assess the risks of the project and allocate each to whoever has greater capacity to handle or mitigate it; at least this is the principle involved. It is sometimes the case that the Procuring Authority tries to pass most of the risks to the private sector without providing sufficient guarantees in return. Depending of how uncertain or expensive the bidders perceive the future risks they may or may not accept these terms.

Involvement of the private sector

FIGURE 4 THE PROCESS OF DELIVERING A TRANSPORT CONCESSION

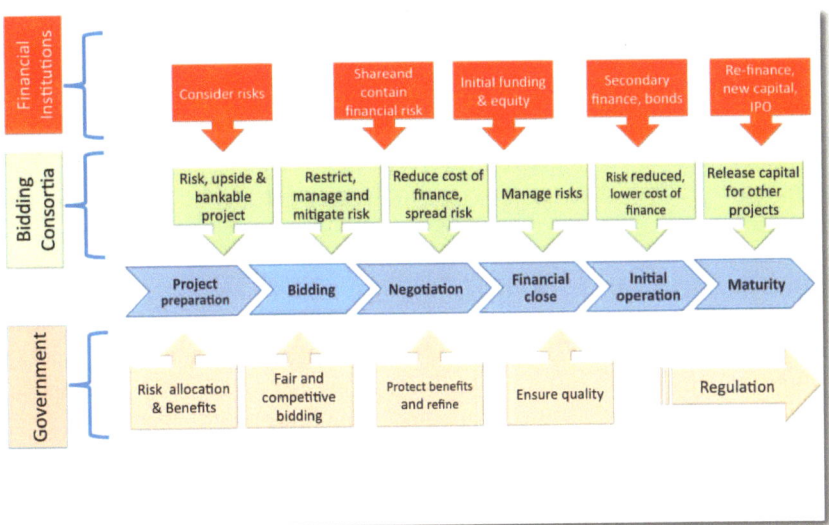

The acceptance of a risk costs money but those who are better placed to manage it are likely to charge less for accepting this responsibility. In many projects revenue risk is transferred to the concessionaire because it is in the best position, through the provision of a good service, to manage it. Sometimes it is not possible to transfer revenue risk in full to the concessionaire, either because expected flows are too uncertain or not strong enough, or because there is a desire to protect potential users from the full cost of paying for the infrastructure.

If it is not desirable to charge users the full cost of the services, shadow prices (or tolls) may be paid directly to the concessionaire by the Procuring Authority. Originally this was based only on actual traffic but later included recognition for good service, for example availability payments (in terms of number of lane-km-hours available to traffic during the year) and perhaps average speeds attained.

For a Public Transport concession revenue may be from the fare box (to retain this incentive) perhaps supplemented by a government contribution/subsidy for bus/train kilometres delivered.

In all cases a *Performance Regime* should be required by the Government to reward or fine the operator for meeting specified service delivery standards. These may be related, for example, to the quality of a road surface or to meeting punctuality targets.

At this stage the Procuring Authority will try to provide a clear and transparent view of risks in order to get good competitive and comparable bids. An integral and essential part of this effort should be the provision of a solid and credible legal framework. Any weakness in this will be perceived as an additional risk, deter long-term investors and limit funding alternatives.

Bidding process. There is often an Invitation to Expressions of Interest (EOI) in the future concession followed by a Request for Qualifications (RFQ) to select a smaller number of bidders (3 to 6 is common). The process involves then an Invitation to Tender (ITT) or Request for Proposals (RFP) to this short list of qualified consortia. During bid preparation each consortium studies the project and its contractual conditions in order to decide how much to offer or to ask for accepting the risks, obligations and compensating revenue streams on offer. The nature of the revenue risk will depend on a number of factors including the requirements of the concession, the award criteria (on toll levels, duration, minimum subsidy/maximum payment, discounted value of revenue stream), potential present and future competitors and conditions to adjust fares and tolls over time. The consortia will try to get a clear view of the risks and determine whether they have a special competitive advantage (faster construction, better finance) that could be exploited in the bid.

Sometimes it is necessary/desirable to constrain the amount of potential losses through the provision of Minimum Revenue Guarantees. The counterpart to this risk containment would be returning to the government a share of (could be 100%) any profits above an agreed threshold: a cap and collar arrangement.

The bidding is usually a Reverse Blind Auction where the lower bid wins the right to build and operate the concession. This tends to favour the bidder with the most optimistic view of the future net revenue streams and project costs. On its own, this criterion leads to the "winner's curse" where the winning bid exceeds the (uncertain) value of the concession. Therefore, most tenders do not use a single criterion to award a concession. A number of complementary factors are used including financial strengths, experience and the quality of the cost and revenue projections.

An alternative to the Reverse Blind Auction is a Swiss Challenge. This is a form of public procurement generally in response to an unsolicited idea or bid for a public project submitted by a private entity. A Swiss Challenge may adopt one of two approaches to this unsolicited bid: either Government purchases the intellectual property rights for a project concept from the proponent and then awards the project through a competitive bidding process in which no bidder has a predefined advantage. Alternatively, the Government can offer the original proponent an advantage in a competitive bidding process. In this case the Government should create rewards or bonuses that satisfy the original proponent while still allowing a truly competitive process. It has been observed, however, that it is not easy to find the right balance between incentives to propose beneficial projects and incentives for third parties to submit counter proposals.

Sometimes the bidding will be in stages concluding with the request for a Best and Final Offer (BAFO). For complex problems some governments prefer a Competitive Dialogue; in this case the Procuring Authority enters into a dialogue with potential bidders to develop one or more solutions for its requirements and on which chosen bidders will be invited to tender. A "beauty contest" is an early version of this idea where the bidder is allowed to submit different solutions or configurations and their assessment is more qualitative.

The Procuring Authority and its advisors will undertake a detailed financial, technical and legal evaluation of each bidder's compliance with the tender criteria specified in the RFP. Assuming compliance with the terms of the RFP, procurers will usually specify a set of evaluation criteria. They will certainly try to avoid been lumbered with a very low bid that almost certainly will fail to deliver a project as this then becomes a procuring agency problem.

Agency theory[13] reminds us that there may be some less than perfect incentives at play. The drive to win is strong in most professionals involved in these transactions; coming second provides no satisfaction. Moreover, staff within organisations is often rewarded with bonuses on winning a project regardless of future profitability. This exacerbates the winner's curse and sometimes begets toxic transactions.

Negotiations. Sometimes these are very short, as the conditions of the bid would have defined the project fully and financial close is assured. Short negotiation periods are generally considered good for the Government provided it has managed to specify the scheme in sufficient detail to avoid problems later in the concession. More often there is a period of negotiation once a preferred bidder has been selected; this period is used to refine the Concession Contract taking into account variations that may have not been envisaged originally. It usually deals mostly with risks other than traffic but it may involve obtaining stronger guarantees from the Government that unexpected alternative routes/services will not be provided in the future. At this stage the concession is assigned to a *Special Purpose Vehicle* (SPV) or company, set up by the consortium to build and operate the project until it is transferred back to the Government. The financial institutions,

---

[13] Eisenhardt, K. (1989). "Agency theory: An assessment and review". *Academy of Management Review* **14** (1): 57–74.

in turn, will try to share and spread the risk among different banks and will press the Government and consortium for guarantees. Rating agencies may play a key role here in assessing project risks. Commercial Close represents the finalisation and signature of the 'head contract' (the concession contract) and the supporting project documentation such as shareholder's agreements and sub-contracts.

Financial close. Here all the funds needed to implement the project are finally secured and made available. This often involves a bridging loan and other facilities, typically from banks. These would include capital expenditure (CAPEX) and liquidity facilities that provide sufficient cushion in the early stages of the project. Often a trust is created to provide debt payment guarantees and financial documents typically establish a "waterfall" in which debt service has first priority after certain CAPEX and Operating Costs (OPEX) requirements are met.

The partners of the SPV provide the rest of the finance as equity. The repayment of this loan is often structured around a lower-cost longer-term finance once the project has matured and is well into operation. Therefore, the financial institutions would like to be confident that this second stage finance is assured. There may be a grant provided by the Procuring Authority to strengthen the financial viability of the project. In the case of existing assets that need rehabilitation and operation over many years, the consortium may offer a payment to the Government in compensation. Financial Close has been achieved when all 'Conditions Precedent' to the financing documentation has been satisfied and the Project Company is therefore able to draw down debt to fund construction of the asset.

Credit risk analysis is very important from bidding to financial close. The scheme is usually financed on the basis of its own worth and the equity contributed by partners of the SPV. Project finance does not rely on the credit strength of the partners whose only liability will be their contribution, usually between 20% and 40% of the capital required. The rest is provided through debt. A number of metrics will be deployed to analyse the credit strength of the project. One of the most important is the Debt Service Coverage Ratio (DSCR, or sometimes just DCR). This is the ratio of net revenues from operations to capital and interest obligations. It will be weaker over the first few years of operations but it will be expected to be safely above 1. A financial package may reduce payments of the principal in early years to satisfy this requirement.

Involvement of the private sector

Credit analysis digs deeper than the direct application of a few intelligent indices. It has to be undertaken in the context of the contractual protections to lenders, insurances and structural provisions.

Second stage finance. Once the project is in operation most risks are much reduced and therefore it should be possible to obtain finance at lower rates; this may take the form of another loan or, more likely, a bond issue depending on market conditions. Often the main remaining risk is associated with the future revenue stream. A review of previous traffic and revenue projections may be needed to offer additional confidence in future revenue streams.

Third stage finance. Once the project is operating well and its long-term financial structure is in place, it is possible to offer equity participation in the market, totally or in part, depending on the terms of the concession and the strategy of the SPV. This may take the form of an *Initial Public Offering* (IPO) or just a private agreed opportunity to invest in the Special Purpose Vehicle holding the concession. This injection of capital will enable the release of some capital of the original investors that they could use in another tender. It is unusual to offer an IPO before the project has a couple of years of successful operations.

Second and third stage finance are just labels as sometimes they may be implemented simultaneously, one of them may be omitted or implemented in reverse order.

The relationship between different agents in this complex field is typified in Figure 5. This is only an example that shows the different actors involved in a typical transaction and the flow of funds, services and contractual obligations between them; the example is based on a toll road transaction, public transport arrangements may be more complex.

2.3   Risks cost money

The overarching issue in forecasting for private and public sector projects is that of uncertainty and risk. Uncertainty has always been present in modelling and forecasting work but the involvement of private investors and financial institutions has given a clear monetary value to the issue of risk. In terms of demand modelling, private investors and financial institutions are interested in a revenue stream, year after year for the duration of a concession, and the degree of confidence that can be associated to these figures. These risks change over time and to understand this we need to start by considering the different stakeholders whose views and perceptions will evolve during the life of the project.

FIGURE 5 CONTRACTUAL ARRANGEMENTS AMONG AGENTS IN A PPP TRANSACTION

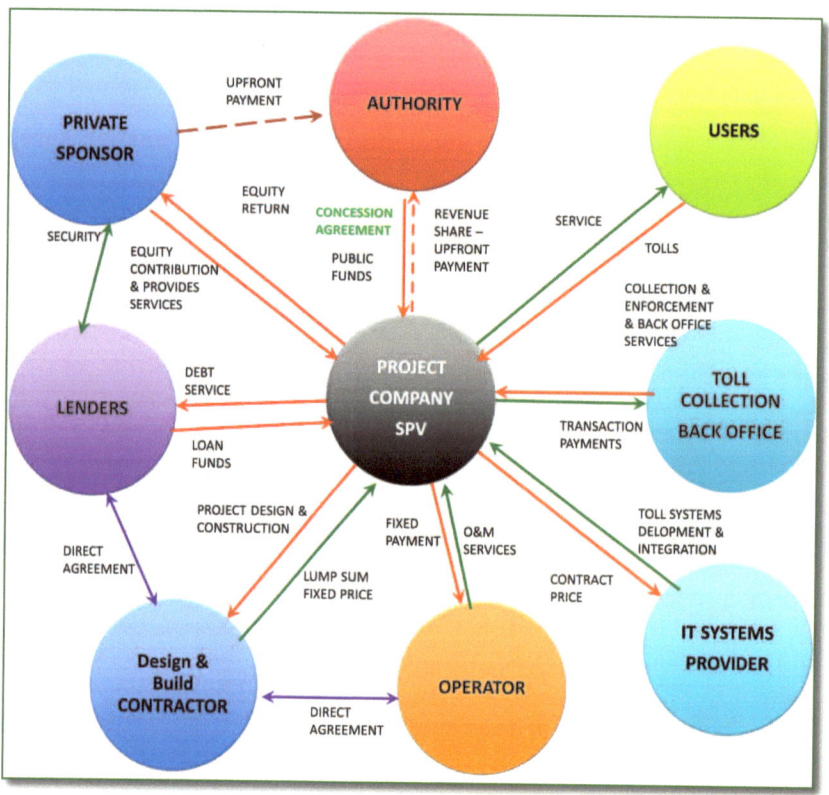

At bid preparation the main sources of risks are:

- Will all the *right of way* required be available and free of encumbrances to the concession in time for construction?

- Are all the *environmental* issues resolved? Impact Assessments, Permits, etc.

- Are all *construction techniques and costs* sufficiently well defined and known?

- Are the *ground conditions* sufficiently investigated, including the possible need to displace utilities?

- Are the costs of *operating and maintaining* (O&M) the future asset well known and quantifiable?

- How confident can one be about the future *traffic and revenue* streams?

Involvement of the private sector

- Are the threats posed by competing services (these may include cars and motorcycles for a public transport project) understood and quantifiable?
- How long and steep will be the period of transition between starting operations and the time when stable traffic levels materialise? The *ramp-up* period.

As can be seen from Figure 6, all of these risks are higher before construction starts. During construction most of these risks are reduced so when the project starts operating the main remaining risks will be some hidden faults in construction, traffic and revenue, O&M and ramp up. Finally the project will reach maturity when traffic levels stabilise and the only remaining risk will be associated with the level of growth, the possibility that competing facilities are provided some time in the future and the advent of a disruptive technology.

FIGURE 6 RISK PROFILE OF A NOMINAL PROJECT

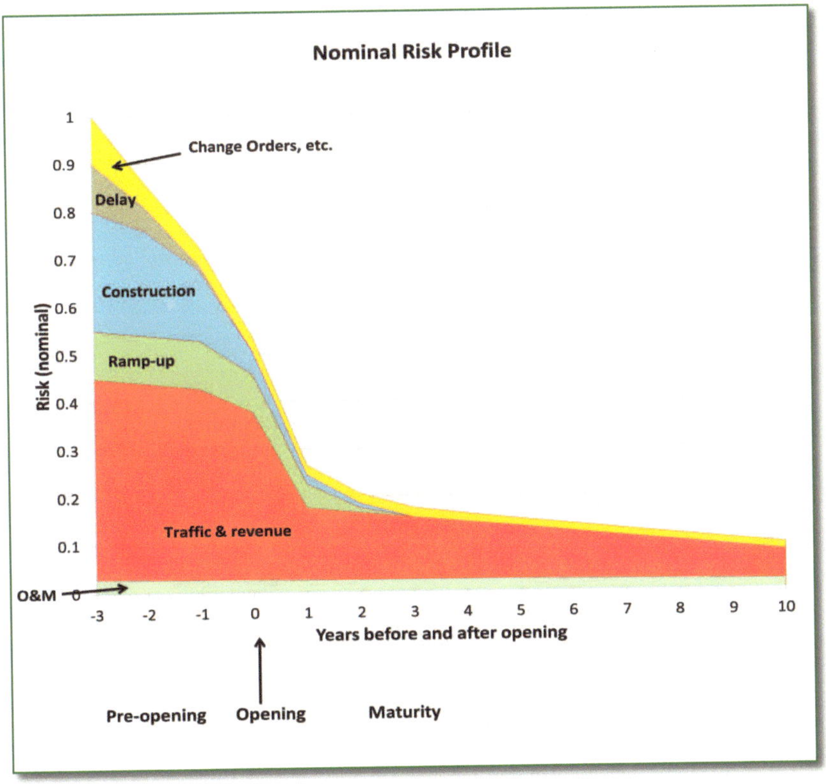

Of course, the full list of risks is longer. These include:

- **General risks**
  - Country
  - Currency
  - Political risks
- **Project specific risks**
  - **Construction**
    - Planning permission
    - Right of way availability
    - Environmental and archaeological issues
    - Ground conditions
    - Design
    - Latent defects
    - Construction costs
    - Cost overruns
    - Delays to start or complete works
    - Change orders
    - Commissioning
  - **Revenue**
    - Traffic volume and composition
    - Competition from other, especially new, facilities
    - Ramp-up or transitional period
    - Growth
    - Toll and fare adjustments
    - Charging technologies
    - Leakage

Involvement of the private sector

- **Legal risks**
    - Legislation and regulatory changes
    - Early termination of contract
    - Insufficient compensations
    - Force Majeure and Business Interruption
- **Operating Costs**
    - Operations and Maintenance costs
    - Service Quality
    - Change Orders

Figure 7 shows how these risks are usually allocated between the Public and the Private sector although there are plenty of variations in this area. For example, in some countries it would be reasonable for the SPV to take the Right of Way risk where in others this would not be acceptable. Some risks may be shared, for example environmental or even financial risks.

FIGURE 7 EXAMPLE OF RISK ALLOCATION IN A TOLL ROAD TRANSACTION

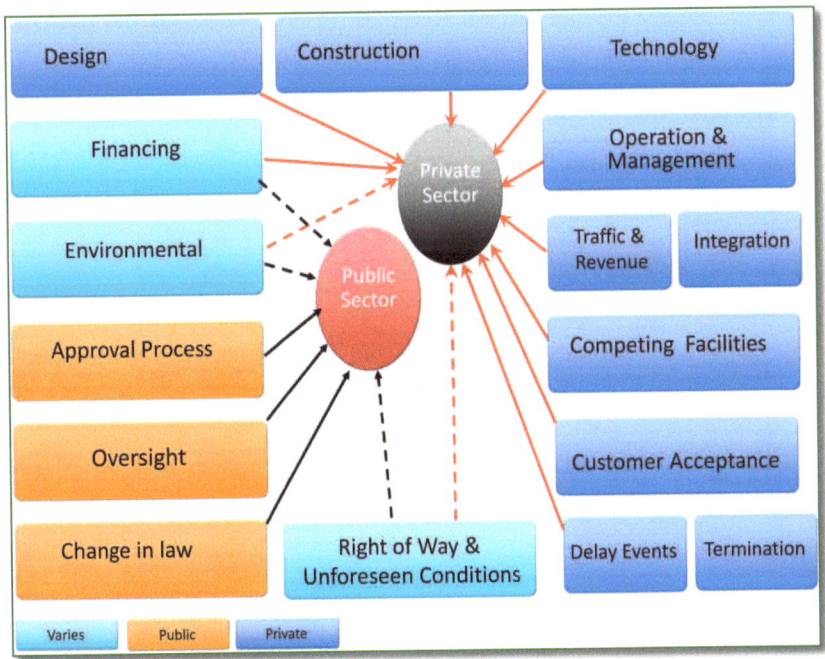

Better Traffic and Revenue Forecasting

2.4 The future is not what it used to be

There is sufficient evidence that the profession has not been very good at forecasting traffic and revenue for private and public sector projects. Standard & Poor's (S&P), the rating agency, collected data for over 100 toll road and public transport projects and compared traffic and revenue projections with the actual outturns in each.

For toll roads, Standard & Poor's[14] concluded there was, on average, a 23% overestimation of traffic and revenue. It also observed that traffic and revenue projections for financial institutions suffered less from overestimation of future traffic. This is illustrated in Figure 8 inspired in the findings of that report:

FIGURE 8 ERRORS IN FORECASTING TOLL TRAFFIC

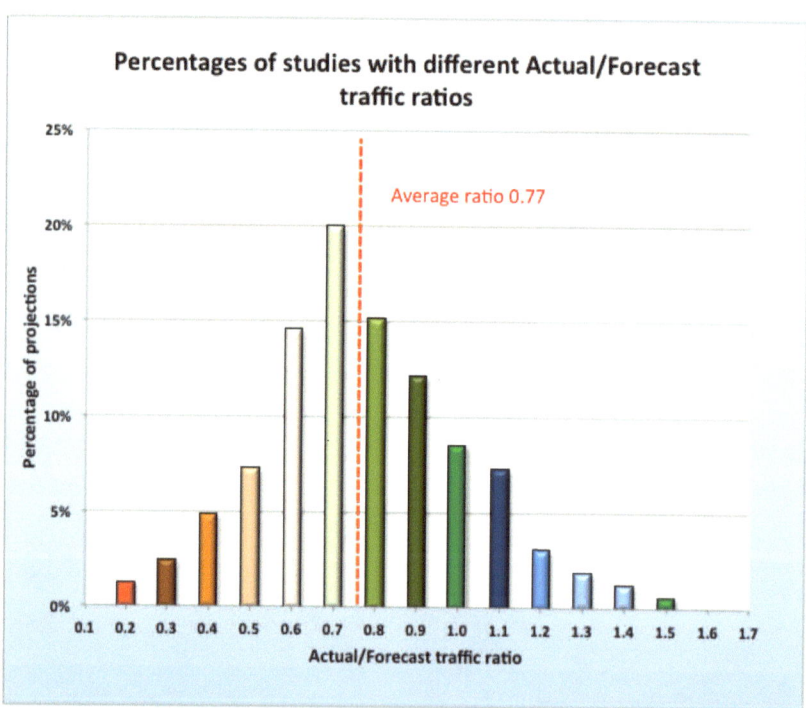

S&P concluded there was an *optimism bias* inherent in most forecasts and that a key element in auditing traffic and revenue projections was to try to compensate for that bias.

---

[14] Bain, R. and Polakovic, L. (2005) "Traffic Forecasting Risk Study Update 2005: Through Ramp-up and Beyond. Standard & Poor's Report, August 2005.

Involvement of the private sector

S&P found similar results when dealing with public transport projects, albeit from a smaller and more local sample[15]. Moreover, the work of Flyvbjerg et al [16] covered over 200 project, road and rail in 14 countries; they found that errors in forecasting rail projects were, in general, greater than for road schemes. They concluded that over 70% of the rail projects overpredicted demand by two thirds. For about 50% of the road projects, the difference between forecasts and actual traffic was greater than 20%.

There have been several other papers contrasting projected against actual flows and revenues; all reach similar conclusions. The most recent by David Hartgen[17] summarises most results and offers some suggestions to tackle these issues; most are in line with what is proposed in this book.

2.5 Optimism bias

Faced with this evidence it is difficult to claim that there is no bias present in our traffic and revenue projections. It can be argued that unless one has an optimistic view of the future no project will ever get implemented. But this is no answer to the question of how best to provide T&R figures for different type of stakeholders involved in private sector projects.

Nevertheless, there are at least three observations in respect of this reported over-prediction bias: nature of the sample, the tendering process and different perceptions of risk.

Sample bias is inevitable in studies of the nature undertaken by Flyvbjerg and S&P. The studies made available to them are those that resulted in implemented projects or successful bids. More pessimistic views of the future led to lost bids or projects that remain postponed indefinitely. Therefore the results do not reflect the whole range of traffic projections but only those that were based on a more upbeat expectation of economic growth and demand.

Most tendering processes are very demanding and also very expensive to bidders. The cost of a tender for a major project may reach 10 million US$; smaller projects cost less but none will be below 2 million US$. This high cost has no compensation unless the bidder is successful. There is a very strong pressure to win for all concerned,

---

[15] Bain, R. and Plantagie, J. (2003) "Fair's Fair? Why tram projects are on a bumpy road". Standard and Poor's Report July 2003.

[16] Flyvbjerg, B., M. Skarmis-Holm and S. Buhl (2005) "Inaccuracy in Traffic Forecasts". Transport Reviews, Vol. 26, No. 1, 1–24, January 2006

[17] Hartgen, D. (2013) "Hubris or humility? Accuracy issues for the next 50 years of travel demand forecasting. Transportation 10.1007/s11116-013-9497-y.

including the independent traffic and revenue consultant. The consultant has to face two conflicting pressures. On the one hand, the independence and integrity that is expected from an advisor of this nature. On the other, good consultants have written into their genetic code a duty care after the interests of their clients, and they make it clear what these are at bid time.

There is always the subtle but real psychological trap resulting from months of hard work preparing a bid. Participants will tend to see the project with more "positive eyes" aware of every possible upside and conceive them as normal base case.

There are different views on risk. The database used by S&P and Flyvbjerg contains projections produced for governments and bidders as well as for banks and other financial institutions. It is not surprising, therefore, that projections are different; generally those for banks are less optimistic than those for equity investors. This is because different stakeholders have different perspectives on risks and rewards. Lenders are aware of a more or less fixed set of rewards associated to a loan: transaction fees, interest rates and repayment of the principal. The risks are failure to receive the full interests and principal payments; all risks are negative.

Equity investors, partners of the bidding consortia, perceive similar negative risks: if traffic is low the future revenue stream may not be sufficient to pay back interest and principal, never mind a suitable return to capital invested. However, they also perceive interesting opportunities and additional profit if traffic turns out to be higher than estimated. There may even be an overoptimistic view that the superior service they will provide will attract more customers. This positive risk, unseen by financial institutions, is bound to colour expectations and perceptions of the overall risk profile from an equity perspective.

Governments are likely to be the most optimistic of the lot. Governments perceive the economic and political benefits of such project beyond revenue streams: accessibility to new areas (and voters), time savings, improved productivity and accident reductions. Procuring authorities are likely to view the future as much more certain and under control than the private sector. Indeed, they may or may not authorise the construction of competitive schemes, the annual adjustment of fares and toll rates. Governments believe they will provide the right of way free of encumbrances and at the right time but reality and unforeseen political initiatives may place obstacles later on.

2.6 Forecasting error

The arguments above may explain the observation of bias in traffic and revenue forecasts, but they cannot explain the wide range of forecasts as illustrated in Figure 8. This, in turn, can have a number of possible explanations: variability in future inputs (population, GDP, etc.) required to run the models for future years, or poor data, modelling and forecasting techniques. In some cases a combination of them.

The case for blaming errors in projected variables that serve as inputs to forecasting models is strong. In most toll roads economic growth, represented by changes in Gross Domestic Product (GDP), is the main driver of traffic growth. In many cases, errors in forecasting GDP alone explain the large majority of differences between forecast and actual flows.

Projections of economic growth are notoriously poor. I remember working with major international banks in 2007 for a large toll road transaction and none of them foresaw the financial crisis that was coming just around the corner.

Figure 9 exemplifies this difficulty. It shows projections of GDP growth in New Zealand undertaken by different institutions in different years. The solid black line shows the actual changes in GDP whilst the coloured ones show the projections produced at any one time. It can be seen that with only a couple of exceptions all projections overestimated economic growth, often by a large margin.

FIGURE 9 GDP GROWTH PROJECTIONS FOR NEW ZEALAND

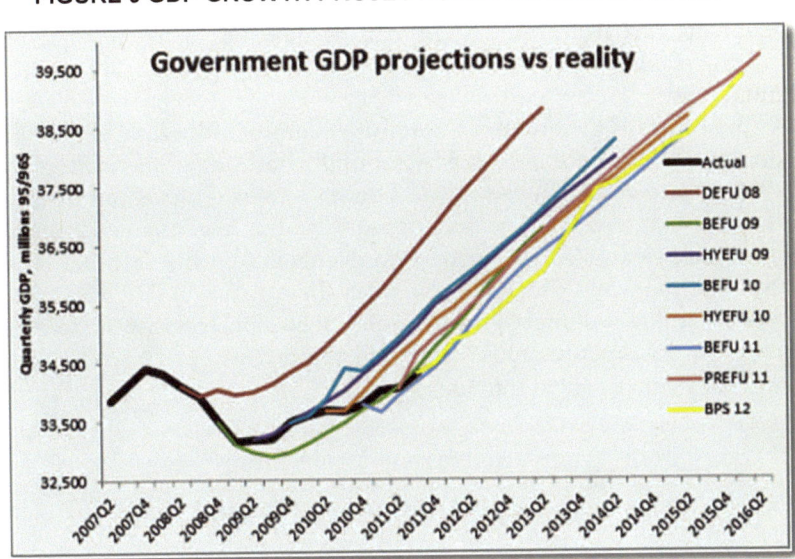

Source: Treasury Fiscal and Economic Updates, and Stats NZ GDP series.

The second source of error is, of course, poor data combined with inappropriate selection and specification of models. Early modelling efforts were inevitably imperfect. They used models directly transplanted from strategic transport planning contexts. I have seen models adopted that were too insensitive to toll rates, one of the reasons behind a failure of many Mexican toll roads in the early nineties. Other modelling efforts have ignored the risk of future competition from other roads or modes.

Modelling techniques have improved since these early years. One of the objectives of this book is to reflect the state of practice in 2014 and show the implications of different choices that can be made in the specification of models to be used in forecasting. Hopefully, this will help in avoiding pitfalls and improving our forecasting ability in the future.

2.7 Summary

We have seen that our track record as professional forecasters of traffic and revenue on toll road and public transport concessions is not good. We must find better ways of:
- Specifying better models to support T&R projections
- Dealing with potential biases in our forecasts
- Handling the inherent uncertainty and risk in any T&R projection

We will discuss the implications of model specification and data collection in Part II whilst Part III will be devoted to the practice of forecasting under risk and uncertainty avoiding, at the same time, potential biases.

As the future is uncertain, no amount of careful modelling work can eliminate risk. What we need is a better understanding of the sources of uncertainty and what can be said, and perhaps even done, about them.

There are indeed known uncertainties and a few unknown ones, Taleb's **black swans**. These unexpected events may result from fat tails of the distributions of some variables like future GDP or from completely unknown interventions. Nobody by 1990 forecast the role of Internet and its repercussions today and tomorrow, even when it was already fully functional at the time.

PART II ANALYSIS

This section deals with the intricacies of modelling to deliver forecasts for traffic and revenue on toll roads and public transport concessions. As such, it will be of particular interest to professionals seeking to develop and improve their modelling and forecasting skills. However, some of it may be too detailed and mathematical for those who will commission consultants or seek to interpret the results from their work. I suggest that those managers should focus on chapters 3, 4 and in particular 5 and 10; if the concession of interest is a mass transit one then chapter 8, on mode choice, would also be relevant.

The classic transport model

"It is utterly implausible that a mathematical formula should make the future known to us, and those who think it can, would have once believed in witchcraft." **Bertrand de Jouvenel**

3. THE CLASSIC TRANSPORT MODEL

3.1 Introduction

Models are simplifications of reality; they are context and problem dependent and what they leave out may be as important as what they include. Transport models are based in some theories of travel behaviour. These may be very simple analogies with other physical phenomena, for example the use of a Gravity Model to represent the allocation of trips to pairs of zones; or more complex constructs based on theories of behaviour, for example Random Utility Theory. In some cases, it may be possible to explain a functional form (equation) from different perspectives; for instance, most gravity models can also be derived from Theories of Random Utility, Information Minimisation and Entropy Maximisation. This equifinality property, however, does not make a model *true*. Indeed, there is no such thing as a true model, only a useful one under certain conditions and purposes.

Data is central to model development; data availability usually leaves little room for compromise in the trade-off between modelling *relevance* and modelling *complexity and realism*. Models predict a number of dependent (or endogenous) variables given other independent (or explanatory) variables. To test a model we would normally need data about each variable. Of particular interest are the *policy variables*, which are those assumed to be under the control of the decision maker, e.g. those the analyst may vary in order to test the value of alternative policies or schemes.

Transport models can be developed to have three different uses:

To improve our understanding of travel behaviour. One hypothesises an analytical model of behaviour and tests it against data to see how much of actual behaviour is explainable by the model.

To test alternatives that cannot be tested in practice. This is the case for most transport interventions. One can test in the model changes to a network, the introduction of new modes, changes in policy and take the model responses to these changes as representative of what will happen in practice. This helps choose the most cost-effective interventions in each case.

To produce conditional forecasts (projections) of what the future of a transport system may look like and perform under different scenarios and interventions. This is the main use of interest in this book, in particular to estimate patronage, traffic and revenue for transport projects.

The academic world is usually more interested in the first of these model applications. Decision makers focus on the second and third use of models. Consortia bidding for transport concessions would only be interested in the last one. Alas, the models and data requirements for each of these uses are likely to be different

In practice, all models require assumptions about human behaviour. Those based on entropy maximisation, for example, ask for very little: travellers are like particles finding their most likely equilibrium subject to a few constrains that reflect behavioural traits (e.g. short or cheaper trips are more likely than long expensive ones). The models with greater behavioural content are conveniently based on rational human beings; the *homo economicus* that considers alternatives and chooses the one that maximises own utility. The key to modelling here is the realistic specification of alternatives and assumptions about the best functional form to represent "utility".

3.2 Behavioural responses

Faced with a new intervention in the transport system, for example the introduction of a new tolled road, travellers may display a number of responses, on their own or in combination:

- Change their route to benefit from the shorter travel time using the new road or to benefit from the reduced congestion now available on the rest of the network.
- Change the time of travel now that the journey can be made shorter. This effect is amplified if the toll rate is different at different times of the day.
- Change the destination of some trips in the short term, for example shopping trips, to take advantage of the new accessibility.
- Change jobs or residence in the medium term, for the same reason. For example, the introduction of a tolled Panamericana Norte in Buenos Aires permitted many residents to move to locations further away from their jobs to enjoy a better and more secure neighbourhood.
- Change mode of travel, perhaps from rail to car or even from car to BRT if this uses the new fast facility.
- Change the make up of the linked trips or tours they perform. For example, it may be possible to go back home and then to play squash rather than directly to the squash club from work.

- Change the number of people that travel together. It may be advantageous to combine trips with family members or neighbours to share the cost of the toll every day.
- Change some of the activities that are undertaken during the week. It may now be worth going to a more distant supermarket to get better food but only once a week rather that buying food more often on the way back from work.
- In the case of an interurban toll road, it may now be possible to go to a destination on business and return the same day rather than having to stay there overnight to get the work done.
- Decide to acquire a car in order to take advantage of the new toll road (travelled by rail beforehand).

Overall, some of these changes result in more trips by car and other in fewer trips and also in changes in overall vehicle-km and vehicle-hours by private vehicles.

It is very rare for all of these behavioural responses to be relevant in any one case. It must be recognised that models that might replicate all these changes will be very complex and required large data sources of very high quality that do not exist at present. One must take a pragmatic view and identify the most relevant (important) responses and focus the model on them. Overcomplicating a model is likely to introduce more errors; we will discuss this issue at greater length in Part III.

3.3   Levels of aggregation

Most transport models are based on zones as representative of origin and destination locations. This not only reduces model execution times but also benefits from modelling groups rather than individuals. Of course, it is possible to take the opposite view and model individuals and obtain the average behaviour and trips later. The results are not the same. The average behaviour of individuals with different income levels is not the same as the behaviour of individuals with an income equal to the average.

Take a toll road that it is only attractive to individuals in the top 20% of income in the zone. They may well decide to use the toll road and generate revenue. However, if we take the average income of this zone it may appear than nobody will find the toll road attractive generating no revenue. Therefore, one must be careful in choosing what level of aggregation or segmentation is the most appropriate.

Having identified the responses that would be most relevant in each case one has to decide the type of disaggregation that is necessary to reflect this relevant behaviour. One disaggregation that pertains to practically all models is by vehicle availability. This helps determine who can choose car as a mode and who cannot. In many cases disaggregation by the number of cars in a household will also be necessary (0, 1 and 2+ cars).

Another common level of disaggregation is the journey purpose and whether this is based at home or not. Journeys with one end of the trip at home are considered to be home-based.

In the case of project where price is a key variable (practically all transport concessions but also Congestion Charging and parking policies) disaggregation by income level, or more precisely by willingness to pay, is usually the dominant factor.

3.4 Trips, tours, purposes

Classical transport models are based on trips, a movement from an origin to a destination that could have one or more stages as discussed before. There has been an increased interest in modelling tours linking activities rather than just trips. It is useful therefore to define more formally these elements:

- An *activity* is a continuous interaction with a service or person, within the same socio-spatial environment. It includes any pure idle times before or during the activity (e.g. waiting at a doctor's surgery).

- A *stage* is a continuous movement using one mode of transport, more precisely one vehicle or walk. It includes any pure waiting (idle) times immediately before or during that movement (e.g. waiting for a bus, searching for a parking space and making parking manoeuvres).

- A *trip* is a continuous sequence of stages between two activities (a trip can have only one stage, for example a car trip, or more in a multi-mode trip).

- A *tour* is a sequence of trips starting and ending at the same location typically home; a *trip chain* is similar to a tour but it may not end at the same location.

- A *trip purpose* is defined by the most important activity undertaken at one of the ends of the trip; it is defined by the activities linked by the trip.

3.5 Generalised costs

Early transport models used distance as the measure of separation between an origin and a destination, for example in the first versions of gravity models. Separation is represented today by the richer concept of *generalised costs*.

Generalised costs are typically represented by a linear function of the attributes of the journey weighted by coefficients indicating their relative importance as perceived by the traveller:

$$C_{ij} = a_1 t_{ij}^v + a_2 t_{ij}^w + a_3 t_{ij}^t + a_4 t_{ij}^n + a_5 F_{ij} + a_6 \phi_j + \delta$$

where

t_{ij}^v is the in-vehicle travel time between i and j;

t_{ij}^w is the walking time to and from stops (stations) or from parking area/lot;

t_{ij}^t is the waiting time at stops (or time spent searching for a parking space);

$t^n{}_{ij}$ is the interchange time, if any;

The last three of these times are sometimes referred to as Out-of-Vehicle-Time (OVT).

F_{ij} is a monetary charge: the fare charged to travel between i and j or the cost of using the car for that journey, including any tolls or congestion charges (note that car operating costs are often not well perceived and that electronic means of payment tend to blur somehow the link between use and payment);

ϕ_j is a terminal (typically parking) cost associated with the journey from i to j;

δ is a *modal penalty*, a parameter representing all other attributes not included in the generalised measure so far, e.g. safety, comfort and convenience; a more general version of generalised costs call this parameter an *Alternative Specific Constant* (ASC) as it could be, for example, an initial resistance to use a new tolled bridge.

$a_1 \ldots_6$ are weights attached to each element of cost; they have dimensions appropriate for conversion of all attributes to common units, e.g. money or time. It is not necessary for these weights to be the same for all modes and not even for different types of journeys within a mode. For example, a_1 may depend on the type of road (dual or single carriageway) or the type of public transport vehicle (with or without air conditioning). In most cases one would expect $a_2 > a_3 > a_1$.

If the generalised cost is measured in monetary units ($a_5 = 1$) then a_1 is sometimes interpreted as the *value of time* (or more precisely the *value of in-vehicle time*) as its units are money/time. In that case, a_2 and a_3 would be the values of walking and waiting time respectively, and in many practical studies they have been taken to be two or three times the expected value of a_1; see chapter 5 for a more thorough treatment of these concepts.

In our case, it is important to make sure the coefficients in this formulation reflect subjective values of time, etc. rather than objective, resource-based, values sometimes specified by the government.

As generalised costs may be measured in money or time units it is relatively easy to convert one into the other. For example, if the generalised cost is measured in time units, a_1 would be 1.0, $a_{2...3}$ would probably be between 2.0 and 3.0, and $a_{5...6}$ would represent something like the 'duration of money'.

Another related concept is that of *disutility of travel*, the negative of *utility*. This is similar to the generalised cost with a negative sign except that the concept of utility is more general. In fact, it allows the inclusion of other terms that are characteristics of the user not of the mode of travel, for example gender or income, plus an error term to account for omitted attributes.

3.6   Zones

A zoning system is used to aggregate the individual households and premises into manageable spatial chunks for modelling purposes. The greater the number of zones, the smaller they can be to cover the same study area.

The first choice in establishing a zoning system is to distinguish the study area itself from the rest of the world. In choosing the study area one must consider the decision-making context, the schemes to be modelled, and the nature of the trips of interest: mandatory[18], discretionary/optional, long or short distance, and so on.

The study area should be somewhat bigger than the specific area of interest covering the schemes to be considered. Opportunities for re-routeing, changes in destination and so on, must be allowed for; we would like to model their effects as part of the study area itself.

The region external to the study area is normally divided into a number of *external zones*. In some cases it might be enough to consider each external zone to represent 'the rest of the world' in a particular direction. The study area itself is divided into smaller *internal* zones.

---

[18] Trips to work and education are considered "mandatory" and the rest "discretionary".

The classic transport model

Private sector projects, in particular toll roads and HOT lanes, benefit from having many small zones to represent route choice better than in strategic planning models. This is also true for public transport concessions where the exact location of stops, stations and their catchment areas is important. However, this is not always possible as the timescales and budgets may preclude the painstaking work of disaggregating zones and the information in them.

For a deeper discussion on the criteria for designing zoning systems and the implications associated to them consult Modelling Transport starting at page 128.

Zones are represented in the computer models as if all their attributes and properties were concentrated in a single point called the *zone centroid*. Centroids are attached to the network through *centroid connectors* representing the average costs (time, distance) of joining the transport system for trips with origin or destination in that zone. Nearly as important as the cost associated with each centroid connector is the node(s) in the network it connects to. These should be close to natural access/egress points for the zone itself. Beware of automatic centroid connector facilities in software that tend to allocate them to junction nodes, an unrealistic arrangement. Centroid connectors are critical to the accurate representation of the network and, at the same time, are very difficult to audit or peer review. It is not too difficult to adjust centroid connectors to influence results in traffic assignment therefore the integrity of the modeller is paramount.

3.7   Networks

The transportation network is deemed to represent what the transport system offers to satisfy the movement needs of trip makers. The description of a transport network in a computer model can be undertaken at different levels of detail and requires the specification of its connectivity, its properties or attributes and the relationship between those properties and traffic and person flows.

Normal practice, however, is to model the network as a *directed graph*, i.e. a system of nodes and links joining them, where most nodes are taken to represent junctions and the links stand for homogeneous stretches of road between junctions. This simple representation is not that useful when dealing with urban congestion or complex interchanges. Links are characterised by several attributes such as length, speed, number of lanes and so on. A subset of the nodes is associated with zone centroids, and a subset of the links to centroid connectors.

The principal source of network data would be one of the many digital maps available for most cities. One should not assume, however, that they are error free. They will need checking, updating, pruning (to focus on the network of interest) and complementing with observations on items like on-street parking, pedestrian friction, bus lanes and other features that may affect their performance.

Sometimes models use network elements that do not correspond to any physical feature but help in defining a charging scheme or some other operational feature, for example complex transit charging structures.

As congestion is likely to be important, link descriptions should also have a formulation for the relationship between flow and speed or travel time. This speed- or cost-flow relationship is critical in a number of ways. The simplest version is a function relating flow on the link to speed. Flow and speed are expected to be related as shown in Figure 10[19], speed in miles per hour and flow in vehicles per lane. A solid line has been added to represent an approximate functional form for the relationship. Note that traffic does not behave naturally along the curve. Individual variations generate this cloud of points that a curve can only approximate.

The top of the curve represents how speed declines slowly with flow until it reaches a critical flow level, the capacity of the lane. Trying to fit more traffic leads to chaotic conditions where flow and speed are below those at capacity. These are the stop-go conditions in a congested highway.

---

[19] US Federal Highway Administration. Quality Control Procedures for Archived Operations Traffic Data: Synthesis of Practice and Recommendations. Visited 3 July 2013
http://www.fhwa.dot.gov/policy/ohpi/travel/qc/images/figure5.gif

The classic transport model

FIGURE 10 SPEED AND FLOW OBERVATIONS POINTS AND A SPEED-FLOW RELATIONSHIP

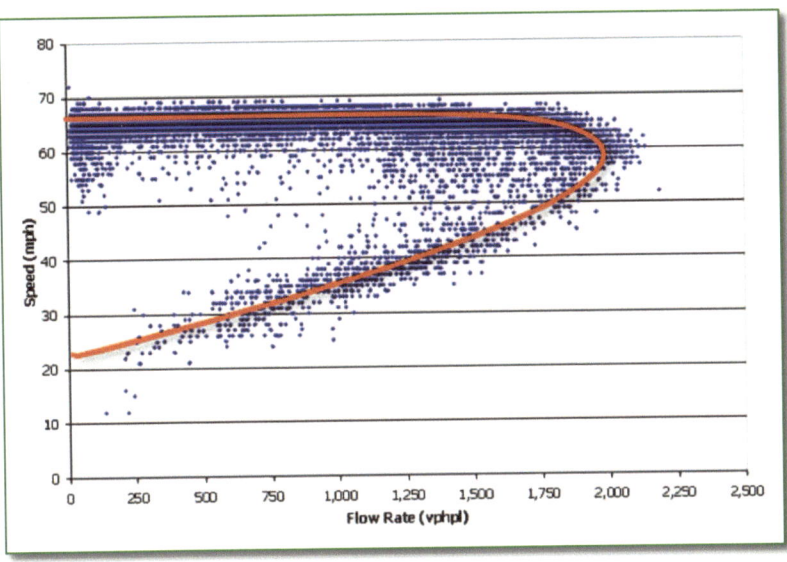

Transport models use a variation on this curve relating travel time per mile or km against flow; note that this requires speeds to be measured over space in contrast with the spot speed measured, for example, by radars and loop detectors.

A frequently used relationship is a BPR formulation:

$$t = t_0 \left[1 + \alpha (V/Q)^\beta \right]$$

where

t and t_0 are actual travel time and travel time under free flow conditions (per km)

V is the actual volume of traffic (per lane per hour or just per hour)

Q is the capacity in the same units as V

α and β are parameters for calibration.

The shape of this curve is represented in Figure 11 for $\alpha = 2$ and $\beta = 8$.

FIGURE 11 BPR TRAVEL TIME FLOW RELATIONSHIP

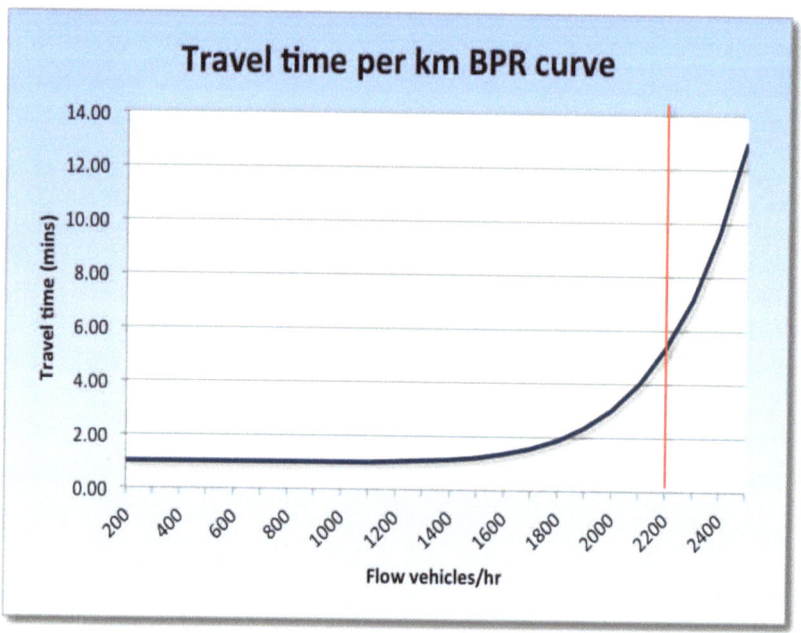

With this type of relationship it is always possible for flows to exceed capacity, something impossible in reality. This condition is needed in order to guarantee convergence in a (static) traffic assignment stage, as discussed later on in this text. It is expected, however, that the travel times for flows above capacity would represent reasonably[20] travel times of the lower part of the curve when that level of flow attempts to join the link. The flow that can exceed capacity is sometimes called the "demand flow" in contrast with "actual flow" that can never actually above capacity. Dynamic Traffic Assignment handles this issue better.

The problem with BPR and similar formulations, despite their popularity, is that they tend to underestimate delays at junctions as they concentrate on the links characteristics. Moreover, they also tend to underestimate delays when demand is close or above the capacity of the link. They are less appropriate in urban conditions where junctions play a more important role in determining travel times than the speed mid-link. Akçelik (1991) has suggested a curve, based on earlier work

---

[20] This will depend on the length of the highly congested period when queues build up.

The classic transport model

by Davidson, which tackles these problems better. When considering conditions close or above saturation the length of the modelling period matters more as it influences the length of the "overflow" curve which in turn drives delay. Akçelik's function applies to V/Q ratios above and below 1:

$$t = t_0 + \left\{ 0.25T \left[(x-1) + \sqrt{(x-1)^2 + \frac{8J_A}{Q_j T} x} \right] \right\}$$

where:
T is the flow modelling period (typically one hour)
Qj is the capacity at the junction; if the saturation flow is Qs then Qj =Qsg/cy
g is the length of the green period at the junction and cy is the cycle length in the same units
x is the degree of saturation = V/Qj
JA is a delay parameter

For a more detailed consideration of flow-delay relationships see MT 351 and following pages.

Considering junctions as nodes implies that all turning movements are possible and at no cost/delay. In practice, some turning movements may be much more difficult to perform than others; indeed, some turning movements may not be allowed at all. In order to represent these features of real road networks better, it is possible to penalise and/or ban some turning movements. This is very important when the network described is an urban one with a variety of junction control methods and banned turns.

In the case of public-transport networks an additional level of detail is required. The modeller must specify the network structure corresponding to the services offered. These will be coded as a sequence of nodes visited by the service (bus, rail), normally with each node representing a suitable stop or station. Junctions without bus stops can, therefore, be excluded from the public-transport network unless they are needed for the accurate representation of delay. Two types of extra links are often added to public-transport networks. These are walk links, representing the parts of a journey using public transport made on foot, and links to model the additional costs associated with transferring from one service (or mode) to another.

The representation of fares in a public transport network can be quite complex depending on the fare structure: flat, zonal, by distance, etc. The representation of a toll or charge is usually done on the corresponding link. It should be represented preferably as a monetary cost, not as an equivalent delay, although software may treat it internally as such. The reasons for this will become apparent as we discuss willingness to pay: different levels of willingness to pay will imply different levels of delay and this creates difficulties whenever the value and location of tolls is to be changed.

3.8   The classic four stage model

The main structure for the classic transport model is represented in Figure 12. This structure is, in effect, a result from practice in the 1960s and consolidated in the 1970s, a period characterised by applying vast amounts of theory to extremely small amounts of data. This approach has remained more or less unaltered despite major improvements in modelling theory and techniques since then[21]. The approach starts by considering a zoning and network system (supply), and the collection and coding of planning, calibration and validation data representing the activity system. These data would include base-year levels for population of different types in each zone of the study area as well as levels of economic activity including employment, shopping space, educational and recreational facilities. These data are then used to estimate a model of the total number of trips generated and attracted by each zone of the study area (*trip generation*).

The next step is the allocation of these trips to particular destinations, in other words their *distribution* over space, thus producing a trip matrix or trip table. The following stage normally involves modelling the choice of mode and this result in *modal split*, i.e. the allocation of trips in the matrix to different modes. Finally, the last stage in the classic model requires the *assignment* of the trips by each mode to their corresponding networks: typically private and public transport.

---

[21] Only now we are seeing the promise of being able to use much larger sampling rates through the use of mobile phone data and other passive sensors; practice is likely to evolve as a result.

The classic transport model

FIGURE 12 CLASSIC TRANSPORT MODEL

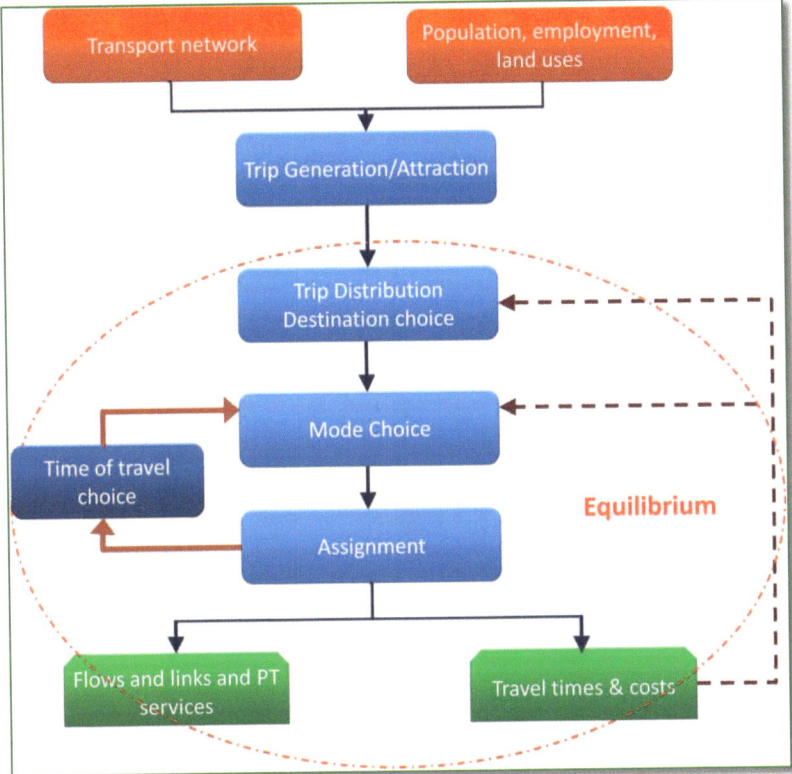

The classic model is presented as a sequence of four sub-models: trip generation, distribution, modal split and assignment plus, when appropriate, a time of travel sub-model. It is generally recognised that travel decisions are not actually taken in this type of sequence; a contemporary view is that the 'location' of each sub-model depends on the form of the utility function assumed to govern all these travel choices. Moreover, the four-stage model is seen as concentrating attention on only a limited range of travellers' responses.

The four-stage sequential model provides a point of reference to contrast alternative methods, even if they are sometimes five-stage or two-stage models. For example, some contemporary approaches attempt to treat simultaneously the choices of trip frequency (trips per week), destination and mode of travel thus collapsing trip generation, distribution and mode choice in one single model.

Once the model has been calibrated and validated for base-year conditions it can be applied to one or more planning horizons. In order to do this it is necessary to develop *scenarios* (defined roughly by the allocation of future population and economic activity over space) and interventions (for example a new metro or toll road). Having prepared realistic scenarios and interventions for testing, the same sequence of models is run again to simulate their performance.

An important issue in the classic four-stage model is the consistent use of variables influencing demand. For example, at the end of the traffic assignment stage new flow levels, and therefore new travel times, will be obtained. These are unlikely to be the same travel times assumed when the distribution and mode choice models were run, at least when the models are used in forecasting mode. This seems to call for the re-run of the distribution and modal-split models based now on the new travel times. The subsequent application of the assignment model may well result in a new set of travel times; in general the naive feed-back of the model times (costs) does not lead to a stable set of distribution, modal split and assignment models with consistent travel times. This problem is treated in some detail in MT 404 and subsequent pages. Consistency is required to obtain unique and interpretable solutions.

It is recognised, however, that the equilibrium so described does not happen in practice. Reality is noisier and travellers lack the perfect information required to reach a stable equilibrium.

3.9 Induced demand

There have been plenty of arguments about the so-called "induced demand", that is new trips that materialise **because** of an intervention, perhaps a new road. First of all, the term is relative to what has been considered in the model. Additional car trips on a corridor may occur because these are trips that have been diverted (changed destination, changed mode, changed time of travel or all of them) to take advantage of a new road. If the responses were not accounted for in the model they will appear as "new trips".

Pure induced traffic is the result of additional trips being generated because of the increased accessibility. This may or may not have been included as a feature of the trip generation models.

Most strategic transport models ignore induced trips but they are sometimes used, without defining them carefully enough, in T&R studies for transport concessions. As such, they will be discussed in Part III.

3.10 Calibration and validation

All useful models need calibration and validation. Calibration is the task of finding the set of parameters in the model that are able to represent reality best, for example finding the best values for $a_{1}...a_{6}$ in the formulation of generalised costs. This concept is related to that of model estimation. Calibrating a model requires choosing a defined set of parameters in order to optimise one or more *goodness-of-fit* measures that are a function of the observed data. Estimation is more general and may include examining some specification issues (e.g. Multinomial or Nested Logit) and the best functional form and parameter set (e.g. eliminating non-significant variables).

Calibration or estimation is not a demanding enough tests for the value of a model. Because the large majority of transport models have been built on the basis of *cross-sectional* data (a snapshot in time when the data was collected), there has been a tendency to interpret model *validation* exclusively in terms of the goodness-of-fit achieved between observed behaviour and base-year model results. Although this is a *necessary* it is by no means a *sufficient* condition for model validation.

The more rigorous version of validation is to use the model to predict a previous state of the transport system, perhaps 10 years ago (backcasting), and compare the results with known conditions at the time. It is rare to have the data and resources to undertake this exercise. A milder version of this is to contrast results of the models with data not used in the calibration, for example a set of traffic counts collected but ignored during calibration. This is often not enough; a second test is to exercise the model with alternative futures and confirm that the responses are logical and explainable.

It must be said that no amount of validation work will ever guarantee that the model is "correct" true or error-free. Over-calibration is particularly dangerous, especially if matrix estimation using traffic counts is employed. Not only it may give the impression of an ability to reproduce reality that is inexistent but it may also distort the trip matrix too much to make it unreliable. Moreover, future conditions are likely to differ significantly from present ones even in terms of solid concepts like car ownership and journey to work.

Sadly, it is not unusual to discover errors in the best model much later, when it is being used in earnest to project traffic and revenue. This is because the forecasting mode "exercises" the model in ways that were not previously tested. It may even be said that most models do contain one or more mistakes in them. They may not be important, as otherwise they would have been found during calibration, validation and forecasting exercises; it is just that no one has teased them out yet.

Surveys to establish the Base Year

> "Oh, people can come up with statistics to prove anything, Kent. 14% of people know that!" **Homer Simpson**

4. SURVEYS TO ESTABLISH THE BASE YEAR

4.1 The Base Year

Any forecasting exercise starts by establishing a strong modelling platform on the Base Year. This is likely to be within 12 months of the tender date and should be based on two key elements: a solid understanding of the context for the project and good data to support the development of a well-estimated model.

Alas, in the transport field we often have to make do with poor and limited data, a somewhat noisy foundation for modelling efforts. This chapter describes the most common sources of data and how this is collected and processed to support our modelling effort.

4.2 Understanding the context

As in any other type of study understanding the context is paramount. The professionals undertaking the modelling and T&R forecasts must get to know the area where the transport concession is to be implemented. One of the key lessons I learnt from my colleagues at Steer Davies Gleave was the importance of "walking the alignment", getting to know the terrain, what type of activities take place in the area, what type of traveller uses the road and public transport systems nearby.

I believe we do not exercise our duty of care to our clients unless we get to understand the area and the context well enough and this usually requires a site visit, accompanied by somebody that knows it well; Street View is not enough. Walking is only possible for relatively short alignments; vehicles will be used for longer ones. It is useful to undertake site visits together with other professionals involved in the tender: financial analysis, road or rail infrastructure engineers and so on. What you learn about the condition of existing infrastructure may help you in modelling future networks and develop alternative scenarios (existing bridges strengthened and widened or remain the same; how dynamic and efficient are incumbent operators).

In the case of a future toll road one would look at the alternatives, tolled or otherwise. Their characteristics, speeds, capacities, gradients, quality of pavement and signage, availability of rest stations and fuel, friction from buildings, road furniture, pedestrians, vendors, parked vehicles. Today it is easy to measure speeds at the same time using portable GPS devices, even smartphones; take some photographs to remind you later of existing conditions (and illustrate presentations). Consider what is provided for public transport and long distance coaches: stops, are they well designed and used? What is going to be provided in the new road? Consider freight movements: current access to plants, warehouses, farms. Any special facilities for lorries? Weighbridge stations? Lorry operating costs are more sensitive than cars to gradients, stops, poor pavement quality.

In the case of an existing toll road you will also look at the operation of the facility itself. Visit the Control Room and the toll plazas; is there any evidence of over manning or poor audit trails for toll collection? Is the toll collection technology working well (detectors, classifiers, computer systems, reporting)? Obviously, very few professionals can observe well **all** these details but in trying you will develop your observation skills and experience.

In the case of a future public transport and rail concession the observations above are still critical. In addition to them you should try to understand the proficiency of the incumbent operators and what they feel about the proposed new service. Are their vehicles in good shape, overcrowded, with good information? Are routes fixed or flexible; how well do they penetrate into residential, education and employment areas? How much are fares and how are they collected, how much (if any) is retained by the driver/conductor? How much are bicycles and motorcycles/mopeds used in the area? Is it safe to walk at all times? What is the condition of the road surface, the level of safety and security of people and goods? These observations will give you ideas on how best to represent the competition to the new mode.

Consider the proposed alignment for the new service. Does it make sense, could it be improved? Is the right of way secured and not encroached? Does it provide access to what really matters or has it been decided because it was easy to provide the land? Is there evidence of solid prospects for new developments near the alignment?

Are the incumbents big companies or owner operators? Is there any evidence or hearsay of collusion and forced protection of routes/services? These issues will give you some idea of how difficult it will be for the Government to deliver on any promises, for example of re-organising services to feed the new mode rather than compete with it. Many semi-informal operations offer a good demand-responsive service; when competing with formal services they reflect unmet demand and are good pointers for where improvements are needed.

All of these observations are mostly subjective but will be extremely valuable in identifying risks, setting up the model and in providing

Surveys to establish the Base Year

T&R projections for the future. It will also be necessary to have solid data to support this understanding.

4.3 Data collation

The Procuring body will normally provide a "data room" as a depository of all the background information and tender conditions that can be made available to bidders and financial institutions. The quality and coverage of this data is very important although it will normally be provided without guarantees to its accuracy. The more comprehensive this data room is, the lower the bidding costs and low bidding costs will encourage greater and more intelligent competition. Poor basic data will be correctly perceived as a source of risk and priced accordingly.

The Government as Procuring Authority can achieve a great deal in terms of protecting the welfare of its citizens through the provision of a well stocked and documented data room. Of particular value will be the provision of the transport model that has been used to design the future concession. This reference model should have been produced in one of the five internationally used software packages (SATURN, CUBE, EMME, TransCAD and VISUM), be well documented and available in a usable electronic format. For obvious reasons it will be offered "as is" with no guarantees to its accuracy or realism. Very often, these models are based on strategic planning efforts and they do not pay enough attention to accurate delay estimation and junction performance; their zoning systems may be too coarse and may not offer sufficient segmentation by willingness to pay. Bidders will wish to refine these models to reduce risk and gain some competitive advantage with more reliable revenue estimates.

Another critical information that should be in the data room are the plans and prospects for population and economic activity growth and, in particular, transport plans. These should describe what is planned in terms of new roads, rail and transport facilities with alignment, characteristics (speed, capacities) and dates for implementation.

Data rooms nowadays are mostly virtual, a website with controlled access, but in a few cases some material will still be available in hard copy only. The fact that data may be abundant does not make it accurate. In my experience, data that is not regularly used for decision-making is more likely to contain errors. This is typically the case for large collections of traffic counts where only a few are really checked thoroughly enough.

One should try to collate other useful information, either because it is not available in the data room or to confirm the accuracy of what is available. Data or reports on the local economy and its prospects as well as income distribution information will be particularly valuable. The same applies to any socio-economic information that can be gathered from census or other surveys. If there has been a household survey in the region this is likely to be available in the data room.

Traffic and passenger counts on permanent sites or ticket turnstiles will be necessary to obtain seasonal variation profiles and to estimate annual traffic and revenue figures via annualisation factors.

4.4　Time series

Time series data are of high value to estimate rates of growth, past and future. This can take the form of traffic counts on different years at the same location, or ticketing and revenue information from public transport operators. Profiles of toll road traffic on nearby facilities help identifying any differences between tolled and untolled traffic growth.

Population growth and location will also be relevant together with evolution of the local economy. What type of activity is likely to locate in the region/area? Any real prospects? The bidding team will scan the news to get the pulse of the area, understand public opinion in respect of the proposed concession and gather low level intelligence on future prospects.

Of particular interest will be vehicle ownership time series, and their reliability. If one is planning an Open Road Tolled facility there will be many other issues to track: validity and currency of the vehicle data base, record of enforcement of fines, use of speed cameras and record of fines collected, general rate of bad debts (credit cards, payment of utilities), legibility of number plates, etc. There may be scope for automatic number plate surveys at key locations to ascertain frequent usage. An alternative to this would be the equivalent Bluetooth surveys, with a smaller and less well defined sample rate.

4.5　Modelled periods

An important early decision is the time periods to model. The objective is to identify time periods where the demand and operating conditions remain reasonably consistent. In the case of an urban project, these are likely to include the AM peak, the PM peak, some inter-peak period, night and one or two week end periods, a total of 5 or 6 periods. The periods may be defined as hour long or perhaps longer to capture most of the relevant demand and flows. Three-hour periods are common. It cases with more complex trip patterns it may be necessary to model additional periods.

Ticketing information, if available, can help define public transport modelled periods but more often than not this information is not sufficiently detailed. The profile of traffic counts will usually helps define modelling periods for all modes.

In the case of interurban projects it may be more difficult to define modelled periods. For very long roads the peak may happen in different places at the same time so a trip may encounter a mix of congested and uncongested conditions en-route. Luckily in this respect, few concessions cover very long toll roads but there are exceptions, like the Autopista del Sol in México and Ruta del Sol in Colombia. In these cases one solution is to expect that congestion is not a main driver and model a nominal hour or 16 or 24 hour day. There are also other solutions that deal with this problem taking advantage of the specific context of each road.

In the case of interurban rail the problem is similar. If the tender is for franchise to operate an existing service then data on its current demand profile will be available. The problem is more difficult for a completely new facility.

4.6 Sampling

In most cases specific data collection requires sampling. *Modelling Transport* provides a good introduction to the issue and this will not be discussed further here. It is important to recognise, however, that all sampling theory assumes that you are making observations from a single population. In our case the population is an assembly of trips undertaken on different days accepting the Activity Regularity Assumption.

Some days in the year are expected to be representative of relevant travel conditions (or representative days). These are usually Tue-Wed-Thu on times of the year when schools and universities are in session, there are no strikes/demonstrations, there are no close holidays and the weather is "normal". Other working days are slightly different but these differences are considered not material enough to require a specific model[22]; in other words, the transport system can cope with these peculiarities in demand without major upheavals.

These assumptions may be acceptable for planning purposes but less so for projects where traffic and revenue forecasts are critical. In these cases it is necessary to collate sufficient time series data to

---

[22] This depends, obviously, on the size of the problem. In some projects it is necessary to model specifically difficult days like the return from Summer holidays, or conditions around major events.

improve decisions on where and when to organise surveys and what set of periods must be modelled.

The next figure illustrates a study area around a proposed new service (toll road, rail or urban public transport) and the main movements generating the relevant trip patterns. The study area is assumed surrounded by a cordon, or at least including a cordon nears its external boundaries. There are different types of trips to be surveyed: residents and non-residents; some move entirely within the study area whilst others cross the cordon. Each type of movement usually requires a different type of survey or at least analysis.

One can specify *internal* cordons as well as *screen lines* (i.e. an artificial divide following a natural or artificial boundary with few crossings, such as a river or a railway line), to be able to intercept more relevant trips.

FIGURE 13 SURVEYS NEEDED TO OBTAIN TRIP PATTERNS

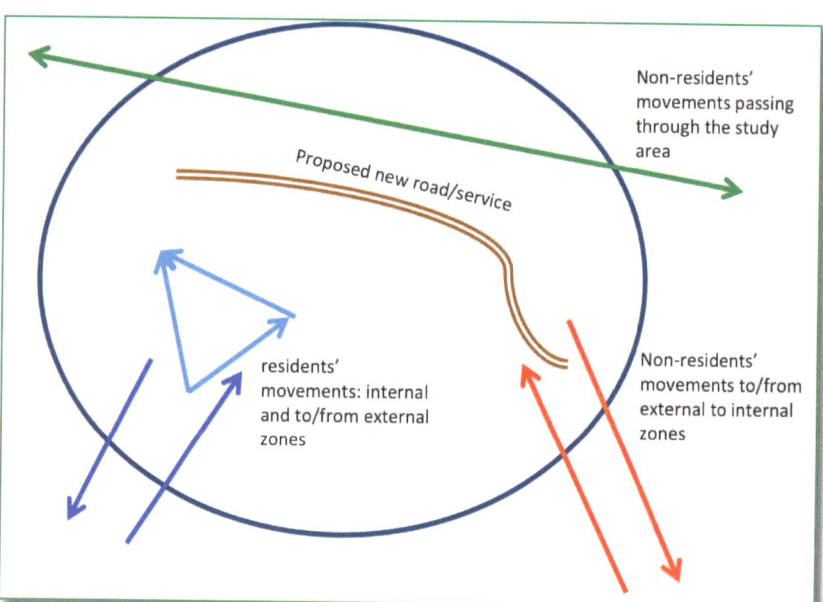

Figure 13 implies that the following surveys would be of interest:
- *Household survey*: trips and tours made by all household members by all modes of transport both within the study area and leaving/arriving to the area during the survey period
- *Intercept surveys, external cordon*: trips by people crossing the study area border, particularly non-residents of the study area.

Surveys to establish the Base Year

- *Intercept surveys, internal cordons and screen lines*: these are required to observe trips by non-residents, to verify household data and to provide a larger sample of trips at reasonable cost.
- *Traffic and person counts*: they are low cost and are required for calibration, validation and for further checks to other surveys.

4.7 Surveys

Surveys are required to establish a set of base year trip matrices, develop a well-calibrated network and gain an understanding of how travellers choose between routes, modes and potentially destinations and time to travel. They are generally expensive and take longer to complete than planned; quality is often poorer than it should be.

Home interviews

These are complex and very expensive surveys that take time to plan, deliver and analyse. They usually reflect samples of 1-3% of the households although a lot can be achieved with smaller sample, as limited as 3000 households. A quick review of these methods is available in MT 75 and beyond. Even with a small sample, they are expensive and some of the most interesting households, the very poor and the very wealthy, are very difficult to interview.

Household or Home Interviews are particularly useful to get complete information about movements in a day, not just intercepting trips. They also capture walking and cycling trips and provide valuable information to estimate motorcycle and car ownership models. In more general terms, trip generation (in contrast with trip growth) models are mostly based on data from Household Surveys.

It is very unlikely that a consortia bidding for a concession would undertake such survey because of the time and costs involved. Even a Procuring Authority will be reluctant to undertake such a task. If such a survey is available, it will be more likely that a city planning effort has required it.

However, if such survey exists, it is also likely that the model based on it will also exist and, in any intelligent situation, this will also be available for inspection and potential use and adaptation by bidders.

In any case, many transport concessions have been studied, and will continue to be studied, without the benefit from household surveys; this has not been the reason for poor forecasts.

Intercept surveys

This type of survey is faster and less expensive method for obtaining trip matrices and other trip patterns. They can take the form of *roadside* or *on-board interviews,* the latter for public transport and intercity rail concessions.

Roadside Interviews. Involve asking a sample of drivers and passengers of vehicles (e.g. cars, goods vehicles) crossing a roadside station, a limited set of questions; these include at least origin, destination and trip purpose. Other information such as age, sex and income is also desirable but seldom requested due to time limitations; however, well-trained interviewers can easily add at least part of these data from simple observation of the vehicle and occupants. In any case, resist the temptation to add more questions to the survey, "just in case they become useful". They will only reduce the quality of the responses.

The conduct of these interviews requires a good deal of organisation and planning to avoid unnecessary delays, ensure safety and deliver quality results. The identification of suitable sites, co-ordination with the police and arrangements for lighting and supervision are important elements in the success of these surveys. It is good advice to insist that a member of the modelling team be present during the execution of these surveys, at least on an occasional basis. There is too much scope for filling in forms on the cheap, anywhere in the world.

In respect of sample size, most texts recommend this table from Modelling Transport:

TABLE 1 SAMPLE SIZE FOR ROADSIDE INTERVIEWS

Estimated observed flow (passengers/period)	Sample size (%)
900 or more	10.0 (1 in 10)
700 to 899	12.5 (1 in 8)
500 to 699	16.6 (1 in 6)
300 to 499	25.0 (1 in 4)
200 to 299	33.3 (1 in 3)
1 to 199	50.0 (1 in 2)

On-board passenger surveys. This is sometimes a misnomer as some of these surveys are undertaken at stations or stops. The objective is the same as roadside interviews and the questions are the same with one exception. It is important to ask also about the availability of a vehicle at home (car and motorcycle). The decision whether to interview on-board or at stops depends on conditions. If buses or trains are too crowded or permission to collect data on-board is not forthcoming, it

Surveys to establish the Base Year

will be nigh impossible to interview. On the other hand if there were too many stations/stops (in particular if they are informal in some areas) it would not be efficient to survey on all of them. Interviews at stops require a different expansion method.

It seems redundant to mention that when undertaking intercept surveys (road and public transport) somebody should be performing vehicle/passenger counts at the same time to obtain an expansion factor. Sadly, I have seen this omitted in more cases than I would like to admit.

Corrections, blending and expansion. Expansion should be undertaken at each site on the basis of the effective sampling rate in each location, that is a different one for cars, motorcycles, buses/coaches (with estimates of passenger loads) and trucks of different sizes. Expansion may also be possible from ticketing or toll transactions if available.

Intercept surveys suffer, potentially, from the problem of double or multiple counting. This happens because the same, or equivalent, trip is intercepted and surveyed two or more times (for example on different days). If one expands the sample by the sampling ratio in each location these doubly counted trips will be over-represented in the resulting trip matrix.

In simple cases it may be possible to correct this by hand on the spreadsheet used to handle the sample expansion. In this case one would use the (weighted) average expansion factor for such Origin Destination pairs. In more complex cases, when there is more than one route between intercept points, the best approach is to apply this correction over a reasonably calibrated network.

In some cases, it will be necessary to combine, blend, trip matrices obtained from different sources, perhaps household and intercept surveys. This is best done weighted by one over expansion factors, but this is not always possible as they may be unknown; for example one source may be an expanded (and perhaps in-filled) set of surveys undertaken a few years back.

This blending is also best undertaken on a solid, well calibrated, network. It may well be combined with trip matrix estimation techniques from traffic counts. To formalise this consider:

T_{ij} is the matrix to estimate;

Na_{ij} is the set of survey locations that intercept the Origin Destination (OD) pair ij;

p_{ij}^{a} is the proportion of trips between i and j that travel over link a;

s_{ij}^{a} is the number of unexpanded trips between i and j observed at point a

r^{a}

is the sampling rate at point a.

The best estimate of the expanded trips is obtained minimising the following formulation:

$$\text{Min} \sum_{Na_{ij}} p^a_{ij} \left(T_{ij} - \frac{s^a_{ij}}{p^a_{ij} r^a} \right)^2$$

The solution to this problem is:

$$T_{ij} = \frac{\sum_{Na_{ij}} \frac{s^a_{ij}}{r^a}}{\sum_{Na_{ij}} p^a_{ij}}$$

Note this is a simple relationship but its application requires estimates of p^a_{ij}. This, in practice, requires a good network and, if congestion is present, a reasonable trip matrix to start with.

Travel time surveys

A good model should be able to reproduce observations of link flows and travel times. The latter are important as travel time savings are the main drivers of new concessions. Travel time surveys serve two complementary purposes. First, they serve to support the views of the analyst about the best travel time-flow curve to assign to each link in the network. Second, they are used to ensure the final model is able to reproduce observed travel times, and therefore route and mode choice, with reasonable accuracy.

To satisfy the first objective it is necessary to undertake travel time surveys during free flow conditions (mostly at a late night, often 2-4 in the morning) and also at other, more congested, times. The second objective requires detailed and accurate travel time for each modelling period.

Travel times can be divided into:
- Running times, whilst the vehicle is moving
- Delays, when the vehicle is stopped because of congestion or traffic control measures (traffic lights, stop signs, to board or alight passengers, etc.)

Signal control and junction delays result in high travel time variability. Therefore, it is preferable to observe travel times on segments covering several junctions, usually a kilometre or so. The most common technique for travel time measurements is known as the "moving observer method". Nowadays this is undertaken using a GPS unit and then mapping times onto a network. This requires a driver only and her task is to maintain the average speed of the relevant traffic: cars, trucks or buses depending on the objective. GPS data can identify stops but not necessarily the reason for this. The observer may be able to record voice messages or press special keys to indicate the cause of the stop. Sometimes this survey can be complemented by video recording to get also an idea of road surface and lateral friction.

As a general rule it is recommended to repeat 4 to 6 times the number of runs for each particular period and section. To be useful for the objective of choosing travel time-flow relationships it will be necessary to count traffic at the same time but this may only be necessary for representative links in each category. More details on the design of these surveys are available in MT 93.

Other surveys

Depending on the project it may be advantageous to undertake other type of surveys. These may include non-resident surveys, attitude surveys, number plate surveys, phone interviews, Stated Preference surveys (discussed in the next chapter) and the use of new technologies. Particularly interesting are passive methods, those that do not require any active participation on the part of the traveller as this is increasingly unwelcomed in most places.

Non-resident surveys. For places with a large number of visitors one needs to consider how best to capture their trips through either just intercept surveys or collecting data at hotels, airports, main stations. Modelling these trips will be a challenge.

Number plate surveys. It is possible to observe the registration or number plate of vehicles at different locations in the network either using human observers or Automatic Number Plate Recognition (ANPR or ALPR for License plates). One would tend to use ANPR either directly or mediated by high quality digital video recordings. Software will then match number plates and times and will construct point-to-point trip matrices and travel times between the places where the number plates were recorded. These partial matrices can then be contrasted with estimated ones to confirm and potentially improve them.

A limitation of this method is the number of locations where recordings can be organised simultaneously. In the end, not all trips are matched (some begin or end without crossing a second point) and therefore not all travel times and trip tables are established. Sample rates, however, are generally quite good.

Bluetooth surveys. It is currently possible to locate Bluetooth sensors in a way analogous to a number plate surveys. The sensors identify the MAC (hardware) number of each Bluetooth device, anonymised if required. Travel times and partial (point-to-point) matrices are obtained in this way. Bluetooth provides a smaller sample than number plates and there may be more than one such device in a vehicle. However, this is a low cost survey method.

Note that both these passive methods require a bit of data cleaning. The raw data cannot differentiate between a long inter-point times because of congestion from journeys where the driver stopped to buy a cup of coffee. These exceptional matches must be weeded out of the data before analysis.

Smart card data. The use of smart cards for payment of public transport and other services generates some valuable data. It is possible, for example, to estimate stop-to-stop matrices using this source. This is easier if the traveller validates both on boarding and alighting the service. If she only validates on boarding (as in most bus services) then the next validated boarding can be used to estimate the end of the first trip. This type of data is seldom available to institutions other than operators and Government. Moreover, processing it requires data mining skills and software not common in our field.

Mobile phone data. The normal operation of mobile phones requires knowledge of where the unit is to route the call or message via the nearest mast/antenna. This information is activated when a call or a message is sent/received and also at some regular intervals or because the phone has moved from one area to another. Phone location, in this sense, is specified in terms of the nearest antenna; many of these are directional and in some cases the information on the strength of the signal can be used to estimate distance to the mast. This information is always anonymised, sometimes twice over. It is always possible to establish a relationship between antenna's location and a transport model zoning system.

Using this type of information is complex and requires good understanding of how a particular mobile phone company operates in this respect. In recent years different companies have tried to offer a service using this information and provide both speeds and trip matrices. Some have been more successful than others and this form of data has already been used in traffic and revenue studies.

The attraction of this type of data is enormous. Companies like Airsage (www.airsage.com) offer this service in the US and can also supply estimates for journey purposes, household income levels and any choice of time periods and days of the year. The activities at each trip end are estimated on their duration, time of day, census data and location land use.

This type of data is likely to revolutionise not only the modelling of traffic and revenue for transport concessions but also more conventional planning and project model development.

Phone interviews. Increasingly unpopular and difficult to control for sampling, this type of survey is cheaper than face to face and may provide useful information. Market research firms have well-established routines for delivering these surveys and can do this at relatively low cost. They may be used to ascertain familiarity with some scheme or facility, attitudes towards charging (of something previously thought free) and even some components from a conventional household survey.

Web base interviews. There are several software packages to assist the implementation of web-based surveys. Conventional attitudinal and Stated Preference surveys can be undertaken in this way. To control for sampling numbered flyers can be distributed to identified population segments and the numbers must be entered to access the survey; this allows correcting for some sample bias.

Other sources. Mapping and Route Guidance companies are starting to commercialise some of the information they collect as a matter of course. It is certainly worthwhile investigating what is available locally taken care to confirm the validity of the data for modelling purposes; not everybody considers speed, for example, in the same way; some measure spot speeds whilst others measure travel times including stops.

4.8   Traffic counts

Classified traffic counts are inexpensive to collect and very valuable to calibrate models. Moreover, they are often available and collected regularly by local authorities to optimise traffic control, organise maintenance, relate to accidents and generally obtain a picture of traffic on the network.

Quality is variable. In some cases axle counts is all that is collected as they are easily obtained from tube detectors. In other cases automatic classified counts are available. These are much more useful, especially if classification is consistent with the proposed toll structure. Classification by spot speed is generally less useful and travel time surveys are to be preferred.

Counts from traffic control systems may be available but it is important to confirm whether they mean the same as manual counts as sometimes they refer to occupancy, a less useful measure in this respect.

Automatic traffic counts need calibration and validation by human observation (e.g. video-based) given the level of errors present in most "ad hoc" vehicle classification and counting technologies. Automatic traffic counts that are not used to make decisions are likely to be less reliable than those used in earnest and therefore inspected with greater tenacity.

Additional traffic counts would be collected to confirm screenlines, especially across the corridor of the prospective facility and also to provide a basis for updating or correcting trip matrices. Data from toll plazas, where available, is particularly useful as it provides a good profile of demand over time.

4.9 Road and service surveys

In some cases it will be necessary to get an up to date view of the quality and characteristics of the road surface, as it will affect speeds and the future re-routing of traffic. This would be accompanied by a review of signage and traffic control devices. In the case of public transport projects, it may be desirable to survey the services offered by current companies, their frequency, quality and reliability.

4.10 Quality

Surveys are usually expensive so it is very tempting to try to cut costs. Saving some money on survey quality will cost many times over in frustrating corrections and supplementary work (if one is lucky to spots the problems) or worse in poor modelling and forecasting (if they are not spotted).

Surveys are usually carried out by local consultants and specialists as they know the lay of the land, the procedures to follow and can recruit the temporary workers more easily and cheaply. Alas, the number of surveys these companies have undertaken is not necessarily a guarantee of the quality of their work.

It is important, therefore, that when specifying the work the local consultants are asked to describe and cost their Quality Assurance (QA) programme. Evidence of good training, constant presence of supervisors during surveys, and a payment system that rewards accuracy, are key. Equally important is the frequent and unannounced presence of the analysts that will use the data so collected. A long elapsed time between data collection and reporting is often an indication of poor quality.

Surveys to establish the Base Year

4.11 Analysis

It is always advisable to allocate resources for data collection, at least to confirm independently the data available in the data room. Inevitably, the analysis of all this information, data room and fresh data, will have to recognise that all data is imperfect and to an extent noisy.

The main products from these data efforts are:
- Origin Destination matrices by the relevant modes.
- Traffic and passenger counts to validate and update trip matrices for different time periods and modes as required.
- Travel times to validate model and potentially to determine the best travel time flow relationships.
- Daily and seasonal demand profiles to identify modelling time periods and annualisation factors.
- Variability of travel times (important for some projects).
- Vehicle ownership, availability and growth data.
- Effective frequencies, load factors and travel times for existing public transport services.
- Collate any information on willingness to pay.
- Collate information on potential competitors, economic development and transport plans.
- Information on land uses, population, employment and prospects for the future.

An effort will have to be made to put all data on a common basis and the most critical will be the production of base year trip matrices.

4.12 Trip matrix building

The production of up to date trip matrices is one of the key objectives for the base year surveys and data collection. They should be constructed for the relevant modes and time periods and disaggregated by willingness to pay tolls or fares, as discussed in the next chapter. This may also involve disaggregation by journey purpose and, in the case of public transport schemes, vehicle availability.

The task of producing these up to date matrices is likely to be finalised using matrix estimation from traffic and person counts methods. These methods are discussed in some detail in section 12.4 of Modelling Transport (MT 435+). All of these methods correct an initial estimate of the trip matrices (from another model, partial surveys or another year) using traffic counts and other similar information, for example independently estimated trip ends or ticketing information. This is a powerful but tricky to use technique.

It is important to recognise at the outset that traffic counts alone are not enough to determine a unique trip matrix. There are always more

OD pairs than independent traffic counts and this means that there will be more than one tip matrix capable of producing the same traffic counts after assignment. There are two possible approaches to define a single tip matrix consistent with the information contained in traffic counts. We can assume a particular model form, for example a Gravity Model, and estimate its parameters using traffic counts; or we can use a probabilistic approach and select a trip matrix because it is more likely in some sense. The first approach can be called "structured" as it needs an assumption about model form (a structure) whereas the second can be called "unstructured" or probabilistic.

Willumsen developed one of the earliest unstructured approaches[23] based on entropy maximisation principles. The estimated matrix can be said to be the most likely consistent with information in the counts and in a prior matrix if available. The resulting model can be used to explain some of the limitations of such an approach. The model can be written as:

$$T_{ij} = t_{ij} \prod_a X_a^{p_{ij}^a}$$

Where t_{ij} is a prior or initially estimated matrix

X_a are adjustment factors, one for each counts a

p_a^{ij} is the proportion of trips between i and j that travel over link a; it takes values between 0 and 1, both extremes are common.

$\prod_a$ indicates the product over all the counted links a.

Note that here the prior trip matrix provides a starting structure and its quality strongly influences the reliability of the result. The original method performed iterative corrections on the prior matrix until a reasonable match to the traffic counts was obtained. Modern software allows greater control, allocating different levels of confidence (weights) to different sources of data and perhaps monitoring the trip length distribution of the adjusted matrix. They will also allow adjusting separate component matrices (by willingness to pay or journey purpose) to traffic counts that do not contain that distinction or adjust only partial matrices retaining as fixed fully observed OD pairs.

---

[23] Willumsen, L.G. (1978) O-D matrix from network data: a comparison of alternative methods for their estimation. Proc. of PTRC 6th Summer Annual Meeting, Vol P168, pp 294-304, Warwick. PTRC Education and Research Services, London

It is advisable to make sure that all traffic counts have a common date adjusting those that do not. It is good practice not to use <u>all</u> available traffic counts to adjust the matrices and to leave some, say 5 - 10% of them, unused for validation of the results.

It is important not to over-adjust the trip matrices. Attempts to match traffic counts beyond their own natural variability (around 10%) are not warranted. See also comments later on in this chapter on the limits to the accuracy of trip matrices; both counts and trip tables are never error-free. Checking that the original trip length distribution is not distorted much is a healthy concern to avoid over-fitting the matrices. For more details on care with matrix estimation check Modelling Transport.

4.13 Calibration and Validation

Calibration of a model is not completed with the estimation of the most accurate trip matrices for the base year. It is also necessary to confirm that travel times are well reproduced and that other aspects of the model that may be relevant, for example mode choice, are also well estimated.

The calibration stage should not be just a mechanical process to improve goodness-of-fit with observed data. It should involve the analyst in gaining a deeper understanding of the drivers of demand in the area, its future prospects and the main sources of future uncertainty. Overemphasis on goodness-of-fit exaggerates the value of a well-calibrated model.

There are several ways to demonstrate the good fit of a model. At the level of the trip matrices, it is useful to show broad travel patterns at an aggregate level superimposed on a map. This could be contrasted with an understanding of how the economy of the region works and identify any apparent anomalies. An example of this for long distance truck movements with focus on one city is shown in Figure 14.

FIGURE 14 LONG DISTANCE TRUCK MOVEMENTS

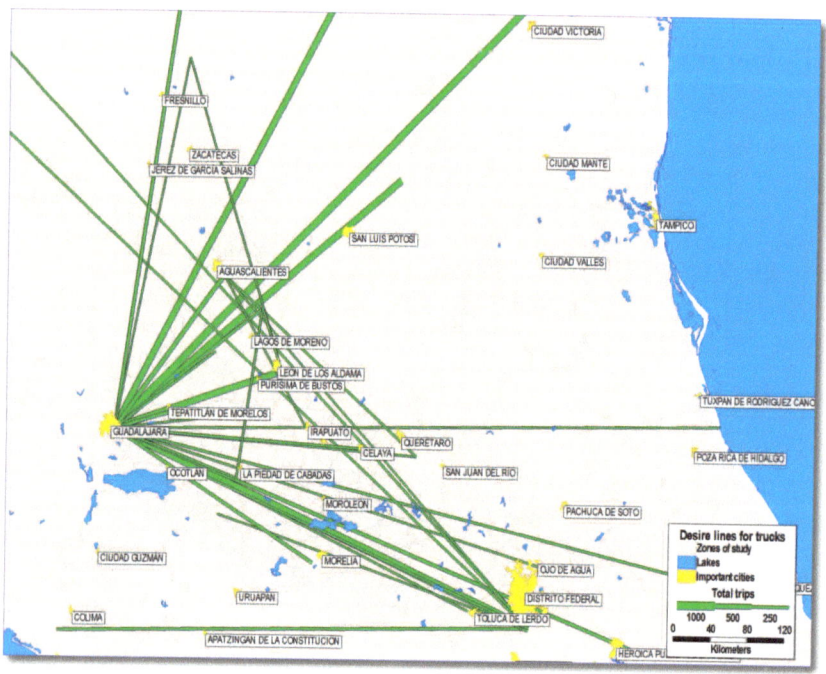

It is also useful to show observations against modelled values, as illustrated in Figure 15 for link flows. It is important to show R^2 (the closer to 1 the better) and the slope and intercept. The closer the slope to 1 the better (here is good at 0.97) and the closer the intercept to zero the better. However, R^2 above 0.98 are likely to indicate that the comparison is against counts that have been used to adjust trip tables; in this case R^2 only shows that the technique has been perhaps over-used. Ultimately, the cloud of points and the parameters above will help identify any bias in the results.

Surveys to establish the Base Year

FIGURE 15 MODELLED VERSUS OBSERVED TRAFFIC

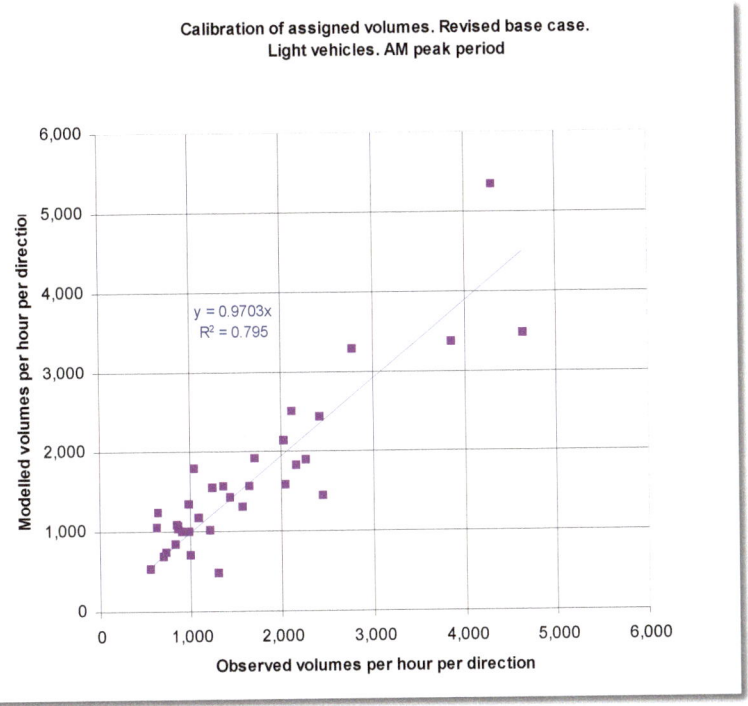

There are several numerical indices of goodness-of-fit, for example the Root Mean Squared Error RMSE

$$RMSE = \sqrt{\frac{1}{N}\sum_{k=1}^{N}(E_k - O_k)^2}$$

Where

E_k is an estimated or modelled value (flow on link k or O-D trips on k pair)

O_k is an observed value (counts on link k or trips observed in pair k).

N is the number of observations

The ratio of RMSE over the average number of counts or trips would be the percentage Root Mean Squared Error %RMSE.

A difficult issue is always how to account for variations in flows in a network when some of the volumes are very large (say on a motorway) and some display lower flows, for example on local links. The GEH "statistic" has been suggested to overcome this difficulty. The GEH measure is discussed in MT 386 and is defined as:

$$GEH = \sqrt{\frac{(O_i - E_i)^2}{0.5 \cdot (O_i + E_i)}}$$

where O_i are observed values and E_i modelled or estimated values for one variable i.

This indicator is not a-dimensional. This means that the recommendation below applies only to hourly traffic flows. If peak period (often 3 hours) or daily flows are used it will exaggerate the acceptability of the results. Equally, the pass criteria below should not be used for other purposes like, for example, total screen-line or cordon flows, for the same reason.

Guidance on what is required for a good model validation varies among countries. In general terms between 60% and 85% of the volumes in a traffic model should have a GEH less than 5.0. GEHs in the range of 5.0 to 10.0 may warrant investigation. If many GEH values are greater than 10.0, there is a high probability that there is a problem with the transport model, the data or both. In the case of screen-lines GEH values greater than 4.0 would indicate poor fit.

However, if the range of flows one is interested in is, say below 500 (an hour/day or whatever), these thresholds would be too generous and a more demanding one should be sought. Figure 16 illustrates how the GEH value changes for different variations in flows (5%, 10%, 20% and 30%) and at different flow levels (50 to 4000 vehicles/hour). This may help in interpreting GEH values for cases different from hourly link flows.

FIGURE 16 GEH VALUES FOR DIFFERENT VARIATIONS IN FLOW LEVELS

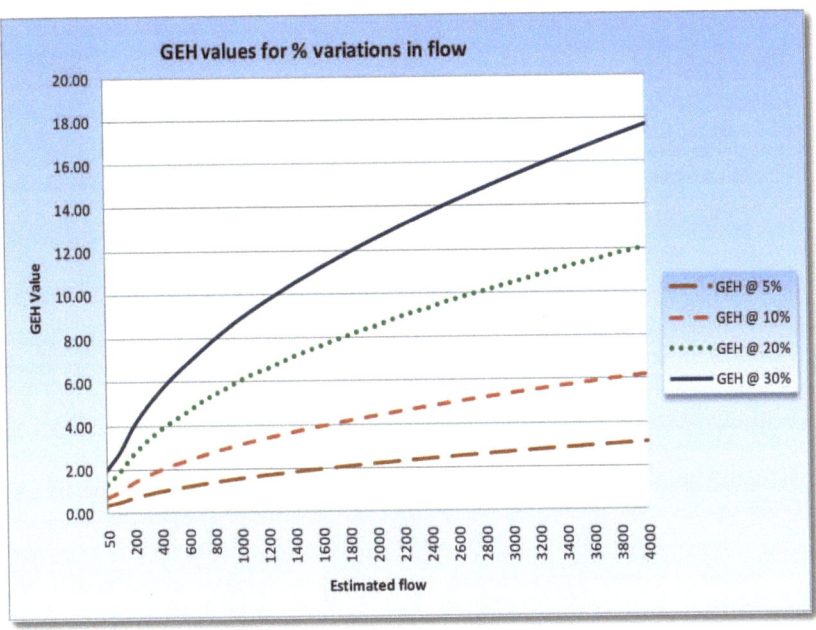

It must be remembered that when validating a trip matrix and model, for example via the GEH statistic, one should not use the same observed flows that were used to adjust and update the matrix in the first place.

The model should also be calibrated and validated against travel time (delays). This is usually undertaken comparing travel time along a route in the model and on an average of travel time runs, probably GPS. The best way of presenting these are to plot observed and modelled cumulative times along the routes travelled during the survey; this is illustrated in Figure 17. Again the R^2 value, the slope and the intercept will help establish an absence of bias in the model, for example that the model is not overestimating travel times on local roads.

FIGURE 17 MODEL VERSUS OBSERVATION TRAVEL TIME VALIDATION

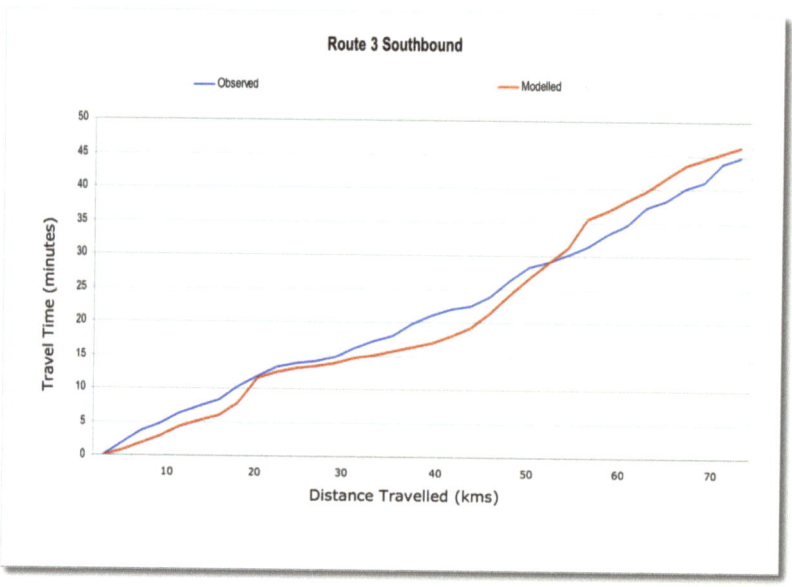

For public transport schemes it will be important to validate the mode choice model, for example using an approach similar to that shown in Figure 15 for OD pairs by mode rather than links. This task is made more difficult by the amount of noise and small sample in the Origin Destination matrices by mode. Therefore, comparisons of modelled against observed data are usually made at a more aggregate level.

4.14   Accuracy of trip matrices

People do not travel according to trip matrices, nor make journeys or tours; these are theoretical constructs by analysts; people just travel. Nevertheless, trip matrices are central to demand modelling so it is worth discussing how accurately we can possibly estimate them. The first problem is that we seldom define our target, a necessary element to any consideration of accuracy. In most areas subject to traffic congestion a good target would be a peak period (an hour or more) matrix; we rarely specify whether this will be a working day average peak period (say of a neutral week in the neutral month of October when schools and universities are active and there are no special festivities), or a representative peak on Monday, or any other choice. It is just a representative peak period. Without defining a true objective we cannot really discuss how accurately we approach it.

Surveys to establish the Base Year

Even assuming that we define our targets clearly there are at least three problems that limit accuracy: demand noise, supply noise and the day-to-day variability of trip matrices. Noise is inevitable but sadly we have not even tried to measure it. By demand noise I include vehicles not moving according to trip matrices: empty taxis cruising for clients, couriers, joy riders, refuse collection and postal vehicles, police and traffic inspectors, etc. We should also include those who would like to go somewhere but get lost or deliver/collect somebody/something on the way. Plus trips that started in the time period but finish their trip in the next one; and those that started before the period and end during it. Until we get better data collection technologies where we can track every vehicle and traveller (anonymously and in aggregate to protect privacy) we will have to accept an unquantified level of noise in our matrices.

Supply noise includes minor incidents (stalled car, delivering children to school, etc.), accidents, changes in capacities and safe speeds due to weather and light variations.

The regularity of trip matrices over time is an issue seldom discussed in transport demand modelling. We know from experience that reality is not entirely repetitive from day to day. We can observe significant day-to-day variations at the level of traffic flows on any link in a network. One would typically expect some 10% variation on flow levels on similar days and on the same day of the week over similar weeks (i.e. excluding seasonal variations). The question is, are these variations in flows due to variations in the trip matrices or something else (changes in route choice, errors in counts).

I was fortunate to have access to carefully collected trip matrices for four consecutive days in the central area of Reading, UK; there were observations for 40 zones and some 80 links with simultaneous traffic counts. It was then possible to obtain day-to-day variations at link flow and OD matrix level using the percentage mean absolute error %MAE, another measure of goodness-of-fit:

$$\%\text{MAE} = 100\% \times \left(\sum_a |V^a - V^b| \,\Big/\, \sum_a V^a \right)$$

for link flows, and

$$\%\text{MAE} = 100\% \times \left(\sum_{ij} |T_{ij}^a - T_{ij}^b| \,\Big/\, \sum_{ij} T_{ij}^a \right)$$

for Origin Destination trips

where the indices a and b relate to *observed* flows V and OD trips T_{ij} on different days.

I found that that typical variations were:

TABLE 2 DAY-TO-DAY VARIATIONS IN FLOWS AND MATRICES

% MAE	Tuesday		Wednesday		Thursday	
	Link	Matrix	Link	Matrix	Link	Matrix
Monday	11%	76%	11%	72%	12%	75%
Tuesday			13%	68%	14%	85%
Wednesday					12%	70%

Day-to-day variations at flow level are consistent with expectations, whereas those at the trip matrix level are much larger. This is partly because, at trip matrix level, we are dealing with small values and sparse matrices, but even then the evidence suggests that variations at this level can be quite significant.

In fact, there has been additional evidence for some time that trip matrices have high variability. One way of verifying this is to record vehicle number plates at the same location on several days and to identify how many are "unique" (appear only once) and how many reappear on other days. Cherrett and McDonald[24] surveyed four different locations during the peak period around Southampton and found that, depending on the road only between 25% and 49% of the vehicles would reappear on subsequent days. Del Mistro and Behrens[25] undertook a similar survey over three weeks and several roads in Cape Town; they found that in arterial roads only 34% to 43% of the vehicles would reappear on subsequent on one or more subsequent days; this percentage increased to around 54% for residential streets.

Although some of these variations me be due just to route changes, these findings provide some evidence that the Activity Regularity Assumption may not be as valid as we would like. It also support questions about what exactly we mean by an "average" or "representative" trip matrix and how much sense it makes to use a single one to forecast traffic and revenue or to design a new traffic management scheme.

---

[24] Cherrett, T. and McDonald, M. (2002) Traffic Composition during the Morning Peak Period. European Journal of Transport and Infrastructure Research **2**, no. 1, pp. 41 - 55

[25] Del Mistro, R. and Behrens, R. (2008) How variable is variability in traffic? How can TDM succeed? Proceedings of the 27th South African Transport Conference (SATC 2008) 7-11 July 2008 Pretoria.

Surveys to establish the Base Year

These results also suggest that efforts to obtain a very accurate single trip matrix may not be warranted, as it will only be a snapshot. As in most cases trip and count observations would be on different days this would be a rather blurry snapshot.

Overemphasis on statistical measures of goodness of fit may, therefore, be misleading. It is equally or even more important to undertake sense checks on the model and input data and to make sure the model is not overcomplicated from the perspective of the problem in hand.

Willingness to pay

> *"A man who dares to waste one hour of time has not discovered the value of life."* **Charles Darwin**

5. WILLINGNESS TO PAY

5.1 Values of Time

The use of a reliable way to model willingness to pay tolls and fares is of course central to any transport project involving price. Willingness to Pay (WTP) represents the amount of money users appear to be willing to pay to gain a particular benefit, generally time savings. Note that this is a model feature to help explain travel choices when money is involved rather than a true property of individuals. Indeed, all individuals will display different levels of willingness to pay at different times. Moreover, some individuals get their tolls and fares paid by somebody else, a relative or the company they work for.

Because it is a model feature, strictly speaking its value depends on the functional form of the model used to determine and use this trade-off between money and time. For the most common Logit formulation, the value of time is fairly intuitive: it is the ratio of the parameter multiplying in-vehicle time over the parameter multiplying price is usually named "value of time".

$$C_{ij} = a_1 t_{ij}^v + a_2 t_{ij}^w + a_3 t_{ij}^t + a_4 t_{ij}^n + a_5 F_{ij} + a_6 \phi_j + \delta$$

Strictly speaking, it should be the (subjective or behavioural) Value of Travel Time Savings, or VTTS.

$$VTTS = \frac{a_1}{a_5}$$

The subjective qualifier is often omitted but it is mentioned here to distinguish it from the Value of Time as used in Cost Benefit Analysis; this is usually an "equity value" selected by the Government to compare all projects and modes on an even basis. In effect, many governments make an explicit decision to treat time savings by all travellers in the same way, with the same value of time, regardless of their income, contribution to society or any other measure. They do this to avoid valuing higher time savings to rich people than to poor communities thus biasing investment in favour of the better-off.

Given its key role in the evaluation of projects VTTS has been the object of much research and academic argument. A reasonable introduction to the issues can be found in MT Section 15.4.

VTTS is a way of converting time into money and therefore it matters what type of time and what type of money are involved. For time, it is usually in-vehicle time under good conditions (uncongested public transport vehicle, good free-flowing dual-carriageway road; but this would depend on local conditions). For money it is usually cash paid specifically for a trip; this is generally a cash toll or fare. Note that other forms of money, e.g. electronic payment, period pass or even the actual cost of operating a vehicle, are less well associated to particular journeys. Whenever payment requires a particular effort, for example topping up a means of payment at a shop or the Internet, there will be an additional cost/nuisance component. Conversely, when payment is very easy, e.g. credit card linked to a tolling account, charges are likely to be perceived as less onerous than cash.

In our case, we are interested in actual and subjective willingness to pay (WTP) tolls (or fares) in exchange for a better journey. In most cases, it is the individual willingness to pay that matters but in some it is their employer's.

Business travellers usually get their travel costs covered by their employer. Any reasonable company would be willing to pay to save their employees time at least the cost of their employment per minute. When the service offers additional facilities like opportunity to work and use WiFi, or to sleep on a long journey, then willingness to pay will reflect that too.

In principle, one could estimate VTTS from direct observations from a situation where there are two alternatives: one shorter and tolled (typically a bridge or tunnel) and one longer and untolled; some people would prefer the shorter but expensive route while others the cheaper one. Those who pay the toll value their time savings at least at that level, probably higher. In practice this means estimating a *choice model* and this is where the problems arise.

It has been shown that VTTS depends on the structure of this choice model (in particular if more than one alternative is involved), on the inclusion or exclusion of variables (for example including fuel costs or full vehicle operating costs and parking charges), the inclusion of quality variables (congested and uncongested travel times, travel time on tunnels or twisty mountain roads, etc.) and also *latent variables* like "Attitude to the payment tolls".

As one would expect willingness to pay depends on income levels, journey purpose and the quality of the service. However, one must remember that we are looking at a generalised cost component, the value of time savings: it is more valuable to save time on travel that is uncomfortable or requires greater effort than on travel that is less demanding. This differential is sometimes called a "motorway premium or bonus" and its complement is a "standard road malus".

Willingness to pay

The opportunity to perform other tasks whilst travelling, for example working on a train journey, should also affect VTTS.

Not everybody has the same willingness to pay; therefore, the use of a single VTTS is not a reliable way to model transport concessions. A single value will tend to exaggerate, one way or another, the real capture rate of any facility. Segmentation is very important and this can be done on the joint basis of journey purpose, income levels and other attributes like travel distance. Trip purpose may be important if differential growth is expected in the future. Income levels, usually expressed as a wage rate, are strongly correlated with VTTS. It is also obvious that people without known income (students, househusbands) are also willing to pay to save time.

An additional and important segment of the travelling population are those who have their costs, including tolls and fares, covered by somebody else usually their employer; they have a high but not unlimited WTP within the travel policies of their companies.

Here we are mostly interested in the central trade-off between time (or rather quality of journey) and money and this pertains to both earners and non-earners as well as employees and trucks carrying goods.

In the case of urban schemes one must also consider that many trips will be made several times a week and the impact of tolls or fares over the monthly budget could not be ignored. Income effects will have to be considered in these cases.

The attractiveness of new public transport facilities will influence WTP, especially if the new mode is better quality, but perhaps more expensive, than existing services.

VTTSs are often estimated using Stated Preference (SP) methods, ideally combined with Revealed Preference (RP) data.

5.2 Stated Preference

There is no doubt that *Revealed Preferences*, observations on how people actually choose between alternatives with different price and other characteristics would be the most reliable approach to establish current VTTSs; "this is what people do and they are likely to choose alternatives in the future in the same way"[26]. The problem is that current reality does not always offer the ideal set of conditions to establish these values. We may be considering a new mode, not present today in the city; or a new type of facility, a toll road that current users are not familiar with. Or even if there are toll roads around they may

---

[26] This will only be true if we are able to identify all factors influencing WTP, today and in years to come.

not offer the range of different prices and travel times to ascertain VTTS for different market segments.

In some cases, we can undertake simple experiments. For example offer some non-users of a toll road a number of discount vouchers and observe how many and of what value are actually used. Or we can run a new LRT service for a few weeks at a discounted fare and make a similar observation. These experiments are easier to organise with electronic tolling and registered tags or number plates, or similarly identified smart cards for mass transit.

Where data from real markets is not available for predicting behaviour or eliciting reliable preferences and experiments are not possible, researchers have to turn to *Stated Preference* (SP) methods. These cover a range of techniques, which have in common the collection of data about respondent's intentions in hypothetical settings as opposed to their actual actions as observed in real markets. The three most common SP methods have been *contingent valuation* (CV), *conjoint analysis* (CA) and *stated choice* (SC) techniques. In transport, SC techniques have tended to dominate and they are often presented as synonymous with SP, an approach we will follow here as we focus on them. For a more general introduction see MT pages 94 and beyond.

In my view, this is one of the most abused techniques in the demand modelling field, sometimes done unnecessarily and often done poorly.

This statement requires some elaboration.

The main problem with SP is that it is very easy to do it cheaply and badly, cutting corners. The task is, in itself, very ambitious and demanding.

In a Stated Choice or Preference study respondents are presented with a number of hypothetical alternatives and asked to choose their preferred one. The alternatives are described in terms of their attributes/characteristics, for example: travel time and its variability, probability of getting a seat or a parking space. These attributes should be different but related to a specific journey of the respondent. The key element in an SP survey is to ensure the respondent not only understand the hypothetical choice context fully but also, and this is of primary importance, she can select an option without ignoring elements of real choices that may not be fully described in the survey.

Hypothetical choice set ups can never fully replicate the real conditions under which individuals make actual travel choices; real choices are affected by, for example, subsequent journeys the same day, repeated trips in a month, the weather, in a hurry or not, travelling with children or large packages, and so on. Good SP surveys will select a recent or present relevant journey by a respondent and offer reasonable hypothetical alternatives for choice. Sometimes, these hypothetical choices involve many alternatives, overloading the

Willingness to pay

decision task compressing in a few minutes decisions that are normally taken over days or weeks.

The process is not without its limitations. Sometimes respondents express their reluctance to pay for something that is currently free, even if in practice they would be willing to sacrifice money to get a better level of service. They are, in fact, expressing their policy bias trying to influence decisions in that way. Occasionally, the respondent may treat the survey as a chore that better be completed as fast as possible and therefore provides quick, perhaps plausible, answers that do not necessarily reflect actual intentions. Treating the survey as a "game" produces similar results. A good analyst should be able to weed out some of these less than helpful responses but it is practically impossible to identify all of them with certainty.

Note that in choosing one of the hypothetical alternatives the respondent has to imagine how satisfied she will be with that selection. This requires the ability to accurately envisioning future conditions with characteristics that have not actually been experienced: a new Light Rail System when currently only an unreliable bus service is available. We make our current choices on the basis of what we remember of the alternatives. Alas, our short and long term memories are not that accurate; in the words of Daniel Gilbert[27] "memory is not a dutiful scribe that keeps a complete transcript of our experiences, but a sophisticated editor that clips and saves key elements of an experience and then uses these elements to rewrite the story each time we ask to reread it". These salient elements can be positive or negative and are mostly remembered because they were different from previous experience or expectations. In Stated Preference the analyst <u>defines</u> these salient elements and requires the respondent to use them to "rewrite the story", to remember forward, in a realistic manner without omitting elements of the reference journey and its constraints; a very difficult task indeed.

The process of constructing effective SP surveys is far from simple and quite time consuming if done properly. For some valuable advice on how to undertake these exercises you can do worse that start at Modelling Transport. This is a specialist field where research experience is particularly valuable.

Extensive qualitative and secondary research is advised to determine the relevant set of alternatives, attributes and attribute levels that will be used to create the hypothetical alternatives. It is usually worthwhile investing in *focus groups* to gain insight into the language used to discuss attributes and choices, and to identify the most relevant

---

[27] Gilbert, Daniel (2007) Stumbling on happiness. Harper Perennial. London

ones. These efforts are often omitted for routine applications; if so, this should be a clear choice rather than a default one.

I believe most of the problems with SP originate at the design and delivery stages; analysis is complex but usually carried out well enough. Cutting corners in the design and quality assurance programme can produce very poor results; with luck, these mistakes will be recognised during analysis and perhaps some correction is possible. The worst case is where the naïve simplifications of the exercise to cut costs result in unrealistic but believable models.

Contemporary techniques for the analysis of SP survey data are particularly powerful and relevant to our case. They recognise that there may not be one VTTS (for a segment of the population) but a distribution of them.

It is generally recommended to use at least 10 categories for WTP for toll roads including at least four for trucks. This is discussed in greater detail later on. In the case of public transport, the level of segmentation could be lower as freight is not an important component of that market. Sometimes complex pricing structure including season tickets and special discounts require additional segmentation. The availability of a distribution of these values of time will help in satisfying this requirement.

5.3   WTP and income

There is a general recognition that WTP and income, or wage rate, are correlated. The wage rate should be that of the relevant population, for example car owning residents; this may be the higher income segments on an emerging country. As suggested, it is preferable to use several VTTS to represent better the range of WTP and this focus attention on income distribution. This should be obtained for the region of interest, a city, province or the country as a whole.

The most commonly used distribution for income levels is the Log-Normal[28], although in general the fit is not perfect. This, plus information on income inequality, like the Gini coefficient, may help develop wage rate distributions if not locally available.

As WTP is correlated with income it is likely to grow with it in the future. How closely VTTS will track per capita income growth is open to dispute. Part of the problem is the difference between cross-sectional and time series income elasticities.

---

[28] http://en.wikipedia.org/wiki/Log-normal_distribution

As income grows people may:
- buy more of the things they already buy (income effect),
- buy new things (substitution effect), and
- change their savings rate.

If the substitution effect is significant then one would expect the VTTS elasticity to income to be less than 1.0; that is people will buy other types of mobility or services. In my view VTTS will grow at between 0.7 and 0.9 times the rate of growth of income per capita of the relevant population; see for example Wardman[29] (2001). Note that some studies have found evidence for values of 1.0 and even slightly higher; the UK Department for Transport has indeed adopted an elasticity of 1.0 for working time and 0.8 for other cases. A unit elasticity would imply either no substitution effect and no changes in the savings rate, or one compensating the other, both rather unlikely in my view.

There is some evidence that WTP also depends on "sentiment" at the time. The recent financial crisis affected this sentiment in a big way encouraging people to shift from being spenders to become savers even in countries where the economy did not suffer much. This shift affects *perceived* and real disposable income and therefore reduced willingness to pay. This adds a subjective element to any estimation of WTP and requires judgement from the analyst in its application.

5.4 Travel time reliability

It has been argued with good reason that new toll roads and new transit modes not only reduce travel time but also improve travel time reliability. Travel time variability is caused by a combination of supply and demand factors. Supply influences include incidents, road works, weather, road geometry and dynamic traffic management. Demand variations within and between days interact with supply to result in congestion effects, queue spillbacks and general variability in travel time.

There are four difficult questions associated with this:
a. What is the best measure for travel time reliability, the one that represents better how travellers consider this element of cost?
b. How to represent travel time variability in surveys and models; how do people perceive and understand travel time reliability?
c. What is the VTTS (or equivalent) that should be applied to this measure?
d. How to estimate in advance how much will travel time reliability change with the new facility.

---

[29] Wardman, M. (2001) Inter-temporal variations in the value of time. *ITS Working Paper 566*, Institute for Transport Studies, University of Leeds.

A priori a useful measure for travel time reliability would be its standard deviation. There are two usual measures associated with it. One is the variance over the mean of travel time; this measure has time units and therefore a VTTS value could be applied directly to it. Another common measure is the Reliability Ratio: the non-dimensional standard deviation over mean travel time.

A third measure that has been proposed is the 95th -50th percentile of travel times. Its relationship with the standard deviation depends on the distribution of travel times that represents the local conditions (usually Normal or Log Normal). For a Normal distribution of travel times the 95th-50th percentile is approximately 1.38 standard deviations.

However, people do not perceive standard deviations but they do perceive lateness; so linking perception to these three indicators is not trivial. Li at al[30] undertook a comprehensive review on the issue of representing travel time reliability in surveys and using these results in models. They noted that there were two successful approaches: either to offer a range of travel times (representing standard deviations) or to express willingness to accept less than ideal departure or arrival times (the schedule delay). These variations around a Preferred Arrival Time (PAT) they termed the schedule delay approach. See a discussion of micro-time choice in MT421-422. There is a cost or value associated to a schedule delay early (VSDE) and one associated to a schedule delay late (VSDL); in general one would expect the perception of one minute SDL to be more onerous than one minute SDE and there may even be a constant component (say δ) of being late. This is illustrated in Figure 18.

---

[30] Li, Z. Hensher, D. and Rose, J. (2010) Willingness to pay for travel time reliability in passenger transport: A review and some empirical evidence. *Transportation Research Part E*, pp 384-403.

FIGURE 18 THE CONCEPT OF SCHEDULE DELAY

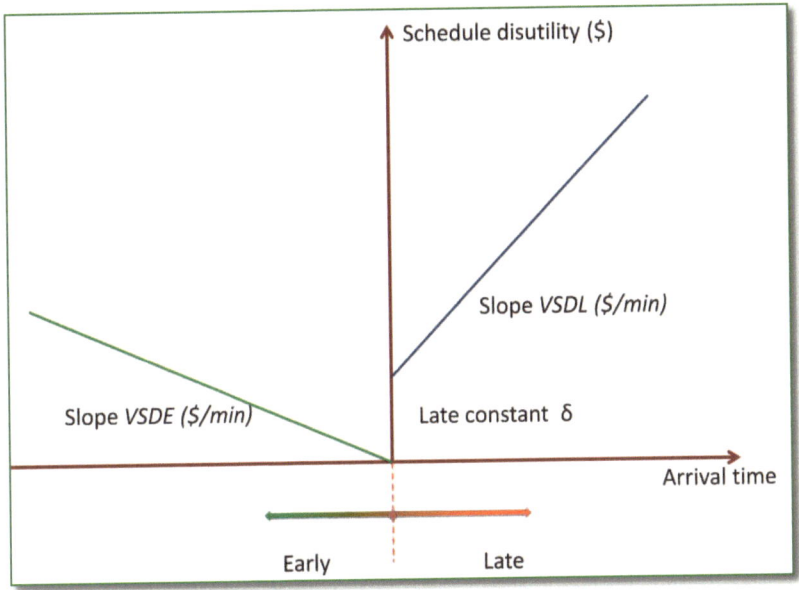

Li et al and Carrion and Levinson[31] have found that the schedule delay representation of reliability in surveys produced more consistent results. In practice, however, it is easier to use the standard deviation formulation in utility or generalised cost functions. It is also useful to see the cost associated to this standard deviation as a multiplier of the in-vehicle-time VTTS. In fact, this applies to most other time-related parameters in the generalised function formulation. In the case of the standard deviation it is not expected that this multiplier would be much grater than 1, perhaps up to 1.3 depending on the importance of reliability on the journey purpose[32]. The possibility of a constant δ is generally ignored.

5.5   Freight

It must be recognised that road haulage is often poorly represented in our models. This is partly because we know much less about freight movements and also a recognition that the intricacies of modern logistics are difficult to model.

---

[31] Carrion, C. and Levinson, D. (2012) Value of travel time reliability: A review of current evidence. Transportation Research Part A 46 (2012) 720–741.

[32] Bates, J., Polak, J., Jones P. and Cook, A. (2001) The valuation of reliability for personal travel. Transportation Research Part E 37, pp 191-222

Freight movements, either by road or rail, can be represented by a similar *generalised cost* concept with allowance for storage and transhipment costs and perhaps other relevant elements like availability of rest and fuelling stations for long distance travel on interurban toll roads.

In principle, decisions on the use of a new toll road would be based on strict economic rationality in the case of road haulage. However, this rationality is not always clearly defined or knowable because of its complexity. In the case of personal travel the assumption that each individual makes its own choices is mostly acceptable; this is less warranted in the case of road haulage. Who exactly makes route choice decisions for a shipment? The shipper, dispatcher or driver? This fuzziness has made the application of SP approaches to ascertain VTTS more complex and less reliable.

In the case of trucks, WTP depends on a number of factors including the size and type of goods hauled (low value goods like bricks are associated to low WTP, high value goods to higher WTP), the type of contract for each shipment (for example *just-in-time* arrangements), company policy and legal requirements (dangerous goods are often required to use the safest road, normally a tolled one) and, ultimately, opportunistic decisions by the driver. I remember an early study of road haulage in Mexico where we found many reasons, some legal and some less so, why truckers often preferred untolled roads. Some road haulage companies, in particular one-man operations, are not fully aware of their operating costs and may be more cash sensitive; these will display a lower willingness to pay for tolls to save time and operating costs than an objective evaluation would suggest.

Despite these limitations, SP seems to be the main source of VTTS for trucks always contrasted with RP data and experience.

5.6   Meta analysis of VTTS

The best approach is to get local values for VTTS that can be used in the model as required. If only a single value is available an analysis of income distribution, perhaps combined with SP, may be sufficient to deliver the range of VTTSs required for the model.

VTTS depends much on context, understanding of the values held by travellers, the opportunities to improve knowledge of vehicle operating costs, and ultimately "sentiment", a latent variable. The introduction of the first toll road in a region is likely to encounter significant resistance and even outrage. This will affect willingness to pay, perhaps for many years, therefore requiring judgment to dilute this influence over time.

Willingness to pay

The means of payment will also affect willingness to pay, as we have all experienced in respect of phone calls and other services that are commonly charged and paid automatically. Separating time of consumption from payment weakens the link between them and makes parting with money less painful. It may well be that for a few people paying a toll for commuting to work becomes part of the fixed cost of living and working at particular locations and is practically ignored in the choice framework; they become effectively "captive" to the tolled facility.

In the case of public transport the availability of season tickets adds a new complication. Once you bought, say, a monthly ticket on the ground that you save money on your regular journeys any additional trip is for free. However, not all season tickets are used in full while others manage to extract maximum value from such a purchase. Willingness to pay as influenced by these choices becomes a very complex task indeed.

There are two valuable research projects that consolidated the results of a wide range of VTTS studies. One has been undertaken by the University of South Florida[33]. The objective of this study was to compile and synthesize current and past research on the value of time and the value of reliability of travel time to "provide practitioners with applicable ranges of estimates". This review covered some 60 articles and reports, mostly from the USA.

The second key synthesis was led by Prof. Mark Wardman at the Institute for Transport Studies, Leeds University in the UK; it covered the meta-analysis of 244 European Value of Time studies using a variety of SP and RP data. This research[34] provides a number of valuable contributions. First, it not only collates monetary values of time but produces also multipliers of a base VTTS for in-vehicle time (or IVT) to obtain the values of related parameters like reliability, walking, waiting, transfer times, parking search and so on. Second, it uses an analytical approach to establish these multipliers so that their consistency, country dependence (if any) and range of values can be determined.

---

[33] Concas, S. and Kolpakov, A. (2009) Synthesis of Research on Value of Time and Value of Reliability. Report BD 549-37. Center for Urban Transportation Research. University of South Florida. http://www.nctr.usf.edu/pdf/77806.pdf

[34] Wardman, M. Chintakayala, P. de Jong, G. and Ferrer, D. (2013) European-wide Meta-Analysis of Values of Travel time. Final Report to the European Investment Bank. University of Leeds.

Better Traffic and Revenue Forecasting

Prof. Wardman and his team were able to determine multipliers for Congested Time, Walk, Access, Wait, Interchange Wait, Search Time, Headway, Standard Deviation for travel time and a few other parameters. They found little if any country[35] specific effects but were able to distinguish how values depend on trip distance, purpose, mode and GDP per capita. The preferred formulation for in-vehicle VTTS in the Report, as the best fit with the data from these 244 European studies, is:

$$VTTS = (e^W) \times D^{0.188-0.048CV} GDP^{0.681+0.128EB+0.039CU}$$

with

$$W = -10.06 + 0.150C + 0.245EBTU - 0.307BU + 0.244AU - 0.061TV + 0.520AV$$

VTTS is expressed in 2010 € per minute. The dummy variables denote the following conditions:

C is commuting, EB is employer's business,

EBTU denotes employer's business for train users

TU, BU, AU and CU are train user, bus user, air user and car user respectively,

TV, CV and AV are train valued, car valued and air valued respectively and

D is distance in kilometres,

GDP is gross domestic product per capita in 2010 euros from World Bank statistics.

As an example, for Malta commuters we would have the following, assuming 25 Km journey: EBTU, BU, AU, TV and AV are all zero but C for commuting is one and hence 0.150 is added to the constant term of -10.060 to leave a figure of -9.91 for W. Given that car valued (CV) is one the distance power is 0.14 (=0.188-0.048). In the GDP term EB is zero but car user (CU) is one and hence the power is 0.72 (0.681+0.039). So:

$$VTTS = e^{-10.060+0.150C} D^{0.188-0.048CV} GDP^{0.681+0.039CU}$$

$$VTTS = e^{-9.91} D^{0.14} GDP^{0.72}$$

$$VTTS = e^{-9.91} 25^{0.14} 16659^{0.72} = 0.0854 \text{ € per min} = 5.12 \text{ € per hour}$$

---

[35] Wardman et al did find a few small country specific effects; this is not surprising as the importance of cultural as well as economic influences on VTTS is well recognised. Refer to the full report for the details.

Willingness to pay

It is interesting to note that the evidence is fairly consistent across Europe and the USA, except perhaps in respect of the value of travel time reliability, where American studies seem to provide a higher value for these multipliers. Part of this difference is the wide range of measures of travel time reliability used in the USA, whereas the European meta-analysis focused only on the standard deviation.

One must be careful, however, not to use these relationships blindly. They are no substitute to appropriate local research. They are useful to provide a range of feasible values and to contrast against results from SP surveys

The following two tables have been prepared based on my own experience and research undertaken by these two groups at the Universities of South Florida and Leeds. The first one covers the values for normal In-Vehicle Time as a function of the local wage rate.

TABLE 3 VALUES OF IN VEHICLE TIME AND WAGE RATES

	As proportion of relevant wage rate	Comments
Base VTTS value		
To Work	0.5 to 0.8	Skewed to lower values
To Education	0.5 - 0.7	Skewed to lower values
During Work	1.1 - 1.3	
Shopping	0.5 - 0.6	
Leisure	0.5 - 0.6	
Other	0.5 - 0.6	

The second table presents the time multipliers, based mostly on the Leeds University work. The values are given as a function of distance travelled (kms) and this facilitates consideration of urban and interurban contexts. For a more complete set of values the reader is referred to the Wardman et al (2013) report.

Note that in most cases there is limited distance effect. The results tend to support the common practice of valuing walk and wait time at around twice IVT. Note that some models use Access Time by whatever mode to public transport where others assume that Walking is the main access mode. Interchange Wait Time is valued slightly higher than the first wait time.

TABLE 4 IVT MULTIPLIERS

Mode	IVT Multipliers								
	CAR			BUS			RAIL		
Distance (kms)	25	100	250	25	100	250	25	100	250
HBWork									
Walk	1.70	1.83	1.92	1.44	1.44	1.45	1.57	1.58	1.58
Wait				1.44	1.45	1.45	1.58	1.58	1.59
Search	1.84	1.84	1.84						
During Work									
Walk	2.02	1.96	1.92	1.79	1.73	1.69	1.57	1.52	1.48
Wait				1.57	1.52	1.48	1.57	1.52	1.48
Search	2.36	2.36	2.36						
Other									
Walk	2.38	2.32	2.26	2.10	2.03	1.99	1.84	1.78	1.75
Wait				1.84	1.78	1.75	1.84	1.78	1.75
Search	1.77	1.77	1.77						
ALL									
Congested travel time	1.90	1.50	1.28						
Standard deviation of travel time	0.63	0.51	0.45	0.63	0.51	0.45	0.63	0.51	0.45

Congested travel time is valued almost double of free-flow time for short trips but only 28% more for long ones. This is to be expected, as congestion is more important in short urban journeys. The standard deviation of travel time appears with a relatively low value compared with other figures closer to 1.

Of course, it is always better to use values determined specifically for each project. But the tables and relationships above may help in benchmarking these values and also in deriving additional components of generalised costs that may not have been possible to estimate locally.

Trip Generation and Attraction

"There are four ways economists can lose their reputation. Gambling is the quickest; sex is the most pleasurable and drink the slowest. But forecasting is the surest." **Max Walsh**

6. TRIP GENERATION AND ATTRACTION

6.1 Trip end models

Classic transport models, as typically used to plan mobility in urban areas, use Trip End models to estimate the total number of trips (or tours if used) generated and attracted to each zone. The main source of data for these is Household Surveys combined with information on Employment, Education Enrolment, Commercial and other economic activities per zone. Projections for these data for each zone will also be needed in order to use them when preparing forecasts for future years. For an introduction to Trip Generation and Attraction models see Chapter 4 of Modelling Transport (MT 139+).

As stated before, it is unlikely that all of these data sources will be available and current in the preparation of traffic and revenue forecasts for a concession; therefore, it is quite common to prepare different growth models as discussed in Chapter 18. Nevertheless, there are two reasons to delve a little into the nature and quality of Trip Generation and Attraction models. The first is that they are likely to be employed in the preparation of strategic models that are often the basis of the Reference Models prepared by the procuring authority; understanding their strengths and weaknesses is therefore valuable. The second is that sometimes the trip-end growth projections, in particular which zones will experience greater growth in the future, help allocating expected growth geographically. This will have to be reviewed by an independent specialist as discussed in Chapter 18.

Trip (or tour) Generation models are generally produced from Household Survey Data complemented with Census (that sometimes contains a proxy for the journey to work) and land use data. Trip Attraction models are generally weaker as there is limited data on how many trips are attracted to each type of land use/zone. These tend to be Linear Regression models based on very limited data.

We discuss here their strengths and limitations as well as the role they may play in T&R projections.

6.2 Trip generation models

The most common Trip Generation model is a household based Category Analysis or Cross Classification methods. These produce daily (or for specific period of the day) trips for different type of households usually classified by levels of car ownership or availability, household composition (residents, ages, etc.) and journey purpose. They may include household income or other socioeconomic data as additional explanatory variables.

Note that GDP is usually not a direct component of these models although this will certainly influence incomes and therefore car ownership and trip making. The number of trips generated by a zone will then be calculated by adding up the number of households of each type in them.

Trips are said to be based at home if one of its ends is there (from home or back home). Usually a distinction is made between trip generation and production. It is said that the residents in a household generate trips, some of which are not based at home. The home zone may produce some trips but also zones without residents, for example shops when the trip is from there back home or to another location.
The most common journey purposes to include are:

HBW: Home Based trip to Work

HBEd: Home based trip to Education (or HBE)

HBSh: Home based shopping

HBL: Home based leisure

HBO: Home based other purposes

HBB: Home based business or in work

NHBB: Not home based business

NHB: Other non home-based

There may be others. Trips to work and education are considered special because of their regularity and the relatively good trip attraction models. They are also considered non-discretionary or mandatory.

Some trip generation models actually model tours rather than trips. This requires first a characterisation of a manageable number of typical tours. Mode choice models are then often based on the complete tour rather than just trips.

In most cities trips to work and education conform between 60% and 80% of the trips during the AM peak. Their contribution is diluted for Off- and PM peak periods as other discretionary trips become important.

A less frequently used type of trip generation model is probabilistic. It attempts to estimate the probability that a given households generates none, 1, 2, 3 or more trips or tours often using a nested Logit formulation.

6.3 GDP growth, trip generation and accessibility effects

Most financial institutions and bidders would expect traffic and revenue projections to depend on economic growth, usually expressed as GDP growth. In the models discussed above, the link between GDP growth and trip making is implicit (via Income and Car Ownership) and it would be necessary to make it explicit and linked to different type of households. This task is rarely undertaken and a different approach is therefore adopted.

Trip generation models are, however, very valuable to show *where* trips will grow thus influencing the shape of the future trip matrices. So, it is not unusual to combine trip generation and attraction models with other, more general, trip growth models; the latter to get an overall trip growth and the former to obtain the differential growth in different parts of the area of interest.

As noted, in general trip generation models are not sensitive to changes in accessibility that may be produced by a new metro or toll road. Early attempts to incorporate accessibility into these models failed because of their aggregate nature: accessibility measures were obtained by zone rather than by household. It is much easier for a traveller to switch from car to metro and make more trips if she lives near a (future) station. The average change of accessibility for a zone is less significant and many households are not really that influenced by the new mode.

This issue is nowadays treated as "induced traffic" in most concessions and discussed later in this text.

6.4 Trip attraction

Trip Attraction models are generally zone based. They represent the number of trips attracted to a zone as a function of attributes like employment, educational registrations, square metres of commercial space, etc. In some fortunate cases employment levels and educational enrolment per zone are available for the base and sometimes future-year projections as well. Models are still needed to convert these into trips at certain times of the day.

For "other purposes" the situation is generally poorer. Land uses may be available, base year and future projections, but household surveys produce very few of these trips and often none to zones that should obviously attract some (because of the low sampling rates). Intercept surveys can partially supplement this BUT it is impossible in practice to intercept all possible trips in an area using conventional methods.

Trip attraction models are mostly zonal linear regression models, see MT 144+. As trip attraction models are weaker than trip generation models it is often necessary to scale trip attractions to match the total number of trips in both generation and attraction.

Some countries have compiled trip generation and attraction databases used mostly to estimate the traffic impacts of new land use developments. They are, of course, useful in the absence of more locally developed rates.

6.5   Vehicle ownership

Vehicle, in particular car and sometimes motorcycle, ownership is a key element in any T&R projection. Greater car ownership will increase the potential market of a toll road and weaken that for public transport. Vehicle ownership is usually expressed as vehicles per person or per 1000 inhabitants.

There are several type of vehicle ownership models, see Section 15.3 in Modelling Transport. Earlier ones were just based on trend extrapolation based on a logistic curve. Key parameters here were a Saturation level S (maximum level of cars per person), the observed growth rate g_0 on a base year and the car ownership level that year C_0.

The car ownership level C_t at year t is estimated by:

$$C_t = \frac{S}{1+[(S-C_0)/C_0]\exp[-g_0 St/(S-C_0)]}$$

This curve has a nice shape as a function of C_0, S and g_0. The next figure shows the nominal case of an emerging country with an initial car ownership level of 5% in 2010. Two potential base year growth rates are shown, 10% and 15% to illustrate their different impact. The saturation level is 61%, close to current best estimates. Bear in mind that these are averages; there will be zones with higher car ownership levels.

Note that the fastest growth rates are experienced for car ownership levels between 0.15 and 0.40 and these are then moderated as they approach saturation. Note also that this model is not particularly useful for T&R projections as car ownership is independent on GDP growth or income levels. A very useful source of models has been developed by Dargay and others[36] using data from a large number of countries.

It is particularly interesting to use models that show the relationship between incomes and different levels of car ownership per household. These are either probabilistic or econometric models, see again MT pp. 503 ss.

FIGURE 19 CAR OWNERSHIP EXAMPLE

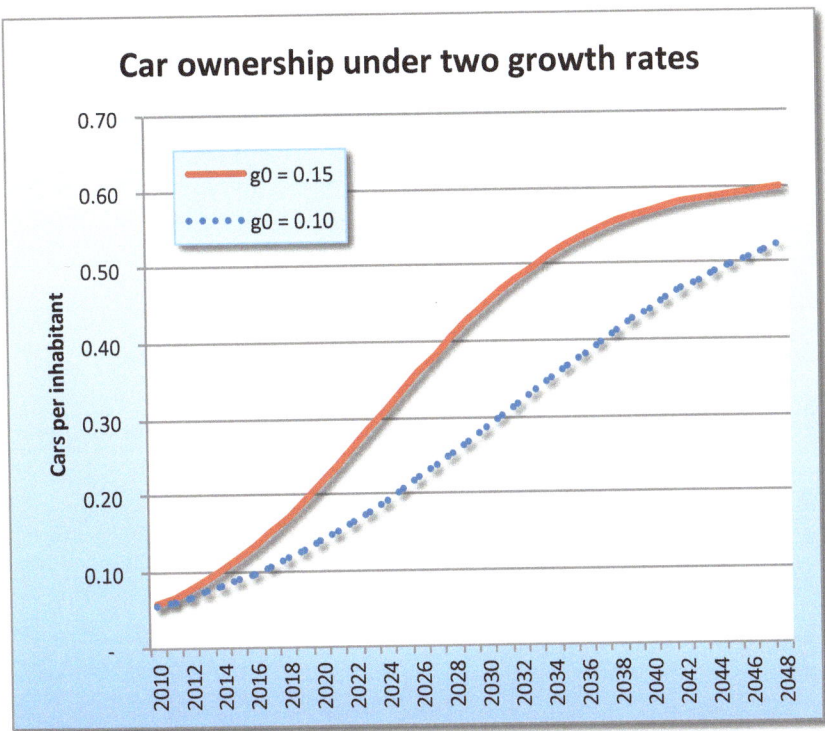

A useful example is a model due to Bates et al[37]. They model the proportion of households having no, 1 and 2+ cars.

$$P_t(1+) = \frac{S(1+)}{1+\exp\{-a_1(I_t/p_t)^{-b_1}\}}$$

---

[36] Dargay, J. and Gately, D. (1999) Income's effect on car and vehicle ownership, worldwide: 1960–2015. *Transportation Research* **33A**, 101–138.

[37] Bates, J.J., Gunn, H.F. and Roberts, M. (1978) A model of household car ownership. Traffic Engineering and Control **19**, 486–491, 562–566.

$$P_t(2+) = \frac{S(2+)}{1+\exp\{-a_2 - b_2(I_t/p_t)\}}$$

where (I_t / p_t) is annual family income (£/week) deflated by a car price index. The model was calibrated using British data for the period 1969-75, yielding the following parameter values:

$a_1 = -7.76 \quad b_1 = 2.26 \quad S(1+) = 0.95$

$a_2 = -3.76 \quad b_2 = 0.04 \quad S(2+) = 0.60$

In many emerging countries it is desirable to model car and motorcycle ownership together as they are ultimately interdependent. One such model was estimated for a city in Latin America with a high level of motorcycle ownership and the resulting figure is shown below:

FIGURE 20 JOINT CAR AND MOTORCYCLE OWNERSHIP

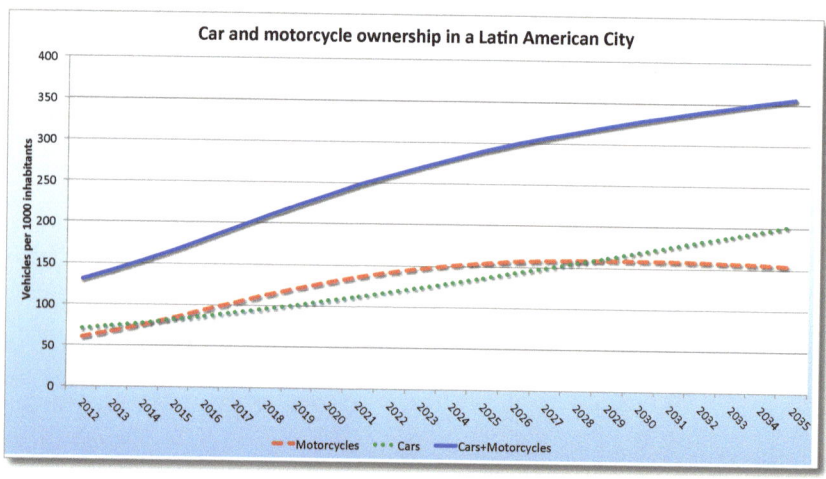

As can be seen the starting point in 2012 is similar to the one in Figure 19 but motorcycle ownership becomes higher than car ownership a few years later. Around 2030 car ownership becomes greater than motorcycle ownership that by then has started to decline. The driver of this model is GDP per capita.

The Wikipedia maintains a reasonably up to date ranked list of countries with their vehicle ownership levels: http://en.wikipedia.org/wiki/List_of_countries_by_vehicles_per_capita . This shows tiny San Marino with more registered vehicles than inhabitants followed by Monaco with almost 90% ownership levels.

Two problems that did not exist 10 years ago surround vehicle ownership. The first one is the idea of "peak car": that car ownership and use has peaked in countries like the USA and Britain and it is now starting to come down. The most important sign of this is a decline in drivers licenses among the young; the under 30 no longer see driving as an expression of their achievements and personality, other technologies now play that role. A good review of this issue is the work of Dutzik and Baxandal[38].

In my view the jury is still out but it seems to be that car usage is not growing much in these countries. GDP and traffic growth seem to be finally de-coupling at high per-capita incomes.

The second problem is Self Driving Vehicles (SDV) that appears to be the most likely name for a wide range of vehicles that eventually will drive themselves without human intervention. They are going to happen, despite the best efforts of some pressure groups and governments to delay their implementation. The main reason for this is that they will significantly reduce traffic accidents, up to 95% for a 90% penetration. The most likely dates for a full SDV hitting our showrooms are 2018 – 2020.

SDVs are going to have a number of impacts, most of which are little understood. They may not be owned but rented by the fraction of the hour like ZipCars, they will reduce parking problems and will certainly pay their tolls or you would not be able to use another one. This is a separate area for speculation and research.

In producing T&R projections we will have to make assumptions about the impact and timing of these two issues: peak car and SDVs.

---

[38] Dutzik, T. and Baxandal, P. (2013) "A New Direction. Our Changing Relationship with Driving and the Implications for America's Future". U.S. PIRG Education Fund and Frontier Group.

Destination Choice

"Essentially, all models are wrong, but some are useful."
George E P Box

7. DESTINATION CHOICE

7.1 Trip Matrices and their growth

We assume that somehow, using the techniques outlined in Chapter 4, one has managed to produce base year matrices and calibrate a model (trip matrices, choices and network) to a sufficient standard. These are not just the synthetic matrices from a strategic planning model but they have been adjusted to current observations (mostly traffic, person counts and intercept surveys) to represent the base year best. These matrices will not remain static; they will change as a result of four broad influences:

- Trends in trip growth driven by GDP and per capita income growth via wealth and higher vehicle ownership;
- The future allocation of population and economic activity over space in the region;
- Changes due to the introduction of new modes, toll roads and Managed Lanes;
- And also other changes to the networks (roads and public transport services) that are outside the control of the concessionaire.

Destination choice, also know a distribution modelling, attempts to replicate these effects, although changes in mode will be dealt with in the next chapter.

7.2 Modelling destination choice

It should not be surprising that destination choice models are the weakest link in the forecasting toolkit. The decisions to select a place of work and/or a place of residence are complex and transport and accessibility are not the only defining attribute. Many other considerations play, in many cases, a more important role in selecting where to live: the quality of the schools for our kids, the amount of green space, where our best friends reside, property prices. In terms of employment: salary levels, the quality of management, the prospects for promotion and the working environment, etc.

Our models are likely to focus mostly in what we can measure and change: transport facilities and perhaps a couple of other variables like type of employment and residential attractiveness for a socio-economic group. For these reasons, we tend to trust less conventional absolute destination choice models often used for planning purposes. Therefore, we prefer to avoid absolute models and prefer in an incremental framework: to estimate *changes* to origins and destinations over an existing and reasonably well-established trip matrix.

There are at least two types of destination choice models in use: aggregate and disaggregate. The classic aggregate approach is the Gravity Model. For disaggregate approaches a multi-nomial logit is the most frequently used. Having said this, given the limited nature of these models most practical applications in the traffic and revenue forecasting arena rely on some version of the Gravity Model.

7.3   Gravity models

The Gravity Model originated as an analogy with gravitational law and was later on interpreted in different ways, for example as the most likely matrix consistent with information contained in trip ends and total costs.

The general form for this model, for a particular trip purpose, is:

$$T_{ij} = A_i O_i B_j D_j f(c_{ij})$$

where:

A_i and B_j are two sets of parameters to ensure the total number of trips originating and terminating in each zone match Origins and Destinations there. For discretionary trips the models are usually singly constrained and in that case all $B_j = 1$.

O_i and D_j are the total trips generated and attracted to each zone

$f(c_{ij})$ is a deterrence or separation function depending on generalised costs between i and j

This function can take different forms:

$f(c_{ij}) = \exp(-\beta c_{ij})$ exponential function

$f(c_{ij}) = c_{ij}^{-n}$ power function

$f(c_{ij}) = c_{ij}^n \exp(-\beta c_{ij})$ combined, Gamma or Tanner function

Note that in the power function $n = 2$ would generate the traditional gravity model. Large values for β will give more importance to distance

Destination Choice

(generalised costs) as a deterrent to travel. This property also helps in the use of gravity models to represent freight movements with commodities of different vales: low value goods are more sensitive to travel costs and therefore will merit a higher β.

β or/and n must be estimated from the household surveys and/or the trip matrices adjusted to the base year information. Note that as n is non-dimensional but this is not the case for β; its units are 1 over the generalised cost units.

7.4 Observed and synthetic matrices

Distribution models produce matrices with values on all cells, even if some of them are insignificant. Observed matrices are, on the other hand, fairly sparse with zeroes in most cells. The gravity model may be one of the best models around but there is little evidence of its capacity to approximate real trip matrices. Additional parameters like k factors (MT 202) can help but it is unclear whether they will remain constant in the future.

Most strategic transport models use trip matrices produced by gravity or other similar models. The argument is that they are trying to model underlying trends and behavioural changes and that the exact base year or future trip matrix is less critical. This approach is not universal as some countries, in particular the UK, place more emphasis in estimating an accurate base year matrix and future matrices are based on incremental changes to it.

Traffic and Revenue forecasts for transport concessions are heavily dependent on the quality of base and future year trip matrices. The use of purely synthetic trip matrices from even the very best destination choice model is a risky approach. Every effort must be made to collect the data to derive the best estimation of real trip matrices. An incremental approach, based on these base year observed trip matrices, is therefore more appropriate.

In many cases, the carefully prepared base year matrices are just expanded to consider future demand levels using a bi-proportional adjustment methods like Furness, i.e. with $\beta=0$ (and $n=0$ if the combined function is used).

7.5 Incremental modelling

Given the limitations of trip distribution models it is desirable to explore how best to retain the observed patterns of the base year matrix and capture, at the same time, some of the behavioural contribution of a destination choice model. The preferred approach is to use the gravity model incrementally.

Incremental or pivot point modelling is a more general approach also applicable to mode choice and even time of travel choice. There are three ways of approaching incremental modelling, all of them useful in practice: analytical, multiplicative and additive.

The first one involves using the exact analytical solution to the problem of estimating the changes in trips due to changes in some of the external conditions. This is simple for a multinomial logit model but more complex for other, more general, model forms.

For example the new number of trips T_{ij} in a singly constrained incremental gravity model can be written as:

$$T_{ij} = \frac{G_i T_{ij}^0 b_j \exp(-\beta \Delta GC_{ij})}{\sum_l T_{lj}^0 b_j \exp(-\beta \Delta GC_{lj})}$$

where

T_{ij}^0 is the observed or adjusted trip matrix in the base year

G_i is the total trips generated at zone i,

ΔGC_{ij} the difference in generalised cost between the base and design years, and

b_j growth factors reflecting changes in the destinations j.

Analytical pivot-point model formulations are helpful, as we only need to account for changes in the generalised costs or utility functions, not their complete values. Therefore, if we are not introducing new modes, modal penalties can be ignored as they cancel out in ΔGC.

Another approach is to use the absolute models (Gravity, mode choice or something else that is relevant) but apply them incrementally. To this end an absolute (usually gravity) model is estimated for the base year $[GM_{ij}^0]$ and then used for a future year $[GM_{ij}^1]$.

One version of this approach is to estimate the future matrix as the observed one multiplied by the ratio of future over base gravity models:

$$T_{ij}^1 = T_{ij}^0 \frac{GM_{ij}^1}{GM_{ij}^0}$$

for all ij

The problem with this version of an incremental model is that those cells that are zero in the base year matrix T^0 will remain zero in the future; this would be unrealistic for zones that are fairly empty in the base year but are expected to have increased activity in future years.

The third approach avoids this problem employing an additive form:

$$T_{ij}^1 = T_{ij}^0 + (GM_{ij}^1 - GM_{ij}^0)$$

This has the potential danger that some cells may turn out to have negative values that should be rounded up to zero, taking care not to artificially increase the total number of trips.

It is worth applying some simple common sense rules to make sure any combination of absolute and incremental modelling works well. Key would be to check whether the model is producing sensible changes in trips numbers in areas/zones of interest that are predicted to have large or new developments.

7.6   Sense checks

Whatever model is applied it is important to make some "sense checks" to confirm that the results are reasonable. This can be achieved in a number of ways and the most appropriate one would depend on the context and the changes expected.

A first sense check would be to compare the trip cost (length) distribution in the base year with that in the future conditions. They should not be too different, and if they are there should be a reasonable explanation for this. This explanation should be based on an understanding of the underlying forces behind movement in the study area, not that "the model equations say so".

Another sense check is to plot where are the most significant differences in trip making, perhaps aggregating zones into some 20 regions to be able to see affects more clearly. This should also be contrasted with any expected changes in land uses, new developments and economic regeneration. Good use of graphics and GIS pay handsomely here.

Note that incremental models tend to retain the pre-existing patterns and some professionals prefer to adopt them only for the medium term and use absolute models for the long term. This is not my preference.

Finally, one should consider whether all these expected changes will happen on the relevant forecasting year or some of them will be lagged in time, for example changes in residence and jobs/educational places. One cannot change jobs or residence immediately in response to a new metro station. Some trips can adapt faster, probably shopping and recreational journeys; but others will take longer. This will be particularly important over the first few years of any concession.

Mode Choice

> *"Demographers can no more be held responsible for inaccuracy in population forecasting 20 years ahead than geologists, meteorologists or economists when they fail to announce earthquakes, cold winters, or depressions 20 years ahead. What we can be held responsible for is warning one another and our public what the error of our estimates is likely to be."* **Nathan Keyfitz**

8. MODE CHOICE

8.1 General concepts

Many toll road studies are undertaken ignoring possible future changes in mode choice; this could be an upside if nothing changes on other modes or a downside if a new mode or public transport service is likely to be introduced in the future. This is generally appropriate. Urban toll roads are probably more at risk from this effect but the role of congestion is so dominant in large cities that it tends to overwhelm any other intervention in the transport system. In the case of interurban toll roads, the main threat may be from intercity rail and air services, in particular if the toll road is long and expensive. In these cases the size of the group travelling together may become important.

Nevertheless, the issue should be at least discussed and any potential competition from new or improved modes should be taken into account, even if to dismiss explicitly their potential threat.

In the case of new passenger concessions, rail or urban public transport, mode choice plays a much more important and critical role[39]. This chapter, therefore, focuses mostly on the introduction of new passenger modes.

First, we must recognise that inducing mode changes is difficult, in particular if car ownership is high.

The most important factors affecting mode choice are those of the trip maker, the journey and the modes:
Characteristics of the trip maker:

- car availability and/or ownership;
- possession of a driving licence;

---

[39] The possible exception is the replacement of one conventional bus service with a new one. This is true even if the new services claims to be a BRT, as the debacle of the Transantiago system in Chile proved.

- household structure (young couple, couple with children, retired, singles, etc.),
- income;
- decisions made elsewhere, for example the need to use a car at work, take children to school, etc.;
- residential density.

Characteristics of the journey:

- the trip purpose; for example, the journey to work is normally easier to undertake by public transport than other journeys;
- time of the day; late trips are more difficult to accommodate by public transport;
- size of group travelling together;
- the needs of subsequent journeys (tours).

Characteristics of the transport facility. These can be split into two categories. Firstly, quantitative factors such as:

- components of travel time: in-vehicle, waiting and walking times by each mode;
- components of monetary costs (fares, tolls, fuel and other operating costs);
- availability and cost of parking;
- reliability of travel time and regularity of service

Qualitative factors which are difficult (or impossible) to quantify in practice, such as:

- comfort and convenience;
- safety, protection, security;
- the demands of the driving task;
- opportunities to undertake other activities during travel (use the phone/tablet, read, etc.);
- availability of knowledge about alternatives and means of payment when not cash.

Not all these factors can be taken into account in every practical model. Decisions will have to be made about which are important and which can be ignored in any particular case. I always prefer to concentrate in those factors that will influence most of the demand and leave the rest for a more qualitative analysis.

Mode Choice

8.2 Modelling mode choice

Again, there are basically two major approaches to modelling mode choice: aggregate and disaggregate. The sensible aggregation of individual trips and their probability will yield choice proportions; this task, however, is not trivial. Most of chapter 9 in Modelling Transport is devoted to it.

Random Utility Theory is currently the best theoretical framework for mode choice modelling and supports directly disaggregate or discrete choice models. Random Utility. Random Utility Theory assumes a rational human being with perfect information and capability to compare large number of alternatives. This is a demanding assumption as real homo sapiens is imperfect in this sense. Some theoretical applications have thought to depart partially from these assumptions but the most common implementations of mode choice models still retain this requirement of full rationality and omniscience.

8.3 Discrete choice modelling

The most important advances in mode choice modelling have been achieved with discrete choice based on Random Utility Theory. This is a disaggregated approach at the level of the individual provides clarity on what is involved and the assumptions that are required to underpin this type of approach even at zonal level.

In zonal based mode choice we deal mainly with the proportion of trips (with choice) the selects a particular mode or alternative. In person based disaggregate approaches we deal with the *probability* that a particular representative individual will choose a mode or alternative. Note that in both cases the alternatives may not just be a mode but a more general one: route, method of payment, destination, time of travel, etc.

In the case of disaggregate models it is better to discuss them in terms of *utilities* rather than generalised costs, to include characteristics or attributes of the individual as well as the journey itself.

An introduction to mode and discrete choice models is provided in Chapters 6 to 9 in Modelling Transport. We focus here on some of the implications for T&R projections for transport concessions.

Random Utility Theory postulates that:
i. *the probability of individuals choosing a given option is a function of their socioeconomic characteristics and the relative attractiveness of the option; and*
ii. *that individuals have good information, compare alternatives in their choice set and choose the one that maximised their utility.*

The task of the analyst is to estimate the best representation of these utility functions based on observations of actual or stated choices and data describing each alternative (in terms of travel time, costs, etc.) and the traveller (income, car ownership, etc.).

In doing so we can distinguish an observable or systematic utility and a part that is not observable as it correspond to attributes of the alternatives and the traveller that we have not allowed for in our models; this unobservable component translates into an error term ξ with standard deviation σ in our models. Therefore we write the utility for alternative j for a representative group of individuals q as:

$$U_{jq} = V_{jq} + \xi_{jq}$$

Where V_{jq} is the Representative or Systematic component, and ξ_{jq} is an error term accounting for all other unobserved characteristics or attributes.

To derive an analytical model we need assumptions about the distribution of errors, the unobserved part. The assumption that errors are distributed Gumbel leads to the Logit formulation; if they are distributed Normal the probabilities of a particular choice are represented by a Probit model, much more difficult to handle than Logit. It is usually assumed that these error terms are *homoscedastic* (a useful word to use in an emergency). This means that all the error terms have the same variance regardless the size of the systematic component. This is a useful but debatable assumption; for example, one would expect this variance to increase with trip length.

8.4   Logit models

The general form for a Multinomial Logit (MNL) giving the probability p of choosing alternative j among many others is, omitting individual q:

$$p_j = \frac{e^{\lambda V_j}}{\sum_j e^{\lambda V_j}}$$

where λ is a scaling parameter related to the error term as:

$$\lambda^2 = \frac{\pi^2}{6\sigma_\varepsilon^2} \quad or \quad \lambda = \frac{\pi}{\sigma_\varepsilon \sqrt{6}} \approx \frac{1.28}{\sigma_\varepsilon}$$

in other words, the greater the standard deviation σ_ε the smaller should be the scaling parameter.

Mode Choice

One would like to incorporate all reasonable explanatory variables in the systematic utility V to reduce the size of the error term. On the other hand, the coarser are our measures of access, waiting and travel time (and any other attributer in V) the smaller should be λ. This observation gains relevance, for example, when moving from Stated Preference (with individual locations for origins and destinations) to zonal models.

Systematic utility functions contain, in general, an Alternative Specific Constant (ASC) that it is actually measured against the best alternative whose constant is assumed zero. The ASC tries to capture all other systematic factors the users consider in their choices. It is, however, a rather blunt instrument and other aspects of individual choice will be represented by the error term. If there are reasons to believe that this error term may be different for each mode or demand segment then a different scaling parameter for each may be appropriate. This may happen when the more subtle attributes influencing the choice of public transport are different from those consider to choose car, taxi or active modes.

The effect of having an ASC is to displace the curve of probability from the central point. Different values of the scaling parameter, on the other hand, will affect the sensitivity (elasticity) of the model with respect to changes in utilities or generalised costs. This is illustrated in the next figure for a binary (two alternatives) Logit model.

Note that the Logit formulation with linear in the parameters utility functions (the most common form) is sensitive to only utility/cost differences. This has the unwelcome property that a 5 minutes saving in a 30-minute journey has the same effect on choice as a 5 minute saving in a 5-hour journey, something intuitively implausible. There are ways of compensating for this property, for example, the use of VTTS as a function of trip length as presented in Table 4.

Another issue of contention is whether fares and tolls should enter as such or divided by income[40]. The second approach would be desirable if one average VTTS is used. Otherwise, most studies conclude that the direct introduction of price works better provided suitable market segmentation is used. This highlights, once again, the importance of market segmentation in the analysis of traffic and revenue projections.

---

[40] It is sometimes divided by the natural logarithm (LN) of income

FIGURE 21 DIFFERENT SCALING PARAMETERS FOR A BINARY LOGIT FORMULATION

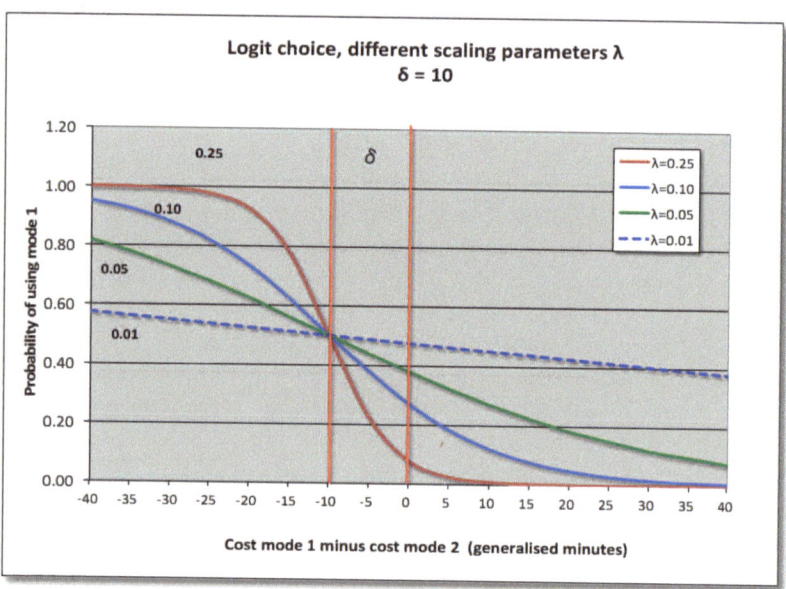

The point elasticity is extracted directly from a MNL. That is the percentage change in the probability of choosing alternative A_j with respect to a marginal change in a given attribute X_{jk}, is simply given by:

$$E_{pj,Xjk} = \lambda \, X_{jk} \, (1 - p_j)$$

This is a useful relationship to bear in mind. It shows, for example, that the elasticity to self price changes is greater for high prices but lower if the proportion currently paying it is high.

The incremental form of the Multinomial Logit (MNL) is, with sub-indices i and j omitted for simplicity:

$$p_k^1 = \frac{p_k^0 \exp(GC_k - GC_k^0)}{\sum_j p_j^0 \exp(GC_j - GC_j^0)} = \frac{p_k^0 \exp(\Delta V_k)}{\sum_j p_j^0 \exp(\Delta V_j)}$$

where

p_k^1 is the new proportion of trips using alternative k;

p_k^0 is the original proportion of trips by alternative k; and

Mode Choice

$\Delta V_k = V_k - V_k^0$ is the difference in utilities (or generalised costs times λ if used in the model)

Note that multiplicative and additive version of incremental mode choice models are also usable.

In order to deal with the limitations that 5 minutes savings are worth the same in short and long trips some incremental models use percentage variations in trip lengths and sometimes a combination of absolute and incremental mode choice models. I find this more difficult to defend preferring to segment the market also by trip length and adopt values of times sensitive to this.

One must remember that incremental models tend to pivot on existing travel patterns. This may be a problem in places with initial low levels of usage of a mode that is to be radically improved; the incremental version may not fully capture the shift in sentiment that may accompany the introduction of a new public transport mode. Common sense checks will be needed to ensure one is not exaggerating nor dampening likely choice changes.

8.5 Limitations

The MNL model is subject to a property called the **Independence of Irrelevant Alternatives** or **IIA**. This is because when any two alternatives have a non-zero probability of being chosen, the ratio of one probability over the other is unaffected by the presence or absence of any additional alternative in the choice set.

$$\frac{p_j}{p_i} = e^{\lambda(V_j - V_i)}$$

and this is independent of any other alterative

This is a useful property when estimating models with many alternatives. It is unrealistic, however, for some choices; for example it would normal to expect that the choice between car and bus be affected by improvements to the metro system.

The IIA property is to blame for the **blue bus/red bus conundrum:** painting half of the buses red and the other half blue increases the choices and reduces the car share, see MT 214.

8.6 Nested Logit

Nested or hierarchical choice models have been used for years to overcome this difficulty. The aim is to put together choice sets that are more similar in a hierarchical structure, for example as illustrated in Figure 22 for mode choice.

These models are slightly more difficult to estimate but retain a good deal of the choice realism and reduce the effect of the IIA property.

As described in Modelling Transport, there are other even more useful mode choice models, in particular Mixed Logit that allows a distribution in the values of some parameters; this is attractive and very practical when dealing with WTP.

Estimating these models is not as easy as estimating trip generation formulations. It is tempting to assume values for the parameters in the utility functions, in other words transferring parameters from other contexts, and calibrate only λ and δ. However, it is better if the full utility functions are estimated first and **then** contrasted against standard values borrowed from other sources.

FIGURE 22 HIERARCHICAL LOGIT STRUCTURE

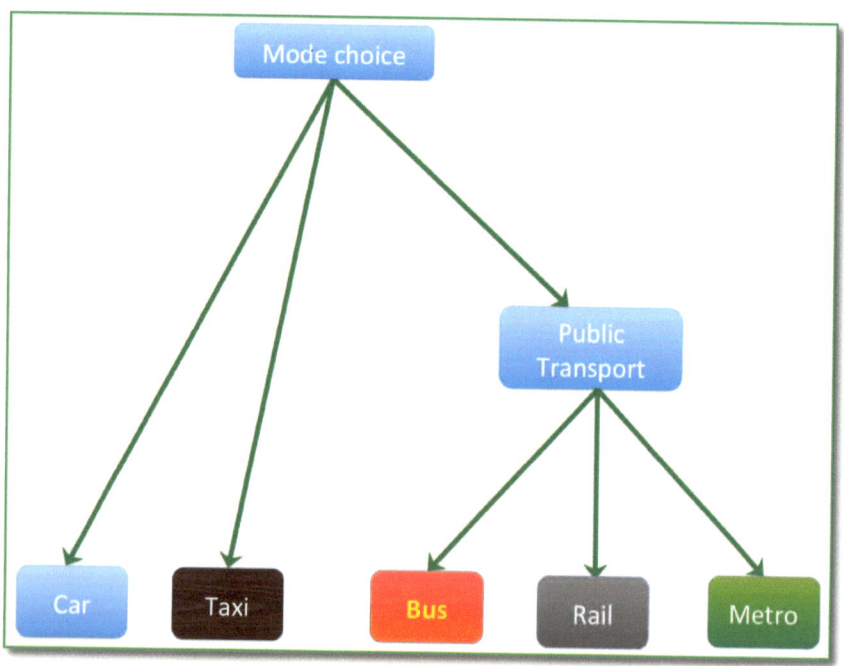

Mode Choice

During the process of model estimation one is likely to encounter some problems, in particular with the sign of some parameters or whether they are statistically significant or not (for example t Student's test). The following table shows what the conflicts may be depending if the variable is a key one and whether it has the correct (intuitive) sign or not. A key variable is one we cannot do without, for example those for price or in-vehicle time in transport concessions.

TABLE 5 SELECTION OF VARIABLES AND STATISTICAL SIGNIFICANCE

Variable selection cases		Variable	
		Key	Other
Correct Sign	Significant	Include	Include
	Not Significant	Include	May Reject
Incorrect Sign	Significant	BIG PROBLEM	Reject
	Not Significant	Problem	Reject

In my own experience whenever a new set of models is to be estimated from raw data (RP or SP) the process takes longer than expected. The initial models are unlikely to be acceptable and it will take some cleaning of the data, omission of outliers and other techniques before a usable model emerges. The quality of the resulting model depends on the experience and judgment of the analysts supported by a battery of goodness-of-fit indices.

8.7 Other choice models

Some software offer alternatives to Logit formulation that may be of interest. Some effectively overcome the extreme effect of small time savings over long journeys. One of them is Kirchhoff's formulation. The proportion of trip makers between origin i and destination j that chooses alternative k as a function of the respective generalised costs C_{ij}^k is given by:

$$P_{ij}^k = \frac{(C_{ij}^k)^{-n}}{\sum_1^k (C_{ij}^k)^{-n}}$$

where n is a parameter to be calibrated or transferred from another location or time (values for n between 4 and 9 have been suggested for both mode and route choice models of this nature). With a judicious choice of n this formulation produces a curve not too dissimilar from the equivalent Logit equation. This model makes choice a function of generalised cost ratios and not cost differences. It is claimed, for this reason, to handle long and short trips better.

8.8 Sub-mode choice

An alternative to hierarchical or nested Logit is to model only the choice between car and public transport and perhaps taxis if they are important in number. The choice among public transport modes is then undertaken as part of an assignment task. This is equivalent to a sub-mode choice model with large scaling parameters making the differences in travel costs dominant at the sub-mode choice.

To be fair, some public transport assignment models allow for more than one route to be taken from an origin to a destination, either because of congestion (overcrowding) or simply because of stochastic effects.

Sub-mode choice by assignment would work better if there is sufficient disaggregation (segmentation) of person types with different WTP and preferences for comfort or frequency or avoidance of transfers.

This type of sub-mode choice may tend, to overestimate the number of people transferring from other public transport modes to a new and better one. On the positive side, it is simpler to implement and supports a more transparent interpretation of the results, a key element in dealing with uncertainty.

8.9 Sense checks

The estimation of a model with satisfactory goodness of fit is not enough. We need to make sure the model makes sense, the parameters are not too wildly different from others we know from experience, and that when used in earnest it will not produce strange and exaggerated (or insensitive) responses.

This is an area where international benchmarking can help despite the difficulties of finding comparable contexts.

Mode Choice

Sensitivity analysis, discussed later in this text, can go a long way to ascertain the robustness of the results of any application of mode choice modelling. Small changes in new mode travel time or fare should not have a disproportionate impact on mode choice. Sensitivity analysis can provide elasticity estimates and these can then be compared with elasticities found elsewhere, see for example to compilation at the Victoria Transport Policy Institute[41]. For example, it has been found that fare elasticities to transit ridership are in the range -0.3 to -0.5 in the short-run, and -0.6 to -0.7 in the long-run (based on British and French data). However, these values depend on the quality of the alternatives, the actual mode share and, of course, on levels of congestion and cultural values. Another useful source of elasticities is Balcome et al[42].

This distinction of short and long-term elasticities is interesting as it implies that certain behavioural responses take longer to materialize, as commented in respect of job and residential changes. It is unclear which elasticity is implied in the classic models. They are estimated with cross sectional data containing a mixture of short and longer term changes as reality is never in equilibrium. This is again a case where noise in the data detracts from the quality of the models, in particular to distinguish between short and long term travel responses.

---

[41] Litman, T. (2009) Transportation Elasticities How Prices and Other Factors Affect Travel Behavior. Victoria Transport Policy Institute

[42] Balcombe, R; Mackett, R; Paulley, N; Preston, J; Shires, J; Titheridge, H; Wardman, M; White, P.(2004) The demand for public transport: a practical guide. Transportation Research Laboratory Report TRL593. Transportation Research Laboratory: London, UK.

Time of travel choice

> *"When one admits that nothing is certain one must, I think, also add that some things are more nearly certain than others."*
> **Bertrand Russell**

9. TIME OF TRAVEL CHOICE

9.1 Background

All large cities experience the phenomenon of "peak spreading". As congestion increases, some drivers choose different departure times to avoid the worst delays and therefore the duration of the peak is extended. Something similar happens when public transport is overcrowded.

The change of departure time is often recognised as the second most likely response to changes in travel conditions, the first one being the change of route. This change is driven by efforts to avoid the worst of congestion but may also reflect pricing structures in toll roads, parking and public transport. Greater flexibility in working hours facilitates this spread of departure times.

Despite its importance, a large number of transport models actually ignore time of travel choice as a behavioural response treating it very simply, if at all. Denying its existence does not make it go away. However, we must recognise that cross-section data collection methods do not capture this behaviour, only a noisy snapshot.

It is interesting to note that this issue has received little attention in most Traffic & Revenue studies. There is often too little time to look into it. Ignoring it may exaggerate congestion on the rest of the network and increase the apparent attractiveness of toll roads and mass transit facilities.

9.2 Macro and Micro Departure Time Choice

It is useful to distinguish between macro and micro time of travel choice. Macro time choice involves the selection of travel between broad time periods; say travel during the AM Peak or mid afternoon. Micro departure time choice is more closely related to the phenomenon of peak spreading and involves small changes in the start of a trip. Both behavioural responses are thought to be active at any one time.

9.3 Micro Departure Time Choice

A basic concept in micro departure time choice is that travellers have a *preferred time* of travel and any shift away from it incurs disutility, known as *schedule disutility*. The preferred time of travel may be defined as the preferred departure time or preferred arrival time, the second one being more important for certain activities (e.g. work with a fixed starting time, business meetings, theatre). The schedule disutility can be added to the travel time disutility to express a combined utility function for travel with variable departure time, see MT Section 11.5.

Estimating these parameters is extremely difficult with current data collection methods. Stated Preference would help but requires a difficult experimental setting for this type of question, in particular sample expansion.

It is not surprising, therefore, that most applications simply attempt to model the duration of the peak; this can be done using time series of the proportion of the peak period traffic that takes place in the peak hour and extrapolate the trend to future years.

The problem becomes more complex if an urban toll road is to be provided and in particular if it is to have different toll levels at different times. The addition of new capacity will enable some trip makers to change their time of travel to a more preferred one, thus reducing their schedule disutility. This may be partly compensated by a higher toll at peak periods. A more explicit time of travel model may be required, even if its parameters are difficult to estimate. MT 424 suggests some practical ways to implement this.

If tolls remain constant during the day the problem becomes less difficult as it could be argued that those who shift their departure time will end up paying the same toll anyway and revenues would be unaffected. However, the issue of estimating the most realistic level of congestion in any time period remains and this would affect the size of time savings using the tolled facility and therefore its attractiveness and revenues.

9.4 Macro time choice

Almost inevitably this will result in discrete choice models (discretising time into periods) albeit with parameters that are difficult to estimate. They should only be applied to discretionary trips or tours. It is recognised that there will be long-term responses for non-discretionary travel but these are better handled as part of destination choice changes.

In principle, macro departure time choice can be modelled as a Logit choice between travelling at different periods. Travelling in each period will be more or less desirable and will incur in different levels of travel

Time of travel choice

time and cost (fares, parking, tolls and/or congestion charging). However, if the demand models use the typical division of time into two peak periods and an inter-peak, the freedom of most trips to transfer between them will be limited. Few work trips, for example, could move outside a three-hour peak periods entirely, and such a mechanism might be applied predominantly for discretionary trips rather than those to work or education.

To model macro choices, it is necessary to know what proportion of each type of trip takes place in each period. This information is best collected from household survey data that contains complete tours. At a macro level, trips must be allocated to a discrete time period even those that start and finish in different periods. An incremental Logit model can then be used to modify the total number of trips of each type in each time period according to the changes in the generalised costs.

In my experience most transport concession studies ignore macro time choice. This is in part because the new facility will increase capacities (public transport or road) and therefore rather than displacing trips to other times it will allow some individuals to travel at their own preferred time, whether they are paying the new fare or toll or benefiting from the reduced congestion. This is perceived as a potential, often ignorable, upside.

9.5 Simplified approaches

It is possible to adopt pragmatic assumptions about the duration of the peak in the future and how expected demand is going to be spread over this period. This requires only simple factoring of demand for future peak periods in order to generate reasonable levels of congestion and delay. To estimate how much it will change in the future one may use historical traffic count data to track the evolution of peak duration.

9.6 Sense checks

As with other stages in the modelling process it will be important to perform sense checks on the results of any time of day choice. As there are few elasticities available for contrasting results the tests should take a different form and rely more on experience, logic and intuition.

It will be useful to compare results of the model system with and without time of day choice, both in terms of traffic and in terms of daily revenue. If the difference is large then a logical explanation must be found and this should satisfy the modeller, any peer reviewer and the financial institutions involved.

Assignment

> *"Conventional economics is mistaken when it views the economy and society as a machine, whose behaviour, no matter how complicated, is ultimately predictable".* **Paul Ormerod**

10. ASSIGNMENT

10.1 Principles

Route choice and assignment are probably the best understood of the travel behavioural responses, at least in principle. They play a critical role in the study of any type of transport concession and are particularly important for toll roads.

During this stage the mode matrices estimated in previous models are assigned to the network obtaining flows and travel costs, for both vehicles on the road network and passengers on public transport modes. People choose routes in a number of different ways. In dense road networks the number of possible routes between A and B is very large but most drivers will seek to minimise travel time and cost or a combination of both. Other factors will also matter, for example signage (in particular for the occasional user), complex driving manoeuvres at some junctions and travel time variability. In the case of public transport the number of routes is much more limited. However, there are many other attributes to bear in mind in addition to travel time: fares, walking and waiting, number of interchanges, reliability of services.

Congestion affects both private and public transport users. In the case of cars, traffic approaching capacity will slow down speeds and eventually generate queues and delays. The nominal capacity of 2000 car-equivalents (passenger car units or pcus) per lane is much restricted at junctions. In the case of public transport users congestion can take two related forms. The first one is the discomfort of travelling in crowded conditions; a nominal capacity of 6 persons per square metre is considered a reasonable limit but not a comfortable one. The second form is the inability to board a bus or train because that capacity has been reached. The first form translates into a disutility of discomfort and the second one a disutility of delay.

In the case of public transport, assignment is more complex as often the mode of access is very important. For example, in dealing with the introduction of a regional rail service in Mexico it was necessary to design feeder services to make the new system competitive with geographically more flexible (but slower and less reliable) inter urban buses and coaches.

10.2 Modelling vehicle route choice and assignment

Real traffic is made up of discrete units with size (vehicles) moving on roads with lanes and junctions, and obeying "rules of physics and rules of the road". These features are handled well in micro-simulation models, mostly used for local problems. However, for consistent and realistic route choice modelling in larger areas some simplification is required. The most common approach is to treat assignment as a steady state or static system where all traffic entering the network will clear it (reach their destination) within an allocated time period, say one hour. Under this treatment the flow rate on each link is uniform during this period and may exceed physical capacity. This ignores the dynamic nature of traffic with demand varying over time; moreover, the influence of traffic control modulates these variations thus affecting delays at junctions and over the whole trip. In practice, queues build up at intersections with delays changing depending on the time of travel. Dynamic Traffic Assignment (DTA) attempts to represent these features without the level of detail of micro-simulation.

The distribution of WTP is accounted for in assignment with multiple user classes, that is demand segments with different VTTS. A classification of static assignment methods is outlined in Table 6. The methods are classified according to three distinctions: whether one or multiple user classes are used, whether congestion is modelled to calculate travel times as a function of flows and whether one allows for stochastic effects. The latter aims to model the fact that not all people think the same nor perceive costs in the same way.

As willingness to pay is critical in estimating revenues the most relevant of these methods are Wardrop's User Equilibrium and Stochastic User Equilibrium, both with multiple user classes.

Dynamic Traffic Assignment adds a layer of complexity to this classification recognising queue building and enforcing physical capacity constraints. This leads to Dynamic User Equilibrium (DUE), with or without stochastic effects, as discussed later in this chapter.

Assignment

TABLE 6 CLASSIFICATIONS OF STATIC ASSIGNMENT METHODS

		Stochastic effects included?	
		No	Yes
Single user class	No Capacity restraint	All-or-nothing	Pure stochastic: Dial's, Burrell's
	With capacity restraint	Wardrop's user equilibrium UE	Stochastic user equilibrium SUE
Multiple user classes	No Capacity restraint	All-or-nothing with multiple user classes	Multiple user classes stochastic: Dial's, Burrell's
	With capacity restraint	Wardrop's equilibrium with multiple user classes	Stochastic user equilibrium with multiple user classes

10.3 Equilibrium assignment

Under user equilibrium assignment all routes chosen between an Origin and a Destination have the same generalised cost for each user class. If one route was better some people would switch to it and change the flow pattern. This equilibrium solution is unique on link flows and travel costs and there are well-understood conditions required to identify it. The main requirement is that:

The cost-flow relationships must be monotonically increasing functions of their own flow

This condition is met by the cost-flow relationships in use and the assignment of fixed matrices with different user classes and VTTS. It is customary to pre-load bus services on their fixed routes. Trucks can also be pre-loaded but it is more common to assign them together with cars albeit with different generalised cost functions. Trucks may be banned from using certain links during a modelled period and this must be reflected in the network.

Static equilibrium assignment with multiple user classes produces a solution that is unique on flows and travel costs but not unique on route flows and user-class flows on links. As more than one path is generally used to connect O and D it is possible to swap travellers between paths without changing total flows and costs (or swapping 3 cars for one truck between routes). This is not a problem in most cases except in identifying the user classes that use particular links, some of which may be tolled; this is, in our case important as it creates two issues. First, the use of matrix estimation from counts cannot uniquely adjust a multiple user-class prior matrix. Second, and more important, as trucks pay higher tolls than cars any estimates of tolling revenues is subject to some additional uncertainty as we cannot be sure of the traffic make-up at the toll plaza.

Boyce and Xie[43] have added a condition of proportionality (the proportion of vehicles on each of two equal cost alternative path segments should be the same regardless of user-class, origin or destination) that removes this non-uniqueness. This is a reasonable condition and may be applied if this problem becomes critical. However, in many cases this will not be necessary as congestion may not play a key role in heavy vehicles route choice and/or the toll rate of heavy vehicles is related to their car equivalence (pcu value) rather than the probably greater damage they cause to the roads; in this case the revenue at the toll plaza will be the same.

All commercial software have efficient algorithms to achieve Wardrop's User Equilibrium and recent years have seen improved efficiency (speed of convergence) in them. User equilibrium is, in my view, the preferred approach for modelling toll roads. The main reason for this is not that equilibrium happens in practice; it does not. User Equilibrium is a reasonable approximation to real congested networks that facilitates interpretation of results, a key element in any practical application.

Convergence and run times are critical in most models. Computation follows, up to now, Moore's law. But assignment, and in particular if its resulting costs are fed back to other models in an iterative arrangement, takes a very long time to converge to adequate levels. Convergence is usually defined in terms of changes to flows (or costs) on all links in the network as this is important to deliver reliable results.

---

[43] Boyce, D. and Xie, J. (2013) Assigning user class link flows uniquely. Transportation Research Part A 53, pp 22-35.

Assignment

10.4 Limitations of conventional assignment

Assignment methods suffer from a number of limitations that must be borne in mind. Many of them apply to any assignment technique and understanding them helps in the interpretation of results. The most important limitations are as follows:

Limitations in the node-link model of road networks

These include the absence of penalised turns at node-junctions and 'end effects' due to the aggregation of trip ends into zones represented by single centroids.

The representation of junctions as nodes is only possible as a coarse approximation. Most junctions in congested areas are controlled and this means that some turning movements may "cost' more than others or even be banned. Node junctions can be expanded into representations of turning movements whose delays will depend on the junction control scheme. In most cases this means that delays on one movement depend on its flows and those on other approaches to the junction. In static assignment this is handled by steady-state junction delay models. Note that this makes the flow-delay relationship non-separable and may even prevent convergence to a unique equilibrium solution; see MT 414 ss.

Imperfect capacity constraint

Conventional flow-delay relationships generally allow flows above capacity on a link or junction. This is unrealistic even if the travel times are approximately well represented. In reality a queue is formed at these locations and it may not clear in the modelling period. The residual queue will be passed onto the next modelling period that will start with an initial queue delay for this reason.

Some static models accommodate some elements of these effects, for example blocking-back at junctions, but in general this is a problem that is best tackled with mesoscopic assignment models as discussed under dynamic assignment.

Not all trip makers perceive costs in the same way

The modelling of multiple user classes (each with different willingness to pay for a better service) is a good way of tackling this issue, provided there is sufficient disaggregation to capture the most important elements of travel behaviour.

In practice, at least 10 user classes are need to achieve this but better models may use up to 20, six for trucks and the rest for different type of users. In the context of toll roads, some users may have high willingness to pay for services because their costs are covered by their employers; others may be very price-sensitive because of personal income or cash flow constraints.

The assumption of perfect information about costs in all parts of the network

This is one of the most significant simplifications. Drivers have only partial information about traffic conditions on the same route last time they used it and on problems in other parts of the network depending on their own experience, disposition to explore new routes, the use of GPS route guidance and traffic information services. Even then, the best vehicle navigation system will not be able to accurately forecast any incidents in the network that may affect drivers. Imperfect information can be reduced but never eliminated.

There is evidence that many drivers are heavily influenced by road signs in their choice of route and that sometimes the signed routes are not the cheapest. Equally important in our context is the fact that unless well signposted a new toll road will not be "discovered" immediately by drivers.

Day-to-day variations in demand

The trip matrix represented in most models is an "average" of different days, even if we do not fully understand what type of average this is. Wardrop's User Equilibrium is at best an average assignment that does not correspond to any particular day.

In the same vein, there are time variations in demand and flow within each day. A 5-minute delay in departure for the same journey may produce a greater delay on arrival at the destination because of increased congestion in the network. The costs on links change dynamically in response to traffic: some drivers understand this well and plan their journeys accordingly; others lack the necessary experience.

Wardrop's equilibrium solution, however, has enough desirable properties of stability and interpretation to warrant its use in practice; however, it is still only an approximation to the traffic conditions on any one day.

Instant response and no search costs

In common with the rest of the classic models, Assignment assumes instant response to changes in the network. There are no search-for-new-routes costs that in practice imply a degree of "stickiness" in the routes actually chosen.

This limitation is handled, again, through ramp-up post modelling adjustments discussed later on in Chapter 13. It takes time for travellers

10.5 Dynamic Traffic Assignment

Most classic assignment methods assume the existence of a trip matrix that is valid over a modelling period, say one hour in the peak. Traffic is then assigned onto the network under the assumption of steady state conditions over that period; this implies that all traffic entering the network during the period actually reaches its destination within the same period. In practice, however, traffic behaviour is dynamic and "steady state" is only a useful simplification. Consider, for example, a road that provide access to a town centre and that most drivers will like to reach it around 9:00 AM. Figure 23 represents an idealized diagram of traffic along this road starting from a place 60 minutes away from the town centre. There is a section that limits the capacity to some 4000 cars/hour at a distance of 30 min from the town centre. In this case, not all traffic will be able to get through the bottleneck in one go; queues will build up that will be cleared once demand falls below the 4000 cars/hour limit.

A further dynamic effect is due to interaction between time-varying flows at junctions; for example, good signal coordination reduces delays by timing greens to the platoon of vehicle moving along an arterial.

FIGURE 23 IDEALISED DYNAMICS OF TRAFFIC ON A RADIAL LINK

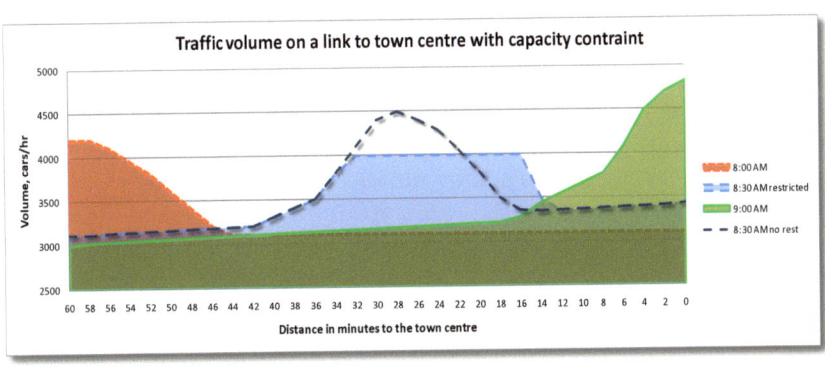

It is possible to develop simplified approaches to this problem using extensions of the static assignment treatment. The first improvement is to discretise time into smaller time slices, typically 15 minutes; this requires disaggregating trip matrices to the same time slices. The second improvement is to treat absolute capacities and queue building in these time slices, passing on residual queues (and delays) to the next period. These extensions of static assignment are available in most commercial packages.

A better approximation to true DTA is to recognise the physicality of traffic adopting a mesoscopic approach. This no longer treats traffic as a multi-commodity fluid described in terms of vehicles or passengers per hour. They handle traffic as platoons (SATURN) or packets of vehicles (AVENUE, DYNASMART). Platoons have been successfully used to model traffic and optimise systems of traffic signals, for example in TRANSYT. Packets are also used in mesoscopic assignment models; they occupy space and interact with each other. Micro-simulation models use individual vehicles together with rules for accelerating, braking, overtaking, changing lanes and so on.

Mesoscopic models are the most commonly used approximation to dynamic assignment as micro-simulation models still find it difficult to handle route choice consistently for large networks. Their objective is more focussed: to model traffic in complex and congested local situations.

If realistic representation of congestion is paramount in estimating the flows on a future toll road then the use of mesoscopic simulation models may be the best way forward; see MT 411 ss. Data collection capable of capturing these dynamic effects will be necessary. Good software offers the facility to select the areas of the network where mesoscopic simulation is applied while the rest is treated in a more conventional fashion. Moreover, packages like DYNASMART and AVENUE offer facilities to model Managed Lanes in a more realistic form than macroscopic static models.

Micro-simulation is a very powerful modelling tool dealing with vehicle-by-vehicle movements (and some can also model pedestrians and two-wheelers at the same time). They usually display traffic movements and performance using advanced graphic animation tools. They support models with a large number of parameters to account for different rules of the road, different driving styles and attitudes, different vehicles and different levels of skills in driving. Their calibration takes a good deal of time as parameters like gap acceptance, aggression and anticipation need to be established for a particular context. This calibrations is often based on indicators like travel time, queue length and, in particular, that the associated animations showing the movement of vehicles on a network, is reasonable. Once calibrated, they become very persuasive software tools as decision makers can visualise, in the animations, the modelled results of alternative interventions.

The main micro simulation software packages like AIMSUN, Paramics and VISSIM are particularly attractive to deal with road and junction design issues. They can account for the dynamics of traffic

Assignment

better than any other approach. However, they are, as yet, less useful in modelling larger networks and situations where route and perhaps mode choice are essential.

For the purpose of toll road modelling the DTA features of mesoscopic modelling suites like SATURN, DYNASMART and AVENUE are generally more suitable.

10.6 Stochastic effects

Stochastic user equilibrium models (SUE) or simply stochastic methods attempt to represent the effects of imperfect knowledge and differences in perception of link and route costs; see MT 361. There are several approaches to this and most software packages include at least one or two of them in their toolkit. They all produce assignments that spread routes a bit wider than strict equilibrium as some OD pairs use less than optimal (from the analyst perspective) routes.

One group of methods is based on Monte Carlo simulation. Random sampling is used to create a range of link costs following an assume distribution for them in each link. Then, successive iterations are performed with different sets of randomised costs.

Proportion based methods seek to approximate discrete choice models to route choice selection. A general problem is that there are numerous routes available and normally these cannot be enumerated (identified). This requires some assumptions to select attractive routes that could reasonably be considered.

Some modellers prefer stochastic assignments methods, usually SUE, because of its claimed greater realism with fewer user classes. I prefer strict UE methods with a larger number of user classes to capture most of the variations among individuals. Stochastic methods make interpretation more difficult and this detracts, in my view, from their value.

10.7 Travel time reliability

Conventional assignment techniques include travel time and costs as the two components of generalised costs. It can be argued that the reliability of travel time, as discussed in section 4.4, should also be included.

It is relatively simple to include the standard deviation of travel time as part of the generalised costs and use SP methods to estimate its value. Failing this, the coefficients discussed in Table 4 can be used to estimate the corresponding values.

Another issue is to estimate how this variability of travel time will change when a new facility is included. This requires a model of travel time variability most likely related to the levels of congestion that in turn amplifies the role of incidents in affecting travel time.

I was involved in research trying to achieve precisely this (MT 413). The resulting model was a function free flow travel time (FFTT) and a congestion index, defined as
CI = Average Journey Time/FFTT.

This resulted in the following model to estimate future standard deviation of travel time, as a good compromise between simplicity and realism:

$$\sigma_t = 0.9 \, FFTT^{0.87}(CI-1)$$

In practical terms this model offers a simple form for relating the standard deviation of travel time to network conditions and is relatively insensitive to trip length. One advantage of this treatment is that journey time variability can be estimated after assignment and then incorporated into other choice models (time of day, mode, and destination choice). Complex interactions between congestion, travel time variability and route choice are then avoided.

More recently, work for the UK Department for Transport[44] used distance d and the Coefficient of Variation CV of travel time (σ/mean) and recommended the following formulation for a particular modelling period:

$$CV = \propto CI^\beta d^{-0.39}$$

Where α is in the range 0.1 to 0.19 (expected value 0.16)

The range for β is 0.50 to 1.37 (expected value 1.02)

The reason behind this variation is the nature of the links and junctions in each route.

Note that both models were developed originally on the basis of route travel time variability. In practice, it is easier to handle link travel time variability as a component of generalised costs in assignment. This is an area deserving further research.

The estimation of future travel time variability often assumes perfect ($\sigma = 0$) reliability for the new facility whereas existing services retain their observed values. This overestimates the advantages of the new

---

[44] Department of Transport (2007) Forecasting Travel Time Variability in Urban Areas Deliverable D1: Data Analysis and Model Development. UK Department of Transport

Assignment

scheme, as σ will not actually be zero. A better assumption is to relate future travel time reliability to flow and congestion on all roads.

10.8 Modelling tolls

As suggested before, tolls should be included in the generalised cost as monetary costs although some software requires it to be represented as an equivalent delay (toll/VTTS). The general equation for generalised costs for a particular user class on a link a would be:

$$C_a = VTTSt_a + \Delta VTTSt_a \delta^a + VTTR\sigma t_a + bd_a + Toll$$

Where t_a is the normal travel time and VTTS is the value for that particular user class

$\Delta VTTS$ is the additional value for congested or poor roads, say 30% of VTTS

VTTR is the value of travel time reliability and σt_a the standard deviation of travel time on that link

δ^a is a 0/1 dummy to indicate if this link is heavily congested or not dual carriageway, etc.

bd_a is the product of the distance on the link by the perceived operating cost b

Toll is the price (if any) to be charged per vehicle in the same monetary units as *VTTS*.

The application of this relationship requires some care. The starting point is the value of *VTTS* for a particular demand segment. If this is the value of time savings on good quality uncongested roads then it would be appropriate to add a penalty (a *malus, ΔVTTS*) to travel costs on normal congested roads. If *VTTS* is based on normal congested roads then it would be appropriate to apply a motorway *premium* or *bonus* (a reduction in *VTTS*) when using high-quality, dual-carriageway, uncongested roads. Sadly, the basis for each VTTS estimation is not always made clear and the issue is resolved during calibration.

The use of a reliability factor *VTTR* is trickier. It requires *VTTS* to be established on the basis of entirely, or at least, fairly reliable travel times. Otherwise the effect of variability in travel times would have been included in the *malus* or *bonus* above. This is discussed further when dealing with specific toll roads issues in Chapter 14. It is important to get a good understanding of how these parameters have been chosen or calibrated under present conditions otherwise one risks "overcooking the books".

The application of this formulation with at least 10 user classes and VTTS should satisfy many requirements. Six of these user classes would correspond to cars and the other four to different types of trucks; more details again in Chapter 14. Greater segmentation may be necessary and desirable for complex conditions. The different values of time will produce a spread of routes and, more importantly, will allocate to a toll road only those with the ability to pay thus assisting interpretation.

Another alternative, offered by several software packages, consist in identifying at least two routes for each Origin Destination (OD) pair, one is the best (fastest) using toll roads and the other using only untolled links. Then a choice model is applied to these alternatives. To obtain the first and fastest route toll prices are ignored but they are included in the application of the choice model. This approach requires fewer user classes.

A related approach is provided by the module TRIBUT[45] in VISUM. These allow explicitly for the lognormal distribution of VTTSs and allocate trips to good alternative routes.

My personal preference is to use a stochastic approach only when unavoidable, as results are more difficult to interpret.

10.9 Public Transport Assignment

This is more complex than private vehicle assignment because of the nature of networks, fares and the different characteristics of each service. The network includes, as links, sections of the bus or rail services running between two stops or stations. The concept of link capacity is associated to the capacity of each unit (bus, train) and its corresponding frequency. Travel time has an in-vehicle component as well as components for waiting at stops and walking to and from them. Many of the public-transport sections will use road links, e.g. most buses and some Light Rail Transit (LRT) services with street running; in these cases there will be an interaction between public and private transport speeds. There will be other public-transport sections or services which will use completely different links, e.g. busways, segregated rail track, etc.

Passengers can access public transport in different ways; they can walk to a stop, interchange between two services and even drive part of the way to board a public-transport service later. This calls for the need to provide and specify walk and transfer links between different services, different public-transport modes (bus, rail) and between public-and private-transport facilities (e.g. 'Park & Ride').

---

[45] Ptv (2010) VISUM 10.0 User Manual. PTV

Assignment

Fares introduce another level of complexity. Modern payment systems based on smart cards or mobile phones allow complex fare structures: fares variable with distance, flat fares (independent of distance travelled), zonal fares (for one or more specific geographic zones), combination and transfer tickets (valid for two or more services), time limit fares (e.g. valid for any number of boardings in an hour), daily, weekly and other period (season) tickets for a fixed service or covering one or more zones and modes.

For these reasons, it is easier to define the generalised cost of travelling between two points rather than incrementally on each link, as defined in Chapter 3:

$$C_{ij} = a_1 t^v_{ij} + a_2 t^w_{ij} + a_3 t^t_{ij} + a_4 t^n_{ij} + a_5 F_{ij} + a_6 \phi_j + \delta$$

where

t^v_{ij} is the in-vehicle travel time between i and j;

t^w_{ij} is the walking time to and from stops (stations) or from parking area/lot;

t^t_{ij} is the waiting time at stops (or time spent searching for a parking space);

t^n_{ij} is the interchange time, if any;

The last three of these times are sometimes referred to as Out-of-Vehicle-Time (OVT).

F_{ij} is a monetary charge: the fare charged to travel between i and j;

ϕ_j is a terminal (typically parking if Park & Ride is used) cost associated with the journey from i to j;

δ is a *modal penalty*, a parameter representing all other attributes not included in the generalised measure so far, e.g. safety, comfort and convenience; a more general version of generalised costs call this parameter an *alternative specific constant* as it could be, for example, an initial resistance to use a new payment system to access a new mode.

$a_1 \ldots _6$ are weights attached to each element of cost; they have dimensions appropriate for conversion of all attributes to common units, e.g. money or time.

In-vehicle travel time depends on the speed attainable and the number and duration of stops en route and these will be affected by the operational design of the new service. Walking time, which depends on proximity to the best stop, is in some cases approximated by an average value for a whole zone. Interchange time depends on station/stop configuration and separation. Waiting time depends essentially on the frequency of the service and its reliability. A general formulation for waiting time is:

$$t^w = \frac{(h^2 + \sigma^2)}{2h}$$

where h is the expected headway of the service and σ its standard deviation (the less regular a service, the greater the expected waiting time). This formulation assumes that passengers arrive at random at the stop and that no passenger fails to board the next service because of lack of space in it.

If the service is perfectly regular, i.e. $\sigma = 0$, then the expected waiting time is half of the headway. It is known, however, that if the frequency of the service is low, passengers will try to arrive just a few minutes before the next departure, thus setting an upper limit to the expected waiting time of perhaps 5 to 10 minutes; how close to the timetabled departure are passengers aiming to come will depend, of course, on the reliability of the service.

Corridors with many services offering similar routes pose a particular problem for assignment as an "all-or-nothing" solution (all prefer the most frequent service all other attributes being equal) is patently not what happens in practice. Different software packages solve this problem in slightly different ways to produce more realistic results.

A full review of the most suitable algorithms for public-transport assignment is outside the scope of this book; we discuss here some of the issues that affect patronage and revenue projections.

When the frequency of a public transport service is reasonably high travellers will not use or memorise a timetable (if it exists) but just turn up at the stop more or less at random. In these cases the frequency of the services is a sufficient descriptor to estimate waiting times. For longer intervals between services the timetable becomes more important to reduce waiting times. The availability of mobile phone apps that tell you when the next service is due allow even shorter waiting times even for frequent services.

One way of handling this is to introduce a cap on waiting time to a maximum of, say, 10 minutes with no app and 5 with app, depending on context. However, this fails to take full account of the opportunity to provide well-coordinated services even under low frequency schedules; for example, timing a half-hourly bus service to a rail station to arrive there 5 min before the train departs for a main destination. In all these cases Timetable or Schedule Assignment is a more appropriate modelling tool.

Assignment

Transit assignment methods can then be divided into:

- Multi-path approaches, for example the allocation of trips to paths proportional to the perceived service frequencies as outlined above.

- Equilibrium assignment methods with or without a stochastic element in them; these focus on congestion effects on public transport systems.

- Both based on service frequency; and

- Timetable assignment that may include some of the effects above.

The basics ideas behind these methods are discussed in MT Section 10.6.

In the case of very complex fare systems some approximations may be necessary as it may be impractical to try to model all their features. These may be based on the most common type of ticket used. For example, in the case of a zonal fare system assignment may be performed on the basis of time alone and the fare cost added at the end. This may still ignore the importance of season ticket holders but is probably good enough for places like London.

An additional task in Traffic and Revenue studies is the allocation of fare revenues among the different operators in a system. This is usually undertaken post modelling together with any other adjustments for period and discounted tickets.

Public transport assignment suffers, in general, from similar limitations to those identified for road networks. Furthermore, it is fair to say that congested assignment is less well developed for transit networks. There are two effects in play here: first, the limited capacity of the units (buses, trains) may prevent some travellers from implementing their optimal choices, thus increasing their travel times; second, there is interaction between public transport and private cars sharing the same road network–increased traffic on one mode will affect travel times on the other as well.

10.10 Within public transport mode choice

Mode choice, as discussed in the previous chapter, is applicable to both the choice between private (car, motorcycle) and public transport (bus, metro, rail, taxi, para-transit) modes and also between modes in a nested Logit framework; this is sometimes called sub-mode choice. The handling of the main and sub-mode choice in a nested formulation allows direct use of results from Stated Preference surveys that usually arrange choices in that way. It also simplifies the inclusion of mode specific constants in the choice models.

When the new mode in question is very different from existing public transport modes embedding the whole choice process in a nested framework is probably the best approach as it would capture the attractiveness of the new mode and its potential impact on destination changes more clearly. This approach also allows a more natural handling of fares when a significant proportion of users have season tickets; they can be treated as a different segment of travellers. However, this process becomes very complex when most origin destination pairs require one or more mode changes to complete their journeys, as there would be several paths for consideration.

It is also possible to process sub-mode choice through public transport assignment. This is usually more transparent and easier to interpret and therefore preferred by many practitioners when producing traffic and revenue forecasts. Nevertheless, this poses a problem for handling sub-mode specific constants, as they do not fit neatly into the assignment process. A better approach in this case is to do away with mode specific constants and re-estimate the models allowing VTTS to depend on the mode used. In this way the quality of each sub-mode is recognised; more attractive modes will have a lower VTTS.

10.11 Sense checks

There are several ways in which one can test how reasonable results are:

For the opening years:

- Check the capture rate, that is the proportion of in-scope traffic that the model assign to the toll road or new LRT; too high rates are suspicious

- Display the sources of these trips; is it reasonable to abstract trips from these modes, roads? Are routes reasonable (no back-tracking, not too diverted)?

- Check the user segments attracted to the toll road/new mode. Are they the high VTTS user? Other?

- Check the capacity offered by the new mode and estimate passenger densities: too high?

Assignment

For future year projections:

- Are flows on the new facility too close to capacities (or even beyond)?

- Is congestion in the rest of the network too high? If so, there would be more peak spreading and/or additional new capacity not yet planned and one should make reasonable assumptions for these. Check whether strict capacity constraints based on today's figures creates these conditions. Capacities after 2020 will increase with self-driving cars.

- Beware of the effects of stochastic assignment. It may increase or decrease flows on new facilities. If used, check flows against equilibrium assignment and seek to explain the differences.

Induced Demand

> "I collected optimistic data, put it in the context of bad analogies, seasoned it with saliency bias, added herd instinct, a pinch of confirmation bias...and here's your strategy." **Dilbert to his boss**

11. INDUCED DEMAND

11.1 Background

There is plenty of argument about the existence of *induced traffic or demand* and how to estimate it. Strictly speaking, induced demand and traffic are the completely new trips as a result of a new road or transit service; those that were not made before.

There is some evidence that new roads built induce new traffic that takes up part of the additional road space very quickly. Large part of this evidence comes from very congested conditions that had previously suppressed demand: congestion acting as a rationing device. Induced demand has also been used as an argument to weaken the case for more road building and strengthen the case for introducing more efficient public transport modes. There is a potential for a policy bias in some of these research results.

It is useful to distinguish demand that is captured from other routes, modes or destinations from that resulting from income and population growth. Both of them can be modelled using conventional approaches.

Then, there is potentially an additional demand, a trip generation effect, as a result of improved accessibility; here we call this pure induced demand and its counterpart is suppressed demand, those trips that do not take place because of the difficulty or high cost of travel.

In the context of this book, general induced demand will be any residual demand that has not been explicitly modelled. In other words, if the model for a toll road covers only assignment, there may be some additional traffic from changes in destination and mode and one would have to argue the case for considering each; it may be unlikely, however, that there would be any changes in trip generation or pure induced demand. But whether these elements of induced traffic exist will depend on how much have trip costs changed in the area as a result of the new facility and a persuasive narrative will have to be developed to support the argument for induced demand.

11.2 Methods for estimation

The first step in the estimation of any induced demand must be a reasoned argument that justifies its inclusion. Induced demand is not something that you can automatically include in any traffic and revenue forecast. *The default expectation must be that it will not materialise.* One needs to show that induced demand is likely to happen, not using models but an appropriate narrative partly based on what the current model excludes and partly on a deeper understanding of the area that will be served by the new facility and what impact it may have.

Having established that there might be a case for estimating induced demand one should consider how to. The first step should be to identify either a general reduction in travel costs in the study area or specific reduction in generalised costs for particular Origin Destination pairs. It is the size of these changes that may justify induced traffic.

Mode choice. It would be very difficult to persuade a peer reviewer (or at least it should be) that a new toll road will attract customers that previously used public transport, rail or air services. In the case of public transport schemes the mode choice model should have picked up this component anyway.

Destination choice. This might play a role, in particular for shopping and leisure trips. In this context an origin constrained gravity model will give you an estimate of redistributed leisure and shopping movements. A new toll road or metro system will not affect commuting and on-business trips until a suitable time lag, some 5 to 10 years. If an appropriate doubly constrained gravity model is used to estimate this effect then the results should be suitably lagged.

Pure trip generation. I believe that a new public transport or toll road[46] facility is very unlikely to create completely new trips. There are a few cases where this might happen in medium distance services. Perhaps the opportunity to perform a trip to another city and come back in the same day that was impossible to accomplish with the previous levels of service. But in my view this would need to be justified and specific data collected to support this assertion.

Suppressed demand. This is the counterpart of pure trip generation. If there is strong evidence that current conditions affectively suppress demand there would be a better case to defend induced traffic when these constraints are removed.

---

[46] There would be a better case for completely new trips if the new facility is provided for free, for example a shadow toll or a free public transport service.

Induced Demand

Short run and long run elasticities. Some responses to changes in costs take longer than others. An increase in fuel price may shift car ownership to more efficient vehicles but it will take time before this change takes place. Sometimes a distinction between induced traffic (short run) and induced demand (long run) is made on that basis.

11.3 Benchmarking induced traffic

The best way to benchmark induced traffic is either to compare it with similar projects where it has been possible to effectively identify induced traffic. For example, there is the view that High Speed Rail in Spain generated some 25% of extra traffic. It is evident that low cost airlines have generated a number of new trips that previously went to a domestic destination, or did not take place at all.

Another way to benchmark induced traffic is to compare the effective elasticity produced by the model (the extra trips resulting from the gravity model as a result of reduced generalised costs), with elasticities established elsewhere.

One of the problems is that there may be significant differences between short run and long run elasticities and it is not always clear which ones have been identified in empirical studies. The potential differences may be large (e.g. a factor of three or more).

A good source of these elasticities is Appendix B in the US Highway Economic Requirements System-State Version[47], devoted to induced traffic. This report focuses on the elasticity of vehicle travel with respect to its own price, including tolls, operating costs, and travel time. The report suggests that short-run elasticities tend to fall in a -0.5 to -1.0 range, and long-run elasticities from -1.0 to -2.0. A somewhat older European source is Goodwin[48] delivering fairly similar figures.

Whatever the case, it is important that induced traffic or transit demand is identified and handled separately from other sources. Moreover, it is not just a matter of applying a couple of models or elasticities. It is necessary to build a reasonable justification from an in-depth knowledge of how the region or city works and how its travel patterns have been affected by very high travel costs.

In summary, a well-justified set of induced traffic figures may represent an interesting upside but this is generally, and correctly, ignored in the financial base case.

---

[47] US Federal Highway Administration (2005). "Highway Economic Requirements System-State Version" U.S. Department of Transportation Federal Highway Administration

[48] Goodwin, Phil B. (1996) "Empirical Evidence on Induced Traffic," *Transportation*, 23, N 1 , pp. 35-54.

PART III PRACTICE

This part deals with the specific issues arising with different aspects of transport concessions; they should be of interest to most readers. Chapter 12 deals with issues of uncertainty and risk in forecasting. Chapter 13 tackles the key issue of pricing services and accounting for revenues. Chapters 14 and 15 discuss the special requirements of modelling toll roads and managed lanes. Chapter 16 provides some guidance for congestion charging projects while chapter 17 deals with public transport (rail, LRT, BRT and bus) projects. Chapter 18 looks at the most pertinent issues regarding the future context of transport concessions. Chapter 19 covers risk analysis and chapter 20 the very important communication aspects of delivering a set of projections. Finally, the last chapter provides a personal view of what it takes to become a good forecaster.

Uncertainty, Risk and Forecasting

"That's right! shouted Vroomfondel, we demand rigidly defined areas of doubt and uncertainty!" **Douglas Adams**

12. UNCERTAINTY, RISK AND FORECASTING

12.1 Introduction

The third part of this book deals with the practice of preparing and delivering traffic and revenue forecasts for private sector concessions. The focus is on projects with significant revenue risk to the private and public sectors. The private sector will pay particular attention at revenue risk when transferred partially or in full to the concessionaire. In the case of shadow tolls and availability payments the effort will be similar but perhaps with a lighter touch. The public sector, represented by the Procuring Authority and the Treasury Department, will look into the issue of revenue risk of any concession with similar or greater interest. If this risk is transferred to the private sector they have to make sure this is reasonable and will not result in a concession failure, expensive to society and investors; if the support mechanism is shadow tolls and availability payments these will commit public resources for many years in the future.

This third part is mostly written with the role of the Traffic and Revenue Advisor in mind. This will normally be an independent consultancy, ideally with some international experience. A related role is that of the Peer Reviewer, somebody in charge of providing checks and balances to control for optimism bias; she is normally and independent professional adjunct to the T&R Advisory team.

A slightly different role is that of the Traffic Auditor, somebody that works for a different agent, normally the financial institutions seeking to syndicate loans or other debt instruments. This auditor is often involved only in the later stages of the project and has not been engaged from the outset in identifying risks. This weakens her contribution that tends to be seen as more cautious than necessary.

It has to be recognised that the role of the auditor is a very difficult one. It is practically impossible to technically audit a model fully, checking for example that all centroid connectors are properly coded and that all flow-delay relationships are correct. The auditor has to rely on a checklist like that provided by Bain[49] or our suggestions in Chapter 18. Based on her own experience the Auditor would also specify some tests to be undertaken by the modelling team. These tests will exercise the model in different ways and the reasonableness of the responses would provide some comfort about its robustness and fidelity. Good documentation will facilitate the role of the auditor; poor or no documentation will be considered as a risk.

Finally, the role of the auditor is often cast as part of a due diligence exercise. The buyer or lender needs to ensure that all risks have been considered and evaluated in a transaction. In our case, the key element is revenue risk.

A good and reliable full Traffic and Revenue study requires significant investment in time and money in order to ensure good data inputs and validated results; anything completed in less than three months or by an inexperienced team is considered suspicious.

12.2 Urban and Interurban projects

There are many different types of transport concessions; the characteristics of each scheme will influence data collection and the approach taken to model traffic and revenue projections.

Interurban toll roads nest in sparser networks, have fewer road alternatives. Data collection will be mostly intercept and travel time surveys plus traffic counts. They will generally lack household surveys and therefore traffic growth will be based on models relating past traffic counts to GDP growth and other variables. Congestion may or may not play a role in traffic capture.

Managed Lanes are particularly attractive in locations where it is possible to widen a facility but not to toll all traffic. They may be interurban or suburban and pose a difficult modelling task as tolls are highly variable; the approach to tackle these issues will be discussed later.

Interurban rail concessions face similar challenges. They will have the additional elements of designing services (stop and express, stations served) and allocating paths. Road congestion may be a contributing factor to rail demand therefore mode choice modelling will be required. Timetable assignment is likely to be important.

Urban projects will normally benefit from previous data collection and possibly an existing regional transport model.

Urban toll roads will be difficult to build because of limited land availability; tolled tunnels and bridges are more common in urban

---

[49] Bain, Robert (2009) Toll Road Traffic & Revenue Forecasts: an interpreter's guide. ISBN 978-0-9561527-1-8

areas but places like Sydney, Santiago de Chile and Mexico City have developed quite extensive urban toll road networks. They will generally be Open Road Tolling facilities introducing a raft of new issues to the analysis, most of them interesting and often positive. The technical issues will only be mentioned here in so far as they affect revenues.

Urban public transport projects, trams, LRT, BRT, metro and suburban rail are more complex. Mode choice should not be ignored (as it often is for toll roads) and sometimes it can be a critical aspect of uncertainty, especially if informal services and motorcycles play a key role; in those cases, data is likely to be poor.

Greenfield projects may happen in deserts. They are completely new facilities. The green bit is the fact that there was nothing there before, or at least nothing of that kind (buses but no metro, rural roads but no tolled motorway). Most of them will be interurban projects but there will be a few urban cases too.

Brownfield projects refer either to an existing facility that may be for full or partial sale for a major improvement, or a facility that will be widened and expanded to cope and attract more traffic. In this case, the assessment of the structural conditions of the facility is a key aspect of the due diligence as future CAPEX and OPEX will be affected. The traffic risk is lower than in the case of a greenfield project because its previous existence and flows facilitate projections.

Extensions to an existing facility are sometimes referred to as **Khakifield** projects, not an endearing name; they share some elements of green and brownfield projects.

12.3   Identifying uncertainty and risk

In this book we use the concept of uncertainty as an unquantifiable lack of certainty. Risk is a quantifiable uncertainty, at least in probabilistic terms. There is **uncertainty** about the eventual impact of self-driving cars on mass transit patronage. I estimate the **risk** of these vehicles constituting half of the traffic in the UK by 2030 as one in three.

Any study of a transport concession, whether it is undertaken for a procuring Government or a bidding consortium, develops at an early stage a "Risk Register" and an important component of this is the identification of sources of Revenue Risk. It is particularly useful if the T&R Advisor is involved, at least partially, at this stage. She will not just contribute to the Risk Register but will also understand better other risks and the strategic perspective of the consortium; this will help her guide the data collection and modelling effort. The Risk Register will inevitably evolve over time as understanding of the project improves and sometimes because the Procuring Authority changes Terms and Conditions.

This early involvement will also help understanding the contractual conditions of the concession. Whether inflation adjustment of fares and toll rates is guaranteed or not; is there a minimum revenue guarantee and associated sharing of profits above a threshold? Understanding these other risks will enable the advisor to make better assumptions and deal with risks more effectively.

Sometimes the consortium will benefit from some competitive advantage, for example building faster than usual, or having access to rolling stock that would otherwise take longer to procure; if so, the advisor will focus more on an early start of operations and forecasting in greater detail the first 36 months.

Occasionally, an experienced advisory team may contribute greater confidence in the Traffic and Revenue projections thus containing revenue risk and strengthening the financial case.

Some uncertainties are difficult to translate into quantifiable risks. Technology offers today an example of this. We are entering a level of wireless interconnectivity we have not seen before with implications too difficult to foresee. Self Driving Cars will happen soon and will potentially change how we understand and model the travel market. These uncertainties are better handled as alternative scenarios and sensitivity tests as discussed in Chapter 14

Before considering these aspects it is useful to visualise the main sources of uncertainty and revenue risk in a transport concession. There are four main sources:

- **Accuracy in establishing the base year (size).** This is often more difficult than it sounds because of the limitations of current data collection methods. Travel matrices are a poorly defined "average" of current conditions; VTTS are sensitive to changes in the economy and the mood of residents, perceptions of operating costs are fuzzy, and so on. What matters is the demand that could possibly be attracted to the new facility: the in-scope demand.
- **Uncertainty due to the quality of the model (capture).** Any model leaves some aspects out and includes others; the choices may be imperfect, the assumptions of consistent future behaviour (no change in tastes) may be unwarranted, the level of disaggregation for WTP too coarse, naïve network coding.
- **Uncertainty about future data inputs (growth).** This refers to uncertainty in respect of future growth drivers like population, income levels and economic activity and their materialisation in space and time. The expected evolution of VTTS for the duration of the concession is also part of this risk.

Uncertainty, Risk and Forecasting

- **Uncertainty about future scenarios (competitive context).** We restrict these to changes in the networks (introduction of new competitive services, or old services that re-invent themselves) and also changes in the technologies and attitudes and how they affect travel (Self Driving Cars, remote presence, etc.).

We can reduce, but never quite eliminate, the first two sources of uncertainty with better data and better models. We can use Monte Carlo Risk Analysis to get a better grasp of the risks surrounding growth uncertainty. Uncertainty about the future competitive environment is better treated through Scenario Analysis. These sources of uncertainty are combined to deliver the total level; its notional evolution is illustrated in the next figure:

FIGURE 24 CONTRIBUTORS TO FUTURE UNCERTAINTY

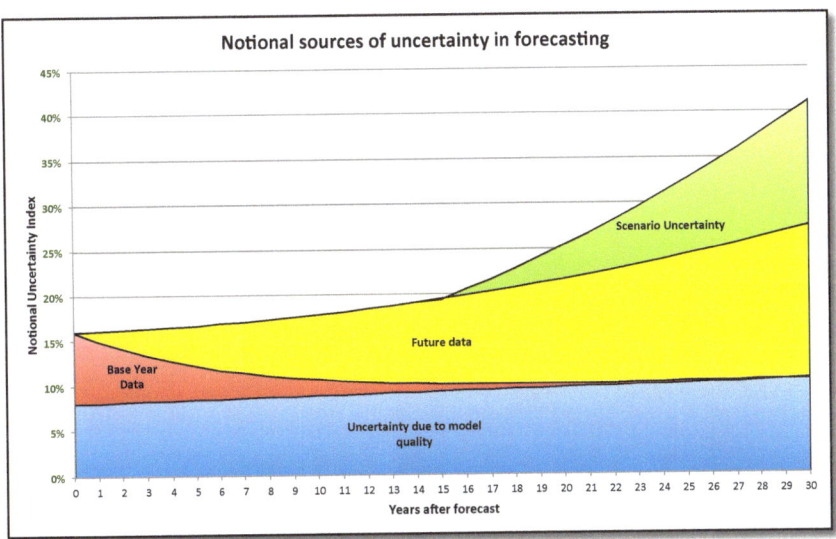

It is said that when a transport concession fails, it fails early. In this case, the most affective ways to reduce the chance of failure are establishing a solid Base Year and delivering a good traffic and revenue capture model including ramp-up estimates.

Having navigated the first few years the focus will shift to opportunities to increase revenue and fend off threats. The delivery of a clearly better service is a key requisite to a successful mature project.

12.4 Steps

The modelling approach adopted to produce T&R forecasts for the first transport concessions mirrored the classic approach employed by the public sector for planning purposes. This use of classic four stage models failed to identify and isolate the key drivers of traffic (and revenue) in a way that recognizes the associated risks. Moreover, the inclusion of less relevant sub-models not only implied wasted resources but also obscured the forecasting process and made interpretation extremely difficult. The synthetic production of trip matrices was particularly dangerous.

A better approach will focus from the outset on what matters most and relies on classic models only as a starting point as illustrated in Figure 25.

FIGURE 25 SCHEMATIC VIEW OF THE FORECASTING PROCESS

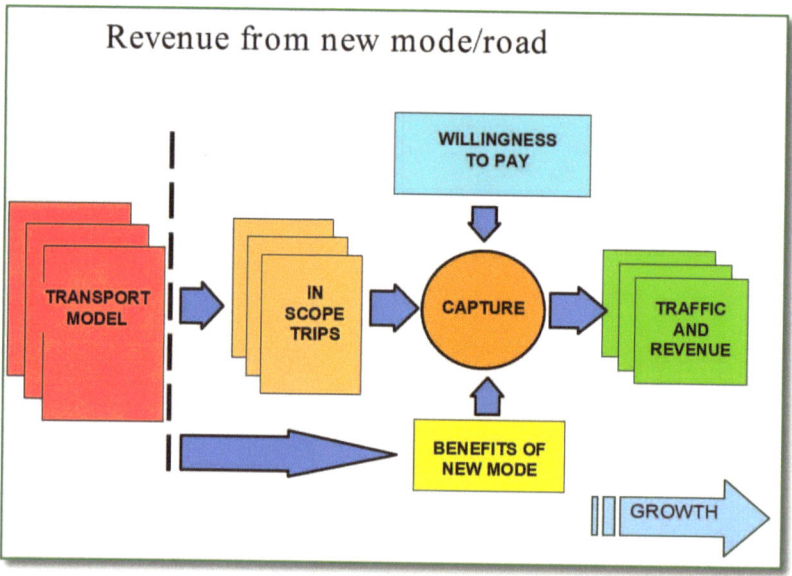

In order to focus the modelling effort we extract from a conventional transport model the main components of in-scope trips; this may mean reducing the coverage of the zoning system, disaggregating some critical zones to gain in precision, disaggregate user classes to capture WTP better or, in some simple cases, just extract the most relevant trip matrices and networks.

The approach will also focus more closely on the advantages/benefits of the proposed new facility, develop an appropriate capture model (with greater granularity) and deal with the issue of growth. Finally, there will be risk and sensitivity analysis and expansion factors to consider. In the case of public transport or other integrated schemes there will be some additional processing of revenues to allocate them to the different entities involved. Each of these aspects will have risks associated with them and it is the task of the modeller to identify and quantify them to provide a more reliable forecast.

In-scope traffic is the demand that *could* be attracted to the new service. As such, it can be considered as the target market for the operator. With a toll road or bridge, it can normally be considered as the traffic that would use the route if no charge were made. For public transport links, it represents an initial judgement on the traffic that could be captured both from other public transport services and potentially attracted from other modes under the most favourable circumstances.

The most reliable way to estimate this potential demand is to undertake a battery of transport surveys (passengers and freight). Investors are more convinced by actual *on the ground* data than by any outputs from elegant and sophisticated models. Origin-Destination (OD) surveys plus traffic counts and travel time surveys, undertaken probably at different times of the year and days of the week, and for at least 16 hours per day, would be ideal. These should be combined with some permanent traffic counting measurements to obtain a suitable profile of demand throughout the year.

12.5 Procuring Authority studies

A procuring Government has more complex objectives than a bidding consortium or a financial institution. The Government is usually interested in tapping the resources of the private sector to achieve maximum benefit to its constituency. Governments can borrow money cheaper than the private sector and in any case, it is the total combined debt of the country that can bring a crisis, not just Public Sector Borrowing Requirements.

Procuring Authorities seek other benefits from private sector involvement: greater creativity and efficiency in solving problems, continuity and effectiveness in asset management, a degree of risk transfer to agents/stakeholders that are better placed to manage and mitigate them. These authorities are interested in tapping into the initiative and good management of the private sector to secure intelligent design, innovative financial packages and to offer a high level of service throughout the concession.

To achieve this, the Procuring Authority has to deliver a competitive and transparent tendering process for a well-designed *Concession*

Package. A good tendering process is assisted by reducing bidding costs and promoting a wide international involvement to bring in fresh ideas and reduce risks of collusion. The Government should retain those elements of risk that it is best equipped to handle, for example securing the right of way in a timely manner.

The Government will seek to maximise welfare and this is generally achieved with good service and low prices, a difficult combination in the absence of a benefactor. Pricing the concession includes the levels of the tolls to be charged, any government contribution to construction costs (there may be facilities already there like an existing road to be widened) and any contribution required from the concessionaire to pay for services or facilities. One or more of these metrics are often included in the criteria to award the concession.

The following table considers the most common risks in transport concessions and how these are often allocated to the public or private sector.

TABLE 7 TYPICAL RISK ALLOCATION IN TRANSPORT PROJECTS

RISKS	Public Sector	Private Sector
General		
Country		Yes
Currency		Yes
Political risks		Yes
Project specific		
Construction		
Planning permission & approval	Yes	
Right of way availability	Yes	Sometimes
Environmental and archaeological issues	Yes	
Ground conditions		Yes
Design		Yes
Latent defects		Yes
Construction costs		Yes
Cost overruns		Yes
Delays to start or complete works		Yes
Change orders		Yes
Commissioning		Yes
Revenue		
Customer acceptance		Yes
Traffic volume and composition	Sometimes	Yes

Uncertainty, Risk and Forecasting

RISKS	Public Sector	Private Sector
Competition from other, especially new, facilities	Sometimes	Yes
Ramp-up or transitional period		Yes
Growth		Yes
Toll and fare adjustments (indexing or real tolls)		Yes
Technologies		Yes
Integration		Yes
Leakage		Yes
Legal		
Legislation and regulatory changes	Shared	Shared
Early termination of contract		Yes
Insufficient compensations		Yes
Force Majeure and Business Interruption	Sometimes	Yes
Operating Costs		
Operations and Maintenance costs		Yes
Service Quality		Yes
Change Orders	Shared	Shared
Financial		
Availability of funds	Yes	Shared
Financing Risk		Yes
Refinancing gain	Sometimes	Yes
Interest rates/conditions		Yes

Revenue risk is very often transferred, in full or in part, to the concessionaire as it can handle it best through good service and pricing. Whether it can be transferred in full will depend on a number of factors: perceived country risk, unavoidable uncertainties, government contributions, strength of the demand and the provision of a well prepared Reference Project. If full revenue risk transfer is not possible, then there are different instruments to retain this motivation but reduce its potential downside. The provision of minimum revenue guarantees (MRG) is one of them. Lenders will often base the debt capacity of a concession on this revenue stream. MRG are sometimes offered over the first few years of the concession and at a level below that of the Base Case scenario. The level of this guaranteed revenue stream is important in determining the debt/equity ratio for the concession.

A counterpart to MRG is sharing concession profits when they exceed a certain level, a cap and collar approach. Estimating this threshold well enough so that it does not discourage bidders but protects social objectives requires a good Reference Study. Governments know that charging more than required (unless they are pricing some externality) simply reduces welfare, transferring it from traveller to concessionaire.

Another factor that helps is the provision of clear and transparent tendering rules and fair and well-described contractual arrangements. It is important to avoid the mistake of awarding the concession automatically to the bidder with the lowest price or most aggressive revenue forecasts. The latter will make the "winner's curse" a real problem and no government benefits from a failed concession.

The procuring Government should undertake a Reference T&R Study that is thorough and well documented. It is required to correctly identify revenue risks and therefore design that element of the concession. This Reference T&R Study should also be made available to all bidders, without guarantees, in order to reduce bidding costs and provide a common base to their efforts. Scrutinising the T&R projections of each bidder will be easier and this is an important task when deciding the award of the concession.

This Reference T&R study should be:

- Undertaken to international standards; this means either an international company or at least a technical audit by one;
- Transparent and well documented; data should be collected with good quality assurance and provided both processed and in raw (e.g. interview records) form;
- Data should cover the relevant periods and be segmented generously; at least a few traffic/person counts should be continuous over a whole year;
- The software packages used to process the data and model demand should be internationally and commercially available;
- The provision of geo-coded data and the whole database in electronic format is highly desirable;
- The study should also detail future plans in the region, transport, economic activities and residential developments.

The bidder would like to confirm this information with its own traffic measurements and other observations, seeking, at the same time, to identify opportunities to obtain a competitive advantage. For these reasons, the Reference T&R Study should be better documented and Quality Assured than a more conventional undertaking. All assumptions should be explicit, all models and sub-models described in detail and ideally available in electronic format for re-processing under

Uncertainty, Risk and Forecasting

different bidder assumptions. Such a well-developed Reference T&R Study will help shorten timescales, procuring authorities are often pressed for time, reduce bidding costs and consequently minimise requests for support or higher toll prices. The benefits of an excellent Reference Study are ultimately transferred to the end-users.

If the future is very uncertain some concessions have been awarded to the bidder requesting the lowest present value (LPV) of the revenue stream discounted at a pre-determined rate. Revenue risk is therefore reduced. Revenue projections are still needed in order to secure financial backing for the project, but they are less critical than in concessions where revenue risk is fully transferred. However, LPV concessions have some undesirable side effects. In them, the focus is on reducing construction costs to the minimum and there is less incentive to offer good levels of service as any increase in Operations and Maintenance (O&M) costs simply reduces profit.

12.6   Bid support model

It is only natural that each bidder will develop its own model and revenue projections. This may be a simple improvement on the Reference Model provided by the procuring authority or a more elaborate task to reduce uncertainties and support a more competitive bid.

The Reference Model should have been provided with a clear focus on the concession to be tendered. It will probably be based on a strategic regional or urban model and adapted to the requirements of a concession as discussed above.

It is sadly true that in many cases this Reference Model is not made available. It will then be necessary to develop a completely new model or to adapt an existing regional strategic model that is perhaps a few years out of date.

The few cases where a model has to be developed from scratch are likely to be inter-urban toll roads. Given the time constraints (often 3-4 months) the model will be inevitably simple. It is also likely that congestion will not play a key role in determining route choice and payment of tolls. The new model may well be a whole day (perhaps the 16 more active hours) model with emphasis on speeds, road surface, single or dual carriageway and operating distances and travel times.

If a model is available, either a strategic regional one or a good Reference Model, the first task of the analyst will be to review its quality and currency. The model is likely to be a couple of years old and a few things would have changed since its development. The starting date for the concession at least is likely to be overoptimistic.

Better Traffic and Revenue Forecasting

During this review the advisor may be required to produce some initial forecasts to start feeding the financial model and provide some basis for strategic discussion. Transport modeller dislike having to provide this early projection and therefore tend to be conservative on the grounds that nobody likes bad news (lower projections) late in the bidding process.

The modeller will also specify the data collection needed to confirm and improve the model to make it a bid support resource. This will include at least some traffic or person counts, some OD and travel time surveys and, if little local information is available on willingness to pay, a Stated Preference survey.

Meantime, the modeller will "walk the line" getting to know the context of the new facility and perhaps refine the data collection task. She will also seek to audit planning and socio-economic assumptions as well as future network changes to be included in the model.

Armed with this information the modeller will refine the model, improving granularity closer to the concession and enhancing traveller segmentation by willingness to pay. She may well decide to remove some modules, for example mode choice for a toll road, to improve running times and, more importantly, the ability to interpret the model. A number of other improvements will be needed and the new model will be calibrated and validated to up to date data.

Pricing

"Price is what you pay. Value is what you get." **Warren Buffett**

13. PRICING

13.1 The complexities of pricing

Pricing transport services has become critical and very complex in the last 15 years. The figure below shows cheapest prices for a train journey from London to Sheffield, a service operating as a concession, on 18th September 2013 (information obtained on 3 September 2013). There are 28 other prices for the same journey reaching £302 for a return trip, all with different restrictions and add-on services. It is said that not two passengers on a plane may have paid the same price for their tickets.

FIGURE 26 DIFFERENT PRICES FOR EQUIVALENT RAIL JOURNEYS

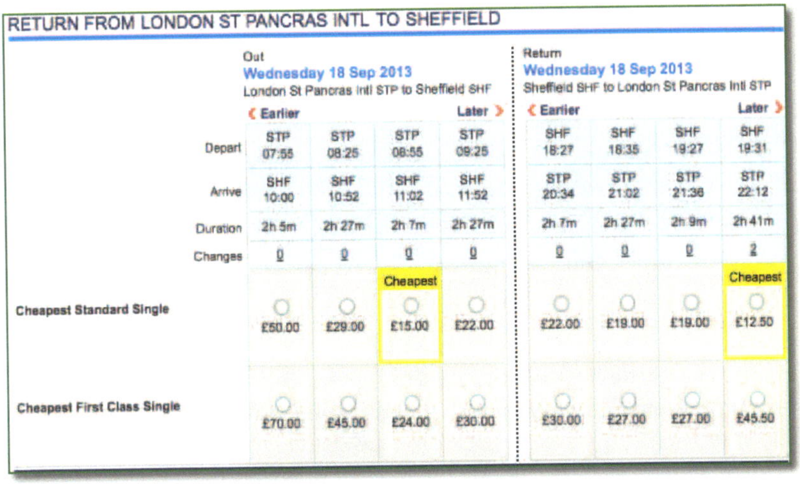

RETURN FROM LONDON ST PANCRAS INTL TO SHEFFIELD									
		Out Wednesday 18 Sep 2013 London St Pancras Intl STP to Sheffield SHF				Return Wednesday 18 Sep 2013 Sheffield SHF to London St Pancras Intl STP			
		‹ Earlier			Later ›	‹ Earlier			Later ›
	Depart	STP 07:55	STP 08:25	STP 08:55	STP 09:25	SHF 18:27	SHF 18:35	SHF 19:27	SHF 19:31
	Arrive	SHF 10:00	SHF 10:52	SHF 11:02	SHF 11:52	STP 20:34	STP 21:02	STP 21:36	STP 22:12
	Duration	2h 5m	2h 27m	2h 7m	2h 27m	2h 7m	2h 27m	2h 9m	2h 41m
	Changes	0	0	0	0	0	0	0	2
Cheapest Standard Single		£50.00	£29.00	Cheapest £15.00	£22.00	£22.00	£19.00	£19.00	Cheapest £12.50
Cheapest First Class Single		£70.00	£45.00	£24.00	£30.00	£30.00	£27.00	£27.00	£45.50

There is less variety of prices on urban public transport systems. However, there are period or season tickets, smart cards, multi-journey, senior and young person discounts, off-peak prices and other clever offers. Yield management techniques reach a number of markets previously impervious to them.

One can think of two boundaries to the price to charge for a service. The upper limit is the value that the service has to each potential customer. In the transport field this varies with the savings achievable and the willingness to pay for them. The lower boundary is the marginal cost of offering the service. This marginal cost is low for toll roads and Managed Lanes but higher if more capacity is required: an extra lane or train to be made available. The marginal cost of an empty seat is, in general, quite low.

The problem with the upper limit is that the service provider is in no position to know the value to each potential customer. Therefore, it tries to segment the market depending on time of travel, how far in advance the ticket is purchased and what restrictions are accepted. These prices can change dynamically thanks to yield management techniques, their objective being to attain high utilisation and revenue without compromising the level of service. In this sense, Managed Lanes and rail travel offer the best opportunities to implement dynamic pricing strategies. Other opportunities do exist, but are less versatile, for toll roads and local public transport.

The prevalence of variable pricing is likely to continue and even extend its reach in transportation. Moreover, many of these prices are converted into revenue not with cash but by means of smart cards, electronic tags/transponders and even mobile phones. This decouples in time use from payment and poses some difficult questions in the field of modelling, namely:

a. Do travellers perceive all money the same? Does the money paid for fuel or road tax have the same quality and invokes the same perception as that paid for tolls or parking? Does it make any difference in respect of route or mode choice?

b. How much the separation between use and payment affects behaviour, as we know it does with telecoms and other utilities?

c. What is the best way of modelling willingness-to-pay (WTP) for transport services and how is this affected by the two questions above?

d. How is this WTP affected by the legibility of the pricing signal? Does it matter that some people may not understand, never mind recall, how much they were charged for a particular journey?

e. How do people that get their travel costs covered by a third party (parent, employer) partially or in full respond to price signals?

f. How does the difficulty of making payments affect willingness to pay?

Prices come in all sort of guises and sometimes they appear designed to be obscure, to encourage us to spend more money than we think we should. The "crispier" concept of price materialises when we

Pricing

need to take money out of our pocket to pay at a tollbooth or ticket counter. Other versions of charging start to de-couple usage from payment: the use of credit cards, payment for period tickets, electronic payment via smart cards or transponders/tags, video tolling charged directly to a bank account and so on.

The cost of operating a car is also blurred to the driver. It is generally believed that the nearest thing to the perceived cost of running a car is that of fuel; other costs like maintenance, taxes and depreciation are mostly perceived as sunk (not variable with usage) costs. However, most of us cannot accurately quote what this perceived fuel cost per kilometre is likely to be; we only know that filling up the tank is more or less expensive than some time ago and may adopt some minor change in travel behaviour as a result. The realistic combination of crisp money (e.g. tolls) and fuzzy money (running costs per km) in assignment models is therefore a difficult task.

Our reaction to a price signal is influenced by how "costly" we perceive it to be compared to a cash equivalent. If we feel that in practice an electronic toll charge is less onerous than the actual payment in cash then our behavioural response will adapt accordingly. In a few cases, some users may feel that they are being charged for more than their actual use of an Open Road Tolled facility; then, they may develop a negative attitude towards using the road and their apparent willingness to pay will drop. This is why it is so important to retain a very good relationship with clients under electronic tolling.

Another important factor is the difficulties involved in making the payment. Automated payments through bank accounts or credit cards linked to a tolling or ticketing account are the least burdensome tasks. Topping up a tag or smart card at shops or other facilities requires some effort. Internet payments are somewhere in between. Topping-up pre-paid public transport smartcards at metro stations is convenient, except for those that only use bus.

Willingness to pay, therefore, is influenced by the normal technical factors (income, journey purpose, level of service), emotional factors (perceived disposable income, trust on the charging process, fairness of the charge) and the burden of the payment task. There is value in reducing unnecessary obstacles to maximise both revenue and customer satisfaction.

With the possible exception of toll roads, the complex price structures in use in Managed Lanes and some public transport services cannot be fully modelled in our classic four-stage strategic software. It is necessary to simplify the price structure in the model and then process, in a separate spreadsheet, the subtleties of the proposed real price regime.

13.2 Optimal pricing

In the context of T&R projections an "optimal price" (toll, fare) is the one that maximises profit for the capacity on offer. This is often the price that maximises revenues. However, depending on the tolling structure, heavy trucks may contribute more to O&M costs than their toll implies; this difference is often ignored.

This optimal price is often established during the model sensitivity tests, something discussed in a separate chapter; it is always a function of the advantages offered by the new facility and therefore depends on how good the alternatives are. This suggests that the optimal toll will change over time.

This optimal toll or price is sought for a couple of reasons. First, during the preparation of a project to the market, the Procuring Authority would like to ascertain how much of the capital costs could be recovered from tolls or fares. The maximum achievable defines this optimal price. However, the toll is usually set below this revenue maximising level. Second, during the bidding stage this optimal price is also of interest, even when the actual toll is fixed in the concession contract; in this case the bidder and financial institutions would like to be confident that increasing prices will still increase revenue. This sensitivity tests may prove that toll or fares have been set too high (perhaps due to an overestimation of WTP) and that more revenue would be collected with lower rates. An example of how this optimal price can be established by running the model at different toll levels is shown in a figure overleaf in some nominal currency. In this case the revenue is calculated per km and day at different toll rates per km. The elasticity at each toll rate is also shown.

The figure shows that the optimal toll rate, in terms of maximising revenue, is around $ 2.00 per km. The demand elasticity is, of course, -1.00 for this value and the revenue elasticity zero. The Government would probably prefer a lower toll level to protect user welfare provided expected revenues cover all discounted costs.

A level below that maximising revenues will give bidders some confidence that prices could be adjusted to improve revenues (after negotiations) and that any inflation adjustment will not result in a reduction of collections. If by mistake the toll rate were set at above $2.00/km, the right hand side of the curve, it would be advantageous to reduce tolls to increase revenues.

Pricing

FIGURE 27 OPTIMAL TOLL LEVEL DETERMINATION

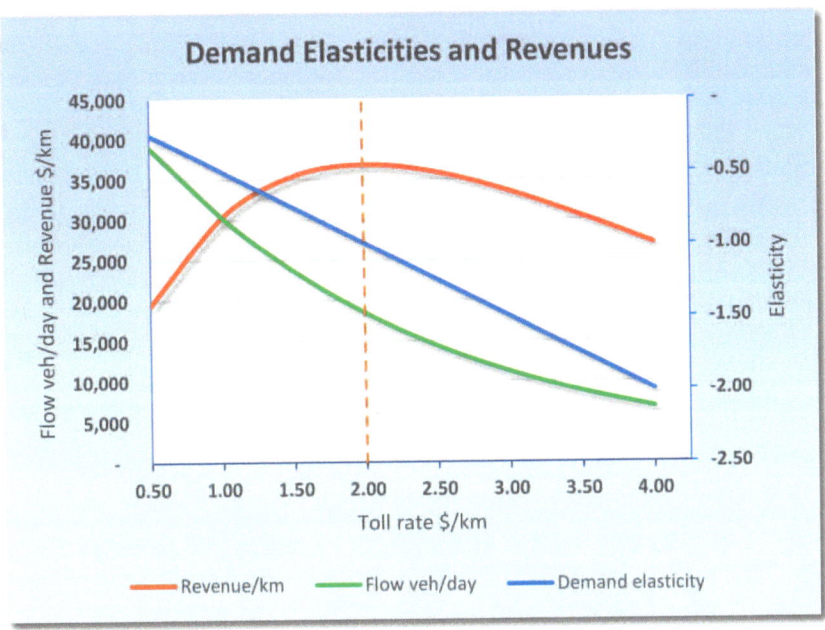

If the set up has some more complex price structures (discounts, period ticketing, etc.) then it would be necessary to find an optimal rate for each of these markets. This is complex because of the mutual interactions between them (single ticket buyers may switch to period ticket if the savings are significant, contrasted with the risk of not been able to use the full period). For this reason alone, this calculation is seldom carried out and an optimal price for the "standard" user is established and the others are fixed by custom, experience or political considerations.

13.3 Price and revenues

It is seldom the case that the price multiplied by the number of customers adds up to the revenues to the transport concessionaire. Not all the money potentially collected gets collected and not all the money that is collected reaches the bank account of the operator. There are taxes and other charges that have to be recognised. In the case of complex interoperable toll systems or public transport networks with integrated fares, there is also the task of allocating revenues to different operators.

There is also the issue of leakage. There is <u>always</u> a percentage of users that manages to avoid paying the toll or the fare. In toll systems with tollbooths and barriers this percentage is small; with Open Road Tolling (ORT) the proportion will be higher. A large number of exempted users always breeds abuse.

Fare avoidance can reach very significant values in public transport systems relying on the honest validation of smartcards. I have seen systems with up to 30% fare avoidance for short periods of time. There will be additional leakage between the toll both/fare box and the bank account. This will be lower with electronic systems but it is never nil in practice.

Lastly, it is also necessary to expand revenues from the modelled periods to the year using annualisation factors.

Therefore, modelled revenues need to be adjusted to account for these effects. This is normally undertaken in a Revenue Recognition model in a spreadsheet.

13.4   Inflation and tax

The prices that are presented to users include any taxes due, for example Valued Added Tax (VAT) if applicable. The model uses these gross prices to influence the choices of travellers. The resulting revenue figures include also a tax element and are not all net to the concession. This must be made clear in presenting revenue streams to the financial group; the financial model should make any adjustments to net out tax components.

However, things are a little bit more complicated when you consider commercial traffic that normally would be able to recover at least some of the VAT. Should the toll rate for trucks in the model be with or without VAT? The simplest approach is to allow WTP by commercial vehicles to respond to toll rates inclusive of taxes (whether they are recoverable or not) and then again let the financial model deal with tax issues. It is essential to make this clear in all documentation and data transfers. Incidentally, the toll or fare may include charges made by an electronic toll collection or smart card operator entity and these must be allowed for in the financial model.

Inflation is another tricky issue. Transport planners and modellers are used to model demand at fixed (real) prices. In principle, inflation should play no role in determining future demand at constant prices. This is also the best approach to follow in dealing with private sector projects: perform all model runs at constant prices.

However, financial modellers always include inflation in their calculations for a number of good reasons. It is best to leave this problem to them and still produce all revenues at constant prices.

Pricing

Inflation may have a subtle effect on demand, in particular in between toll/fare updates. Say that toll prices are adjusted by inflation on the first day of the year (it is usually a few days later). As inflation takes place during the year the cost of the toll in constant money will be eroded and this will generate additional demand. After a year the toll is adjusted again to catch up with inflation. The immediate response is a reduction in demand reflecting the short-term elasticity to price. This is illustrated in the next figure that shows the impact of inflation-eroding prices on demand (and revenue) assuming an opening of the concession on the first day of January and annual toll adjustments on the same date. The top figure shows a projection at constant prices for a Flow Index as a straight line and demand increasing slowly above this reference line to return to it when tolls are adjusted for inflation each year. This is a rather idealised model; in reality toll flows are subject to seasonal variations as depicted in the lower version of the same figure.

This effect is small and a bit theoretical as incomes are not smoothly adjusted for inflation each month; therefore, it is best ignored. It requires guessing future inflation something nobody is very good at.

Some concessions, for example urban toll roads in Santiago and Mexico City, allow for an escalation of prices at a fixed rate above inflation. There are two reasons for this. First it allows increasing future revenues (provided the original toll rate is less than optimal). Second, it compensates for expected increases of WTP over time so that higher prices contribute to maintain free-flowing conditions on the toll road.

In cases with toll rate escalation the model will have to incorporate this rate above inflation in future year runs as well as expected increases in willingness to pay over time. This should also be made clear to the financial team to avoid double counting of toll escalation.

In a few misguided projects, tolls are not adjusted yearly for inflation. This means that the effective toll rate actually decreases over time. This <u>should</u> be incorporated in the model thus requiring an estimate of future inflation, something bidders have no way of influencing. Bidding for this type of project is unusual and generally unwise.

In summary, whenever prices will not be adjusted in line with inflation, the traffic advisor will have to make allowances to incorporate this deviation in the model. Bear in mind that this may also involve adjustments to other prices like fuel, competitive tolled roads or services.

FIGURE 28 IMPACT OF INFLATION ON DEMAND, WITHOUT AND WITH SEASONAL VARIATIONS

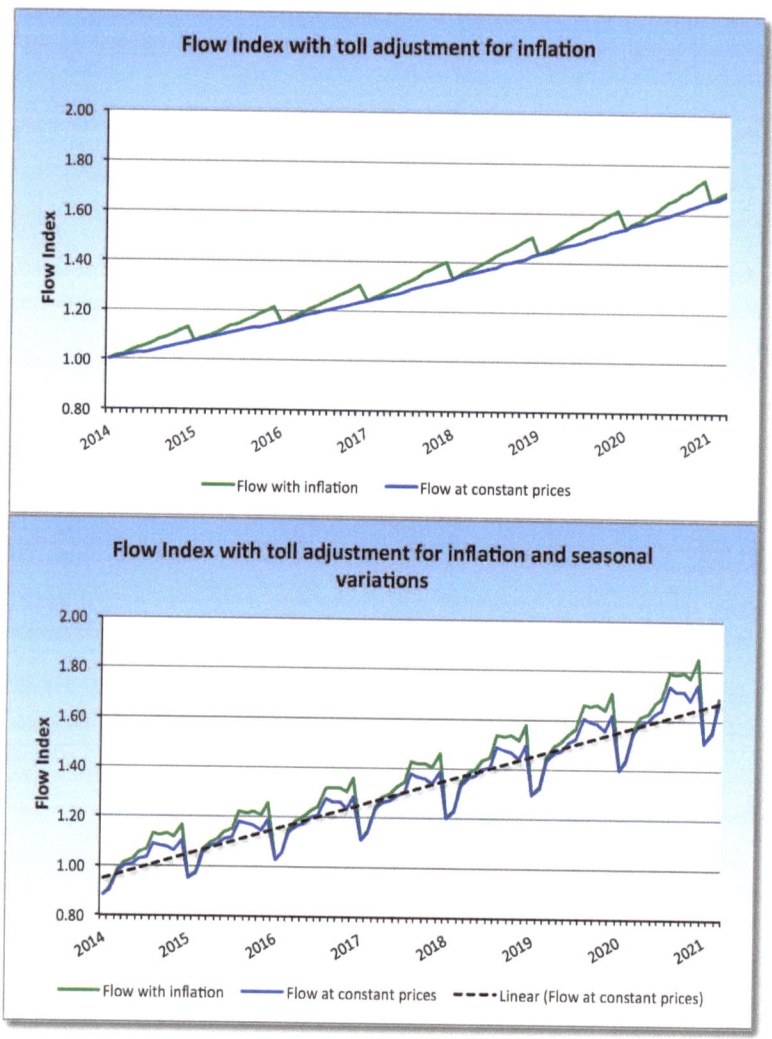

13.5   Pricing different users

Toll roads would normally charge a different rate to cars, motorcycles, buses, and trucks of different sizes. This should reflect both their respective use of space on the road and the incremental maintenance costs that they cause. The contribution to maintenance costs is rarely applied to the differential tolling of trucks; it would create too large a difference with lighter vehicles that is considered unfair or contrary to economic policy.

Pricing

As a general rule, whenever prices are set below the optimal level any reduction in price will lead to a reduction in revenue. This rule holds true for an average of the market more widely than one would like to believe.

However, there may be market segments for which the price is set above their optimal level. In these cases it is possible to reduce prices and increase revenues. The difficulty therefore, is how to identify and isolate these market segments without cannibalising revenue from the rest.

One approach is to distinguish prices by time of day. This is what off-peak pricing does, as the advantage of a faster but pricier route/mode will be reduced in the absence of congestion. This is critical at night and reducing truck tolls at that time may prove advantageous to both toll road and truckers.

Another approach is to award discounts to particular groups of users that could be identified easily enough and within the constraints imposed by the concession Terms and Conditions. For example, the provision of discounts to frequent users, something we discuss in section 14.8. Sometimes discounts are offered to residents of an area, a ploy used to reduce resistance to a new expensive facility. This is a bit more difficult to model than the previous case as it requires different prices or adjustments to residents of an area. This is not the same as trips emanating from zones in the selected area so additional calculations are required to establish the percentage of such trips (and trips returning from other areas) that deserve the discount. For very complex cases this is best handled in a combination of network model and the revenue recognition spreadsheet.

The same is true for different types of ticketing: period (season), off-peak, student's discounts (and any government compensation due, usually delayed). The Revenue Recognition model must account for all of this and be well documented to avoid mis-interpretations by the financial team.

13.6   Transitional period

Classic transport models ignore the fact that people do not react instantly to changes in the network and prices. There is a delay while travellers discover, try the new facility and decide whether any advantage it offers is superior to the price of using it.

This transitional period, usually referred to as "ramp up", may be a few months or a few years long and can be shortened by means of a good communications and marketing strategy.

Better Traffic and Revenue Forecasting

This is an area seriously under-researched, partly because it does not fit neatly into what universities are adept to investigate. Current practice involves finding a similar road in terms of location, type of trips, toll level and significance of the time saving to be achieved, and adopt a similar pattern for the planned road ramp-up.

Douglas Economics has done a useful review of ramp-up profiles for rail projects in different parts of the world[50]. The following table summarise the findings in it.

TABLE 8 RAMP-UP PROFILES FOR RAIL PROJECTS

	Semesters					
	1	2	3	4	5	6
Eastern Suburbs Railway Sydney AU	100%	100%	100%	100%	100%	100%
Holsworthy Station Sydney AU	59%	100%	100%	100%	100%	100%
Joondalup Western Australia AU	45%	72%	78%	82%	88%	96%
Marseille Mass Transit FR	67%	94%	100%	100%	100%	100%
Croydon Light Rail UK	83%	100%	100%	100%	100%	100%
Lewisham DLR Extension UK	78%	99%	100%	100%	100%	100%
Manchester Metro Link UK	57%	82%	91%	100%	100%	100%
West Yorkshire New Stations UK	60%	96%	100%	100%	100%	100%
Auckland Rail NZ	82%	100%	100%	100%	100%	100%
Sydney Airport Rail Link AU	80%	90%	100%	100%	100%	100%
Hongkong Airport Express HK	79%	86%	99%	100%	100%	100%
High Speed Rail Spain E	81%	93%	100%	100%	100%	100%
TGV S.E. Corridor FR	30%	50%	55%	77%	100%	100%
Modelled average	70%	88%	94%	97%	99%	100%

As can be seen, there is a wide variety of ramp-up profiles, even among projects that would be similar in principle: High Speed Rail-TGV. Douglas Economics also fitted a model to represent average conditions; its results are presented in the last row of the table.

It is possible to gather some information for toll roads but it is not so well organised. For example, for Madrid radial toll roads it is possible to form the following table from data published in Wikipedia[51]. The next table is based on such information:

TABLE 9 RAMP-UP PROFILES FOR MADRID RADIALS

All traffic	YEAR			
	1	2	3	4
R4 Madrid Ocaña	56%	59%	81%	100%
R2 Madrid Guadalajara	53%	65%	81%	100%
R3 Madrid Arganda del Rey	65%	83%	99%	100%

---

[50] Douglas, Neil (2003) Patronage Ramp-Up Factors for New Rail Services. Douglas Economics unpublished report.
http://www.douglaseconomics.co.nz/reports.htm

[51] http://es.wikipedia.org/wiki/Autopista_Radial_2.

Pricing

A recent report provides an analysis of ramp-up profile in inter-urban toll roads in Mexico[52]. The report summarises the findings in a table reproduced below. It is interesting to note that different modes present different profiles and the longest one is for goods vehicles.

TABLE 10 AVERAGE RAMP-UP PROFILES FOR MEXICAN INTER-URBAN TOLL ROADS

	YEAR				
	1	2	3	4	5
Cars	42%	78%	92%	100%	100%
Buses	21%	30%	92%	100%	100%
Goods Vehicles	20%	44%	75%	93%	100%

Finally, the following table is based on unpublished reports in Australia. Empty cell indicates lack of information in this case.

TABLE 11 RAMP-UP PROFILES FOR SOME AUSTRALIAN TOLL ROADS

	Period				
Cars	1st month	6 months	12 months	18 months	24 months
M4	78%	88%		100%	
M5	39%	64%			100%
M2	63%	81%		100%	
Eastern Distributor	68%	88%	100%		
Domain Tunnel	76%	87%	100%		

Features that can shorten ramp-up are: good marketing including free rides before commercial operation, good signage, significant time savings, low tolls and frequent users (commuters).

A particular issue with ramp-up concepts is that in some cases the road offers such an advantage that land uses start adapting to the improved accessibility with new developments, sometimes well ahead of plans; this produces an apparent "long ramp-up" over several years that cannot be explained by a transition or learning process alone. This illustrates the difficulties in defining what exactly is ramp-up and what is induced growth. Land use forecasting in response to improved accessibility is a tricky area.

---

[52] Felipe Ochoa Asociados (2010) Estudio de Demanda para la nueva infraestructura denominada Atizapán – Atlacomulco. Report to Secretaria de Comunicaciones y Transportes de Mexico.

13.7 Annualisation factors

A separate post modelling issue is the selection of the most appropriate annualisation factors to convert period revenues into annual ones. Again, this is a poorly researched area and for the same reasons. Ideally we would like to expand each modelled period (AM peak, PM peak, in-between peaks, etc.) by a different annualisation factor corresponding to its contribution to annual flows. Permanent classified traffic counts (or regular passenger counts and ticketing information) in locations close to the prospective facility, would be used to estimate these annualisation factors.

Problems arise because each of these locations will in fact produce its own set of annualisation factors. Moreover, one would expect that a priced facility, like a toll road, will have different demand profiles than a free one. Therefore, the annualisation factors from untolled roads might need to be corrected before applying them to a future tolled facility.

The figure bellow illustrates the seasonal variations in different sections of an ORT with nine different tolling gantries. It is possible to observe that although the general profile is similar there are differences in different gantries, in particular at peaks. These differences can reach 10-15%, a large figure, as normally a single profile will be adopted for a new toll road.

FIGURE 29 WEEKLY TRAFFIC PROFILE ON 9 SECTIONS OF A TOLL ROAD

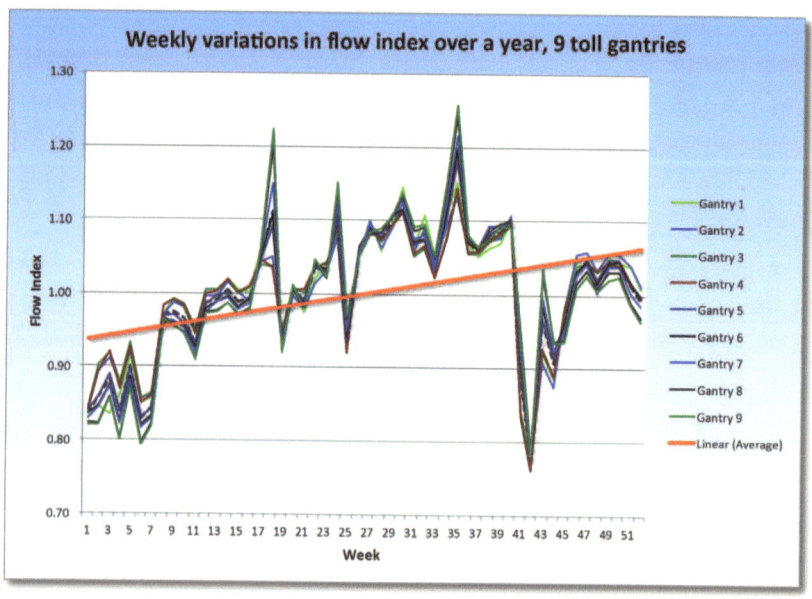

Pricing

A complementary approach is to undertake calculations based on the number of hours each representative period will have in a year. An example of this is presented in the next table for an urban toll road. The flow profiles depend on the context and also the time of the year, in particular the presence or absence of students in the travelling population.

TABLE 12 CONSTRUCTING ANNUAL REVENUES

Period	Representative times	Expansion Factors
Morning Peak	7:30-8:30	879
Off-Peak	12:00-13:00	2057
Evening Peak	18:00-19:00	1382
Saturday	11:00-12:00	925
Sunday	14:00-15:00	1083
Revenue hours		6326
Non-revenue hours		2434
Total		8760

The expansion factors calculated in this way may serve to validate any annualisation factors obtained from continuous flow measurements. Bear in mind that these expansion factors, in the absence of annual counts, are a partial guess as they involve combining different seasons, holidays and other factors affecting demand over a typical year.

This is one of the areas where it is easiest to be optimistic and difficult to argue against particular choices. Therefore, it is important to make clear in any report how the annualisation factors were estimated and on what basis they are considered to be the expected future values.

13.8   Price Elasticities and sentiment

Elasticities are an output from our models and rarely an input to our work. However, it is very useful to compare the price elasticities of demand (PED) resulting from our models with others observed in practice. In other interesting cases, the concessionaire has the opportunity to change prices on an existing facility, either to adjust for inflation, to improve revenue or attract more demand. It is useful, therefore, to be a bit more precise about PEDs, how they are measured and what are the main factors affecting them.

Better Traffic and Revenue Forecasting

Elasticity is a measure of responsiveness of the quantity of a good or service demanded to changes in its price. The formula for the coefficient of price elasticity of transport demand T at a price P is:

$$E_{T,P} = \frac{dT/T}{dP/P}$$

This measure of elasticity is referred to as the *own-price* elasticity of demand to distinguish it from the elasticity of demand with respect to the change in the price of some alternative, a cross-price elasticity; for example the elasticity of demand for rail travel in respect of the price for air travel.

A price elasticity of demand can be estimated in practice whenever a price is changed, say from P_1 to P_2 and the consequent variation in demand T_1 to T_2 measured:

$$e_{T,P} = \frac{(T_2 - T_1)/T_1}{(P_2 - P_1/P_1)}$$

To be equivalent, the changes in this second formulation should be infinitesimally small. This formula also implies that the elasticity to a price increase is the same to that of a price reduction, something not frequently observed in practice at least because the price changes are not infinitesimally small.

The main factors affecting PEDs are:

- **Availability of alternatives:** the better the alternative route or mode the higher the elasticity is likely to be, as people can easily switch from one to the other. This is often the case on urban toll roads or LRT systems resulting in a strong substitution effect. If no close alternatives are available, the substitution effect will be small and the demand more inelastic. This is one of the reasons it is difficult to transfer elasticities from one scheme to another; they depend heavily on the availability of good alternatives. Note that the alternatives must be known to travellers to be really available. Improving knowledge about the advantages of a particular service or toll road will facilitate demand capture and apparently reduce price elasticities.
- **Income effects:** the higher the percentage of the consumer's income that the service price represents, the higher the elasticity tends to be, as people will pay more attention when purchasing the service because of its cost. Tolls and public transport tickets do not represent a high proportion of income but the income effect may become substantial if the service will

Pricing

be consumed frequently, as is the case for commuters. A psychological or real change from "spenders" to "savers" for whatever reason has the effect of reducing (perceived or real) disposable income and therefore strengthening income effects.

- **Necessity:** the more necessary a good or service is, the lower the elasticity, as people will attempt to pay for it no matter the price; commuting again may reflect this need but it will be weakened in the future as distant presence and work offers travel-less alternatives.
- **Duration:** for most goods and services, the longer a price change holds, the higher the elasticity is likely to be, as more and more consumers find they have the time and inclination to search for substitutes. When fuel prices increase suddenly, for instance, consumers may still fill up their tanks in the short run; but if prices remain high over several years, more consumers will reduce their demand for fuel by switching to more fuel-efficient cars, public transport or even move home or job to save on travel costs.
- **Form of payment:** parting with money has different guises. Cash is the standard against other forms of payment can be compared. Electronic payment, in particular when linked to a bank or credit card account, reduces the burden of disbursing money; this is well known and the reason why special deals and discounts are offered to persuade customers to pay by Standing Orders or Direct Debit for utilities and other services. Requiring the customer to pay at specific locations increases the burden of payment. The difficulty of the payment task increases the price elasticity of any service.
- **Brand loyalty and sentiment:** an attachment to a certain brand—either out of tradition or because of proprietary barriers—can override sensitivity to price changes, resulting in more inelastic demand. In a similar vein, the feeling of being exploited by the Government or a transport concessionaire will have the opposite effect thus increasing price elasticity. Trust in the provider of services is most important. The customer must feel that he is not being exploited, that the applicable charges are fair and commensurate with the quality of the service. This is particularly important when use of a service and payment are not simultaneous: the account is topped-up before use or funds collected monthly from a bank account. Lack of trust in the fairness of the charges may put many potential customers off.

- **Who pays:** where the purchaser does not directly pay for the services they consume, such as with corporate expense accounts, demand is likely to be more inelastic; in our terminology, WTP will increase.

The difference between short and long-term elasticities is relevant to transport concessions. A price increase to adjust for inflation will produce a short-term response that will reduce demand. This effect will weaken over time as inflation reduces the impact of the price change. However, in each case there will be some travellers that will seek and use alternatives and some of them may find the alternative acceptable and not come back.

Toll Roads

"If you can look into the seeds of time, and say which grain will grow and which will not, speak then unto me." **William Shakespeare**

14. TOLL ROADS

14.1 Modelling simple toll roads

The simplest of toll roads are those presenting the driver with only two, perhaps three, clear alternatives. This is sometimes the case with major tunnels, significant river or estuarial crossings and some roads in apparently simple road networks like the Chilean Highway 5[53]. In these cases it is possible to build a good model in a spreadsheet to represent actual choices.

When modelling toll roads there are several concepts that need to be treated carefully. It is recognised that travel timesavings are not the only factor determining choice. Drivers also seek to reduce the driving burden. The driving task may be more demanding if the road conditions are poor: limited visibility, frequent stopping and starting and changing gears, uneven road surface, presence of traffic lights and/or speed humps, safety and security concerns and so on. The reliability of travel times is also an increasingly important consideration. In many cases, it will also be important to consider any savings in vehicle operating costs (VOC) that may be achieved on a better route.

In order to capture these influences we can restate the generalised costs formulation for each link a and user class k specifically for toll roads as:

$$C_a^k = VTTS^k t_a (1 + \alpha\, \delta_k) + \beta VTTS^k \sigma_{ta} + VOC^k d_a + Toll_a^k$$

Where

$VTTS^k$ is the VTTS for user class k (\$/minute)

t_a is the travel time on link a (minutes)

α is the additional proportion of VTTS applicable to congested or sub-standard roads, from Table 4.

β is a coefficient to apply to VTTS to value travel time reliability

---

[53] Highway 5, the Pan American Highway, runs North South in an already narrow country like Chile. The free alternatives are often very limited and in some cases non-existent. It is tolled for over 1,500 kms.

σ_{ta} is the standard deviation of the travel time on link a (minutes)

δ_k is a 0/1 indicator that takes a value 1 if the road is sub-standard

VOC^k is the *perceived* vehicle operating cost per km for class k ($/km)

d_a is the length of link a (km)

$Toll_a^k$ is the toll applicable to class k ($/vehicle)

The toll is generally the same for all light vehicles unless one of the classes has special discounts (residents, transponder users). Note that in some roads with steep gradients or many tight curves VOC^k will need to reflect this, at least for commercial vehicles. In many urban cases users may not actually perceive the differences in vehicle operating costs in the alternatives therefore the second term is ignored:

$$C_a^k = VTTS^k t_a(1+\alpha\, \delta_k) + \beta VTTS^k \sigma_{ta} + Toll_a^k$$

In most cases the travel time reliability component is not included and is subsumed in the motorway bonus effect. One must be careful to avoid double counting the advantage of a free-flowing reliable travel time tolled facility. Understanding how the value of VTTS were estimated should help avoid this error.

Example

Take the simple road in figure 30 and a trip between origin O and destination D.

To connect O with D via the toll road (Route A) the driver has to spend 5 minutes to access the motorway, 20 minutes on the tolled road and another 5 minutes to reach D. Using untolled roads (Route B) it takes 40 minutes to connect O and D. The total demand from O to D is, say, 1000 vehicles an hour.

Toll Roads

FIGURE 30 A SIMPLE BINARY CHOICE NETWORK

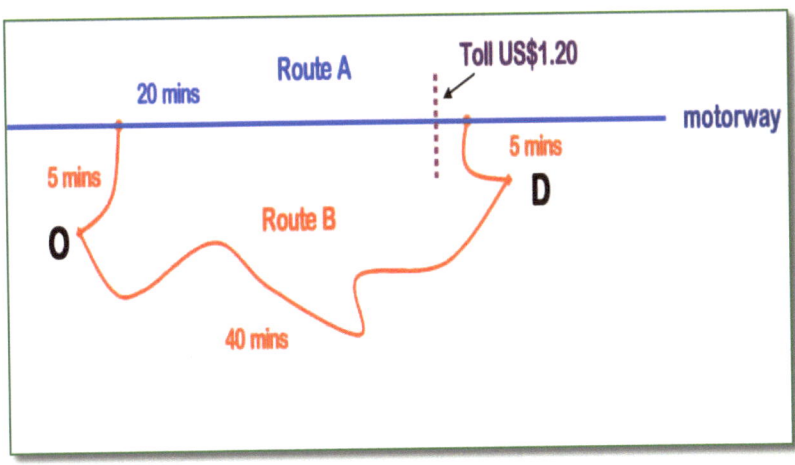

It is possible to model this choice in two different ways: as an assignment task or as a binary choice model. In the case of assignment we can use the same VTTS for both roads or a lower value for the tolled section on account of its better characteristics, a motorway bonus. These two options for assignment are shown in the next table with generalised costs measured in monetary units and VTTS is $ per minute saved:

TABLE 13 ASSIGNMENT WITH TWO ALTERNATIVES

Demand	Type of VTTS	VTTS Mtw	VTTS Rd	Time Rd	GC Rd	Time Mtw	GC Mtw	Toll	GC Route A	Time Rd	GC Route B
						Route A (tolled)				Route B	
1000	Average	$0.10	$0.10	10	$1.00	20	$2.00	1.20	$4.20	40.00	$4.00
1000	Mtw Bonus	$0.08	$0.10	10	$1.00	20	$1.60	1.20	$3.80	40.00	$4.00

With only one VTTS for all roads the untolled facility takes all the traffic. When we recognise that the tolled motorway may be perceived as better and the VTTS associated with its use to be 20% lower; then the generalised cost of travelling via the tolled facility is lower and all 1000 vehicles pay a toll to save time. The revenue will be $ 1,200 per hour.

We have recommended using at least six user classes for cars (and at least four for trucks). The next table shows the results for the same problem when we acknowledge this type of distribution of VTTS (the average is the same in both problems). The number of vehicles in each class is shown on the "demand" column; the corresponding VTTS for each type of road in the next two columns.

TABLE 14 ASSIGNMENT WITH 6 USER CLASSES

Demand	Type of VTTS	VTTS Mtw	VTTS Rd	Time Rd	GC Rd	Time Mtw	GC Mtw	Toll	GC Route A	Time Rd	GC Route B
135	Low	$0.03	$0.04	10	$0.40	20	$0.64	1.20	$2.24	40.00	$1.60
200	Low-med	$0.06	$0.08	10	$0.80	20	$1.28	1.20	$3.28	40.00	$3.20
200	Medium	$0.08	$0.10	10	$1.00	20	$1.60	1.20	$3.80	40.00	$4.00
200	Med-High	$0.10	$0.13	10	$1.25	20	$2.00	1.20	$4.45	40.00	$5.00
200	High	$0.16	$0.20	10	$2.00	20	$3.20	1.20	$6.40	40.00	$8.00
65	V High	$0.24	$0.30	10	$3.00	20	$4.80	1.20	$9.00	40.00	$12.00

Drivers with lower VTTS will select the untolled road whereas the rest will pay the toll to save time. The total flow on the toll road will be 665 vehicles an hour and the revenue $ 799.20 per hour; in my view this is a more reasonable estimate.

The problem can also be tackled as a binary choice model where the generalised costs are exactly the same as in Table 13. The binary choice model can be written to estimate the proportion of trips in each user class that would select the tolled facility as:

$$p_{toll}^k = \frac{e^{-\lambda C_{toll}}}{e^{-\lambda C_{toll}} + e^{-\lambda C_{rd}}}$$

and the total flow on the tolled facility is:

$$V_{toll} = \sum_{all\ k}(V_{toll}^k p_{toll}^k)$$

The approach is illustrated in the figure overleaf and table 15 shows results for different values for λ, the scaling parameter, and for one or six user classes. It is useful to remember the relationship between λ and σ_ε, the standard deviation of the stochastic component of the generalised cost of each alternative:

$$\lambda = \frac{\pi}{\sigma_\varepsilon \sqrt{6}} \approx \frac{1.28}{\sigma_\varepsilon}$$

Good demand segmentation should be able to reduce σ_ε for each user type and therefore increase λ making the difference in costs more significant in determining choice.

FIGURE 31 TOLL CHOICE METHODOLOGY

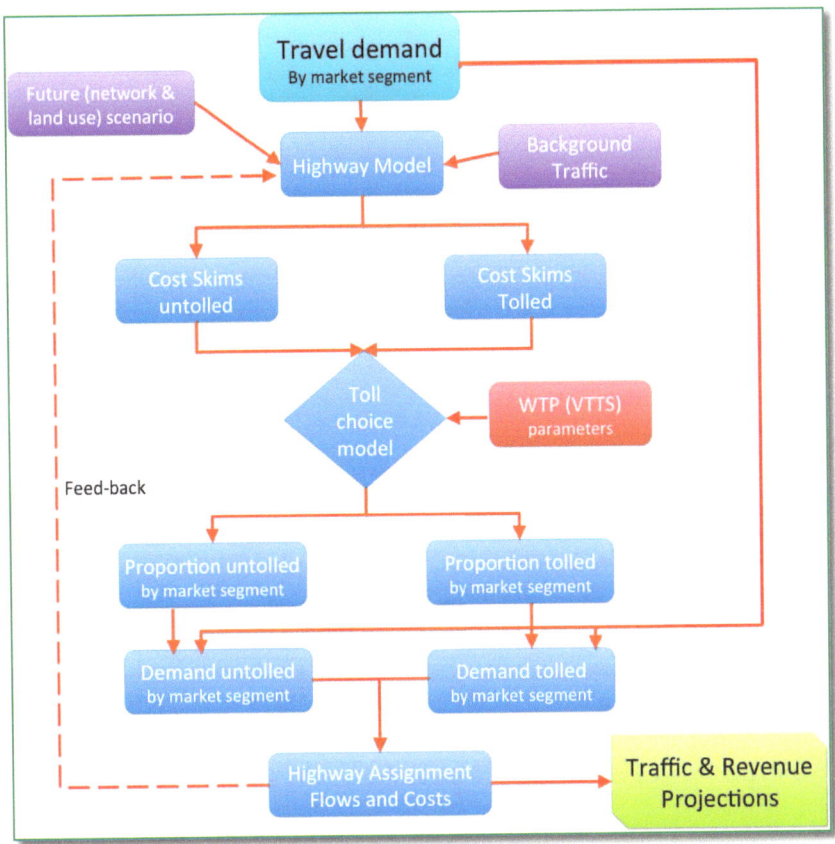

Consider the effect of the scaling parameter. For a single user class a high value (3) generates a solution similar to that of the assignment approach with six user classes. It should not be surprising that when the stochastic formulation is applied to each of the six user classes the results are even closer.

As one reduces the value for λ the closer is the proportion to 50/50 thus removing much of the effect of willingness to pay. In this case it results in a reduction of revenues; however, if the toll road was less attractive (capturing less than 50% of the demand), a lower value for the scaling parameter would increase revenue. The determination of what is the correct value for the scaling parameter λ is not straightforward; it is sometimes chosen so as to reproduce an observed elasticity but rarely a local one. This is one of my reasons to prefer assignment with multiple user classes over stochastic approaches.

TABLE 15 COMPARISON OF ASSIGNMENT AND LOGIT CHOICE ON TOLLED ROAD

Type of VTTS	Total Demand	Assigned to tolled motorway	Prop tolled motorway with λ			Uses motorway with λ		
			3	0.3	0.03	3	0.3	0.03
Average	1,000	-	0.35	0.49	0.50	354	485	499
Mtw Bonus	1,000	1,000	0.65	0.51	0.50	646	515	501
Toll Revenues		$ 1,200.00				$ 775.20	$ 618.00	$ 601.20

Type of VTTS	Total Demand	Assigned to tolled motorway	Prop tolled motorway with λ			Uses motorway with λ		
			3	0.3	0.03	3	0.3	0.03
Low	135	-	0.13	0.45	0.50	17	61	67
Low-med	200	-	0.44	0.49	0.50	88	99	100
Medium	200	200	0.65	0.51	0.50	129	103	100
Med-High	200	200	0.84	0.54	0.50	168	108	101
High	200	200	0.99	0.62	0.51	198	124	102
V High	65	65	1.00	0.71	0.52	65	46	34
Tolled flows	1,000	665				666	541	504
Toll Revenues		$ 799.20				$ 798.00	$ 649.20	$ 604.80

Consider now a slight variation on this problem. The toll is split into two locations and there is a new link that connects X, just one minute before the second tolling point with Y, six minutes away from D.

The two original choices remain the same: 40 minutes via untolled routes and 30 minutes via the toll road paying $ 1.20. There is now a new route from O to D via X and Y and this takes 33 minutes and requires a payment of $ 0.60.

FIGURE 32 THREE ALTERNATIVE ROUTES

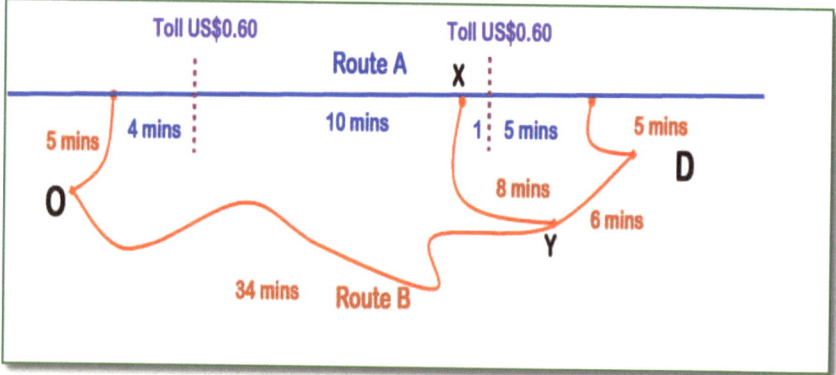

The reader can verify that under these conditions only the lowest VTTS user class prefer the untolled route, the next three classes use the route via Y (and pay only $ 0.60) and the two highest VTTS prefer the fully tolled route for 30 minutes and $ 1.20.

Toll Roads

14.2 Tolled roads on a network

For more complex systems one would use a standard package (CUBE, EMME, SATURN, TransCAD, VISUM) and the facilities included there. Most of them will offer the option of estimating toll road traffic and revenue via assignment with multiple user classes and Wardrop's equilibrium, Stochastic User Equilibrium or binary choice using Logit or Kirchhoff formulation, and perhaps new ones claimed to perform even better in these cases. Some include facilities to approximate some dynamic features of assignment.

The question remains of what should be the values assigned to VOCs, the perceived operating costs, in the generalised cost formulation.

$$C_a^k = VTTS^k t_a(1+\alpha\,\delta_k) + \beta VTTS^k \sigma_{ta} + VOC^k d_a + Toll_a^k$$

This question must be resolved locally. A starting point is that car drivers perceive at most fuel costs. These can be calculated using average fuel consumption for the average car (in each class if you wish to split hairs) and under the conditions of the network (urban, interurban, gradients, average speed, etc.).

In the case of trucks we suggest you have at least two sizes (or more depending on the proposed toll rate structure) and two levels of cost perception for each. One level of perception is for the small, one-man operator, who probably perceives fuel costs plus a percentage added for other costs, perhaps 20%. The other level for large trucking companies that are fully aware of their costs and in that case the full estimation of operating costs should apply.

Many urban toll road studies provide traffic and revenue estimates assuming that there is no perception of VOCs. This is generally a reasonable assumption as the travel distances would not be that different via toll or untolled facilities. However, in interurban studies, where the alternative routes may be quite different, it would be important to add a component of VOCs as suggested above. It would be advisable in these cases to have traffic and revenue projections with and without perceived VOCs added, to understand better what changes when they are considered. To an extent, this is an indication of what could be achieved with a good communication programme.

14.3 Means of payment and delays

There are at least three main forms of payment for toll roads:
a. The classic operation of toll plazas where the driver pays cash to an operator that in turns lifts a barrier to allow the vehicle through; this may include payment via tokens, credit cards and other means
b. Automatic tolling where the vehicle travels at relatively slow speed through a section of motorway with a barrier that is lifted when it is accepted as a valid user; and
c. Free flowing or Open Road Tolling (ORT) where a gantry covering all lanes represents the tolling point and detectors are used to identify the vehicle and charge it with no barrier in sight; the operating speeds and capacities are maintained throughout.

Identification in case (b) may be through a valid electronic tag. In some cases, it may be acceptable to have registered the number plate of the vehicle to a tolling account that may, or may not, be linked to a bank account.

Case (c) always involves Automatic Number Plate Recognition (ANPR) or Automatic License Plate Recognition (ALPR) and in most cases adds electronic tag reading, an efficient and low error method of identification. There are more than 20 such Open Road Tolls (ORT) in operation at the time of writing.

ANPR techniques have improved significantly in recent years achieving very low error rates. However, the claimed accuracies of 98-99% are dependent on locality; for example the quality of the number plates and the use of screws and other fixings affects the actual accuracy on the road. Manual verification for difficult cases is still needed.

Open Road Tolling is particularly attractive in urban areas and for HOT or Managed Lanes as it does not require the additional widening of a toll plaza. Automatic tolling with barriers requires some additional space; the vehicles must slow down and in some cases queue to pass through; sometimes vehicles are rejected for technical reasons and a bypass solution must be found for them. Manual or cash tolling certainly requires a wider toll plaza and delays to get through are unavoidable. These must be added to the link where the toll is modelled.

The appropriate way to add these delays is to consider the proposed capacity of the toll plaza and contrast it with the expected flows. The

Toll Roads

UK Manual for the Design of Roads and Bridges[54] offers the following capacities for all systems except ORT that requires no delays and has the same capacity as the lanes on the road:

TABLE 16 LANE CAPACITIES AT TOLL PLAZAS

Method	Explanation	CAR Throughput vph	HGV Throughput vph
Electronic Toll Collection (ETC)	Transponders, contact-less reading of bar code/stickers, Toll proximity cards, Tags (Low speed automatic – vehicles reduce speed, barrier lifts when transponder/card/tag is read)	450 - 900	300 - 500
Card Payment	Credit, Debit or Charge Cards (Vehicles stop – barrier lifts when card is passed through reader and has been verified – receipt may be given) Note: Throughput will reduce if driver is required to enter a PIN to verify the transaction	200 - 350	150 - 250
Coin Bin	Cash machines/coin baskets (Vehicles stop – barrier lifts when cash has been verified – change and receipts may be given)	300 - 500	200 - 350
Manual (*)	Card/cash/voucher/token (Vehicles stop – barrier operated by attendant; change and receipts may be given)	200 - 450	150 - 250
Note (*): Manual figures adjusted from author's experience	900 vph = 4 seconds per transaction 450 vph = 8 seconds per transaction 300 vph = 12 seconds per transaction 200 vph = 18 seconds per transaction		

Queueing theory can be used to estimate delays but one must also consider the time taken to slow down, pay and accelerate to normal speed. This provides a minimum delay of 30 seconds. Several simulation programs like CORSIM and VISSIM can be used to study this problem in greater detail.

Some concession contracts impose maximum delays at toll plazas (or maximum queues as they are easier to measure) and when these are exceeded the operator is required to open the barriers and let the vehicles through without paying. This is a good management measure and it poses a difficult problem for estimating the impact on revenues. These situations may happen, even for a properly designed plaza, on exceptional days (return from holidays or long week-ends).

14.4 Tolling structures

Many toll roads display a simple tolling structure, just a series of barrier plazas intercepting traffic between junctions. This assumes that the junctions are far apart to compensate for the significant cost of building and operating toll plazas. If junctions are closer then it is always possible to have some auxiliary toll mini-plazas on entries and exits to capture most, if not all, traffic using the facility. These are

---

[54] UK Department for Transport (2008) "Design Manual for Roads and Bridges", Volume 6, Section 3 Highway Features.

generally called "open systems" and the toll collectable at each site reflects the average toll per km and the distance between entries and exits; in many cases this is only approximate.

For an ORT system it is possible to collect tolls at every section between intersections but the cost of each gantry (CAPEX and OPEX) may make this proposition unattractive. Last time I looked into this the cost of a gantry with all the equipment and cabling to the control centre was about 1 million US$.

In these conditions, the T&R Advisor must search for the best combination of gantries and toll revenues. This approach is followed, for example, in all urban toll roads in Santiago.

A closed system is organised so that the vehicle is identified on entry and exit from the tolled road and the toll is calculated as a function of the distance travelled. This can be achieved by issuing (automatically) entry tickets identifying the point of access and then handing this out on exit where the operator calculates the toll. It can also be done through automatic vehicle recognition linked to pre-established accounts. In this type of system every vehicle pays whereas in some open systems parts of the road may be used for free.

Closed systems offer the opportunity to introduce any type of charging structure, not just a basic rate per kilometre. For example, some sections may have a higher charge to manage demand and maintain free-flowing conditions.

By default, open system tolls should always be modelled as monetary charges (not equivalent delays) at the point of collection. Closed systems could be modelled as an additional cost per km if this is the actual toll schedule. Any other tolling structure poses some interesting problems.

Consider first an open system with ORT charges in every section between junctions. In a simple case each charge represents just the distance between junction times the toll per km. Some toll roads establish a tolling schedule with other policy objectives, for example discouraging short trips and supporting longer trips on account of their assumed economic regeneration properties.

This can still be modelled using static congested assignment alone. Consider a configuration of sections, each with a charge of 3 units and a policy to require a minimum charge of 5 units and a maximum charge of 10 units. The travel time on each section is T minutes. This is a complex arrangement but Highway 6 in Israel has it and M7 Westlink in Sydney imposes a maximum cap (but no minimum).

It is easier to configure the network that simulates the capping of tolls to 10 units using a combination of real and virtual networks:

Toll Roads

FIGURE 33 VIRTUAL NETWORK FOR CAPPING TOLLS

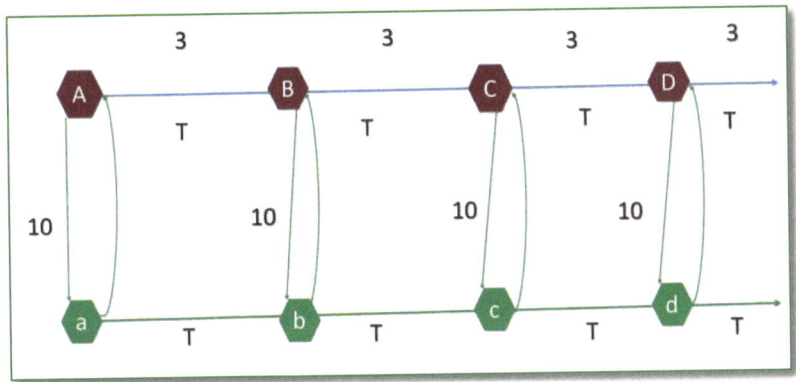

The real toll road connect junctions A, B, C, D etc. The virtual network connect nodes *a, b, c, d* etc. The travel times on both networks are the same; the toll on the real one is 3 units per section. The virtual one has no tolls except to access it, 10 units; exit is free and instant (no delay). For shorter trips the user will travel on the real network and for longer on the virtual one. If congestion on the tolled road is important then one must combine real and virtual links and calculate new speeds.

The configuration for a network with minimum and maximum tolls is more complex. We only show part of such a virtual network here:

FIGURE 34 MINIMUM AND MAXIMUM TOLLS IN A NETWORK

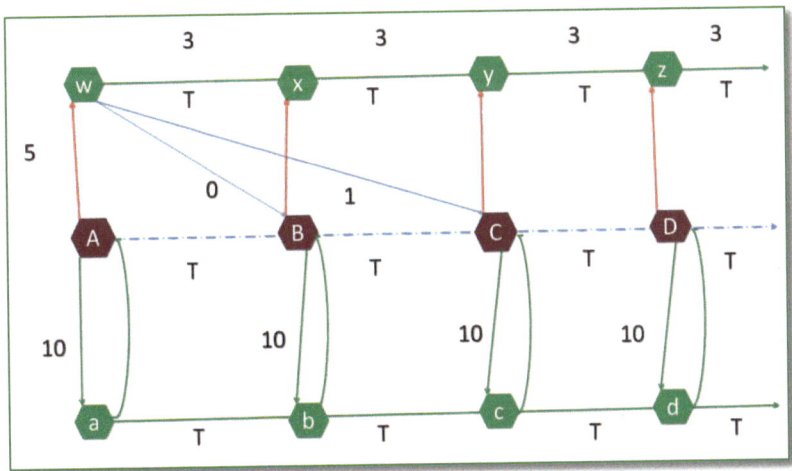

Now the real links are disconnected. There is a new virtual network with tolls of 3 units per section and access costs of 5 units. Each node of this virtual network is only connected for exit to two consecutive real nodes. From w to B at no toll and from w to C at a cost of 1 unit. Again it is necessary to collapse these networks to calculate real travel times on the tolled links.

If this becomes too complex, as it is likely, then it will be necessary to use simpler approaches. One possibility is to connect each point of entry with each exit and allocate the corresponding time and toll charge to this virtual link. Another option is to use the technique of identifying the best untolled route and the best tolled one and split flow among them using a binary choice formulation. Commercial software organises this efficiently.

14.5 Time of day tolling

Some toll roads have complex tolling structures that change with the time of the day. The reason for this is to maintain the tolled facility free flowing. ORTs in Santiago Chile charge three different levels of tolls, off peak, peak (twice that of off peak) and saturation (3 times off-peak). The charges are different per section, direction and each 30 minutes. The decision to switch from one level to the next is based on actual speed measurements over a period of time and the change must be communicated in advance. Most toll gantries display the average charge per km at the time of use. This policy is illustrated in Figure 35.

FIGURE 35 TOLL CHARGES AND SPEEDS IN SANTIAGO

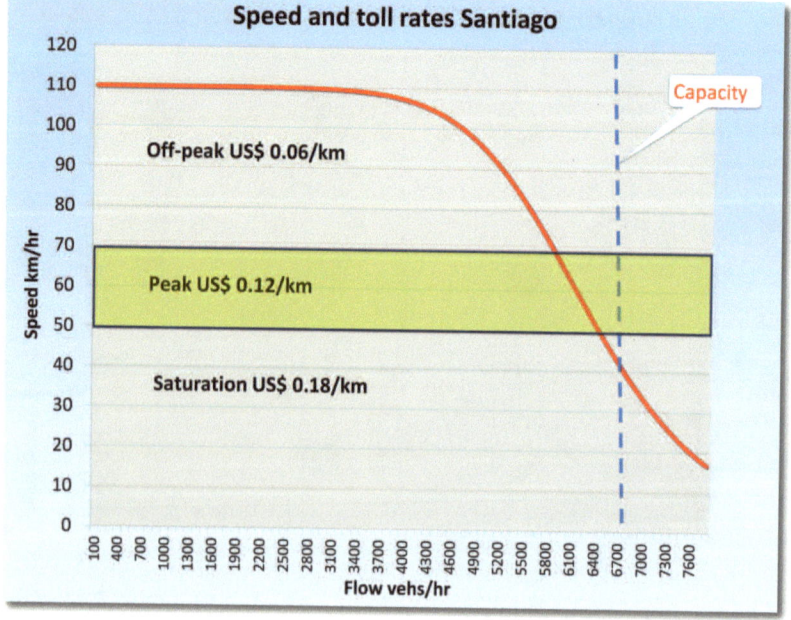

Toll Roads

This is a complex arrangement and estimating future revenues requires running the model iteratively, calculating speeds, deciding whether to increase tolls at any 30 minute period in each section and direction. An example of the complexities involved is illustrated in the next figure. It contains projections for off-peak (TFFP), peak (TBP in yellow) and Saturation (TS in red) for four forecasting horizons, 13 different sections, each direction and for five modelling periods: AM peak, off-peak (FP), PM peak (PT), Saturday (SA) and Sunday (DO).

It must be recognised that these are only averages for each modelled period. Specific half hour slots may have, in general, a higher toll rate than the average over the period.

If these toll rates are difficult to estimate with confidence, consider the route choice task demanded from the driver. He has to be able to estimate tolls and travel times with a combination of toll rates per km (people are not very good at estimating distances) at different times with a subjective indication of a "blip" sound on their transponders when passing under a gantry. This is difficult, similar to other choices like whether to use a mobile phone or a fixed line one to make an x minute call at a certain time of the day.

FIGURE 36 TOLL SCHEDULE URBAN TOLL ROAD

Section	Direction	2006					2010					2015					2020				
		AM	FP	PT	SA	DO	AM	FP	PT	SA	DO	AM	FP	PT	SA	DO	AM	FP	PT	SA	DO
1	NS	TBFP	TBFP	TBFP	TBFP	TBFP	TBFP	TBFP	TBFP	TBFP	TBFP	TBFP	TBFP	TBFP	TBFP	TBFP	TBFP	TBFP	TBFP	TBFP	TBFP
1	SN	TBFP	TBFP	TBFP	TBFP	TBFP	TBFP	TBFP	TBFP	TBFP	TBFP	TBFP	TBFP	TBFP	TBFP	TBFP	TBFP	TBFP	TBFP	TBFP	TBFP
2	NS	TBFP	TBFP	TBFP	TBFP	TBFP	TBFP	TBFP	TBFP	TBFP	TBFP	TBFP	TBFP	TBFP	TBFP	TS	TBFP	TBFP	TBFP	TBFP	TBFP
2	SN	TBFP	TBFP	TBFP	TBFP	TBFP	TBFP	TBFP	TBFP	TBFP	TBFP	TBFP	TBFP	TBP	TBFP	TBFP	TBFP	TBFP	TS	TBFP	TBFP
3	NS	TBFP	TBFP	TBP	TBFP	TBFP	TBFP	TBFP	TBP	TBFP	TBFP	TBFP	TBFP	TBFP	TBFP	TS	TBFP	TBFP	TBFP	TBFP	TBFP
3	SN	TBP	TBFP	TBFP	TBFP	TBFP	TBP	TBFP	TBFP	TBFP	TBFP	TBFP	TBFP	TBFP	TBFP	TBFP	TBFP	TBFP	TBP	TBFP	TBFP
4	NS	TBFP	TBFP	TBP	TBFP	TBFP	TBFP	TBFP	TBP	TBFP	TBFP	TBFP	TBFP	TBP	TBFP	TBFP	TBFP	TBFP	TBP	TBFP	TBFP
4	SN	TBP	TBFP	TBFP	TBFP	TBFP	TBP	TBFP	TBFP	TBFP	TBFP	TBP	TBFP	TBFP	TBFP	TBFP	TBFP	TBFP	TS	TBFP	TBFP
5	NS	TBFP	TBFP	TBP	TBFP	TBFP	TBFP	TBFP	TBP	TBFP	TBFP	TBFP	TBFP	TS	TBFP	TBFP	TBFP	TBFP	TS	TBFP	TBFP
5	SN	TBP	TBFP	TBFP	TBFP	TBFP	TBP	TBFP	TBFP	TBFP	TBFP	TBP	TBFP	TBFP	TBFP	TBFP	TBFP	TBFP	TS	TBFP	TBFP
6	NS	TBFP	TBFP	TBP	TBFP	TBFP	TBFP	TBFP	TBP	TBFP	TBFP	TBFP	TBFP	TS	TBFP	TBFP	TBFP	TBFP	TBP	TBFP	TBFP
6	SN	TBP	TBFP	TBFP	TBFP	TBFP	TBP	TBFP	TBFP	TBFP	TBFP	TBP	TBFP	TBFP	TBFP	TBFP	TBFP	TBFP	TS	TBFP	TBFP
7	NS	TBFP	TBFP	TBP	TBFP	TBFP	TBFP	TBFP	TBP	TBFP	TBFP	TBFP	TBFP	TBP	TBFP	TBFP	TBFP	TBFP	TBP	TBFP	TBFP
7	SN	TBP	TBFP	TBFP	TBFP	TBFP	TBP	TBFP	TBFP	TBFP	TBFP	TBP	TBFP	TBFP	TBFP	TS	TBFP	TBFP	TS	TBFP	TBFP
8	NS	TBFP	TBFP	TBFP	TBFP	TBFP	TBFP	TBFP	TBFP	TBFP	TBFP	TBFP	TBFP	TBFP	TBFP	TBFP	TBFP	TBFP	TBFP	TBP	TBFP
8	SN	TBFP	TBFP	TBFP	TBFP	TBFP	TBFP	TBFP	TBFP	TBFP	TBFP	TS	TBFP	TBFP	TBFP	TS	TBFP	TBFP	TBP	TBFP	TBFP
9	NS	TBFP	TBFP	TBFP	TBFP	TBFP	TBFP	TBFP	TBFP	TBFP	TBFP	TBFP	TBFP	TBFP	TBFP	TS	TBFP	TBFP	TBFP	TBFP	TBFP
9	SN	TBFP	TBFP	TBFP	TBFP	TBFP	TBFP	TBFP	TBFP	TBFP	TBFP	TBFP	TBFP	TBFP	TBFP	TS	TBFP	TBFP	TBFP	TBFP	TBFP
10	NS	TBFP	TBFP	TBFP	TBFP	TBFP	TBFP	TBFP	TBFP	TBFP	TBFP	TBFP	TBFP	TS	TBFP	TBFP	TS	TBFP	TBFP	TBFP	TBFP
10	SN	TBFP	TBFP	TBFP	TBFP	TBFP	TBFP	TBFP	TBFP	TBFP	TS	TBFP	TBFP	TBP	TBFP	TBFP	TBP	TBFP	TBFP	TBFP	TBFP
11	NS	TBFP	TBFP	TBP	TBFP	TBFP	TBP	TBFP	TBFP	TBFP	TS	TBFP	TBFP	TBFP	TBFP	TS	TBP	TBFP	TBFP	TBFP	TBFP
11	SN	TBP	TBFP	TBFP	TBFP	TBFP	TBP	TBFP	TBFP	TBFP	TBFP	TBP	TBFP	TBFP	TBFP	TBP	TBFP	TBFP	TBP	TBFP	TBFP
12	NS	TBFP	TBFP	TBP	TBFP	TBFP	TBP	TBFP	TBFP	TBFP	TBFP	TBFP	TBFP	TBFP	TBFP	TS	TBFP	TBFP	TBP	TBFP	TBFP
12	SN	TBP	TBFP	TBFP	TBFP	TBFP	TBP	TBFP	TBFP	TBFP	TS	TBFP	TBFP	TBFP	TBFP	TBFP	TBFP	TBFP	TBP	TBFP	TBFP
13	NS	TBFP	TBFP	TBP	TBFP	TBFP	TBFP	TBFP	TBP	TBFP	TBFP	TBFP	TBFP	TBP	TBFP	TBFP	TBFP	TBFP	TBP	TBFP	TBFP
13	SN	TBP	TBFP	TBFP	TBFP	TBFP	TBP	TBFP	TBFP	TBFP	TBFP	TBFP	TBFP	TBFP	TBFP	TBFP	TBFP	TBFP	TBFP	TBFP	TBFP

AM: Morning Peak   FP: Off-Peak   PT: Evening Peak   SA: Saturday   DO: Sunday

Price starts to lose its clarity and becomes a fuzzier attribute. It will not be ignored, as the bill at the end of the month will remind the user, but its association to a specific journey and choice is less clear-cut.

In most studies, the T&R Advisor will take a conservative approach and assume that electronic toll collection is equivalent to cash payments (the toll feels equally onerous). If there is sufficient local evidence that electronic payments are less onerous than cash, the following formulation could be used:

$$C_a^k = VTTS^k t_a(1+\alpha\ \delta_k) + \beta VTTS^k \sigma_{ta} + \gamma Toll_a^k$$

Again, one should be careful not to overstate the case in favour of an ORT facility. I do not believe that one should apply <u>all</u> the modelling advantages to ORT; in other words, at least one and probably 2 of the three coefficients α, β and γ should in fact be 1. Alternative values should be used in sensitivity tests to identify potential upsides of interest to equity investors.

14.6 Means of payment and market share

Toll road operators try to offer as many different means of payment as commercially viable to widen their market appeal. Different types of users are attracted (or less averse) to different type of payment methods and contracts.

From the point of view of revenue collection costs, operators would probably prefer all users to have transponders linked to bank accounts or credit cards. However, some users are reluctant to have money collected from their bank accounts automatically, at least initially; others do not wish to use tags because concerns on technology, cost or privacy issues. In some countries, not all users have a bank account (although all may have mobile phones) so a cash payment or a pre-paid tag may be attractive to them. Possible means of payment would include:

a. Systems with barriers and attendants
- Cash
- Credit/debit card
- Tokens

b. Automatic systems with barriers (slow speed) or ORT
- Tag linked to a contract/bank account, post payment
- Pre-paid transponder, various top-up methods
- ANPR, linked to account, pre or post payment
- ANPR linked to a day pass, pre-paid[55]; this allows the driver unlimited use for a day.

In most cases the T&R Advisor will estimate how many customers will use each of the methods of payment as they have different levels of penetration, would affect the ramp up duration and have different costs implications (including leakage).

---

[55] As in the London Congestion Charge, "pre-payment" can be actually effected up to a certain number of hours after usage, depending on commercial policies.

Toll Roads

The future is likely to see innovations in the forms of payment trying to make it as painless as possible.

14.7 Leakage

No form of payment guarantees that all the money potentially collected reaches the bank accounts of the concessionaire. There is scope for losses at every stage in the process: misclassification of vehicles, change errors, in-transit loses, etc. In the case of electronic payments there will be a proportion of bad payers, as for any utility. Some users will avoid paying and become violators.

Some of these loses will be estimated by the financial team with better understanding of audit trails and loss avoidance techniques and technology. But the T&R Advisor may be asked to estimate some losses, as there is interaction with assumptions and model features.

The main reasons for loses in Electronic Toll Collection include:
- Technical System Failure; the system failed, this happens only very infrequently and depends on the quality of the back-up systems;
- Transaction Technical Failure; the vehicle was not, or wrongly, identified;
- Notification failure; vehicle identified and has no valid payment but the notification to the violator fails;
- Database failure; errors in the database (old address/bank account closed) prevent collecting the toll;
- Bad debtor; individual left the country or simply will not pay.

In Figure 37 assess the impact of these failures to develop a "leakage factor" to estimate effective revenue to a concession. A proportion of violators has low VTTS or is involuntary (come from outside the region, strayed into the toll road by mistake). These vehicles would NOT have been modelled as toll users; it is not necessary to adjust expected revenues for them, only for those with higher VTTS that would appear in the revenue projections. Some involuntary non-payers, on the other hand, are recoverable (plus an administrative fee). Of course, it is always necessary to identify and chase payment from all violators, not just to recover some revenue (and surcharges) but also to retain a culture of fairness to paying users.

Better Traffic and Revenue Forecasting

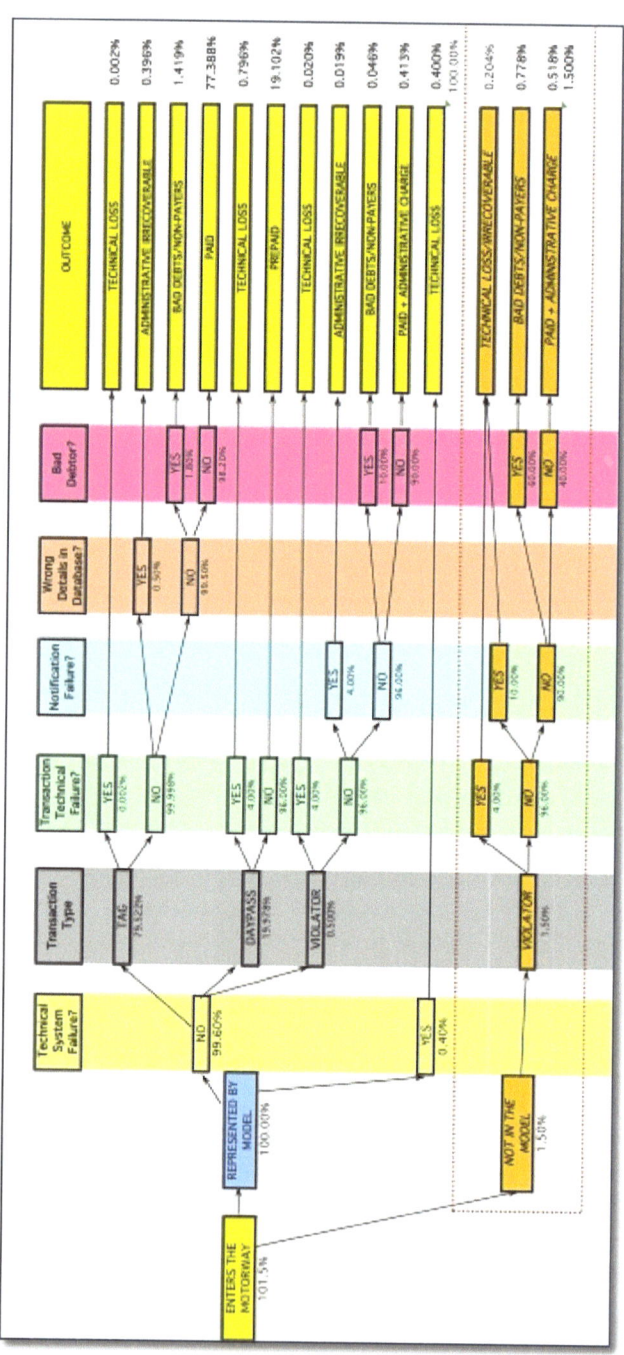

FIGURE 37 ESTIMATION OF LEAKAGES IN AN OPEN ROAD TOLLED FACILITY

14.8 Frequent users

It is intuitively accepted that drivers using toll roads for commuting, say 40 times a month, will have a different willingness to pay than those using it only occasionally. Spending, say, US$ 5, a day is not the same as doing so some evenings; such payments will affect budgets introducing an "income effect". In effect, there is evidence from transponder usage on some expensive toll roads that the proportion of commuter use is relatively low. Many users seem to be opportunistic, using the toll road occasionally when pressed for time. It is therefore important to treat commuters, the most likely frequent users, separately from other travellers.

Stated Preference surveys may help determine this difference in VTTS. However, people are not that good at imagining the impact of doing something for a long period of time (smoking and marriage come to mind). Therefore, it is also desirable to make comparisons with other type of frequent use. For example, comparing the average toll per day paid by commuters with the average public transport fare paid by those travelling in the same area. Other comparisons may be with average Cable TV charges and mobile phone bills.

We were very concerned about these issues when forecasting for the Santiago ORT facilities as all other toll roads in the country were for long distance travel at the time. We assumed that electronic payments were as onerous as cash payments and worked out that as the average toll was only slightly higher than the average public transport fare there would be no "income effects". These, together with other assumptions, turned out to be a good basis and we were not much wrong in our traffic and revenue estimates. The point of this is that one should never "load" all the assumptions in the same direction.

14.9 Sense checks

As in any forecast, it is important to undertake sense checks before adopting any figures. Some of these sense checks are fairly obvious.

a. Check practical capacities on future toll road. Because of the limitations of network representation and flow-delay relationships one must always check that future flows do not exceed practical capacities. This applies critically to flows on the future toll road; modelled volumes that are too close to, or exceed, capacities are not realistic, whatever the model says. They should be checked and corrected as necessary.

b. Check future congestion levels on other roads. Conventional models may allow flows above capacities on the rest of the network and this is highly unlikely to materialise in practice.

Other behavioural responses will be triggered before; the most important of these is likely to be peak spreading or time of travel changes. This will limit the apparent future congestion and moderate the attraction of the toll road.

c. Check for likelihood of other behavioural responses, in particular mode and destination choice (in addition to peak spreading).

d. Check also the assumptions or future network improvements at least because of better traffic control and the advent of self-driving vehicles.

e. Consider whether the region population may be approaching limits to car usage (peak car) and what assumptions are made about vehicle technology and ownership/rental after 2025.

14.10 Future uncertainties

It is easy to blame Google for one of the most important uncertainties facing toll roads (and public transport concessions) from 2020 onwards. Self-driving vehicles (SDV) are going to change the way we view and interact with the automobile and affect congestion in a very significant manner.

It is difficult to forecast at this stage what will actually happen with SDVs. The most likely dates for their appearance in the showrooms for real and legal sales seem to be 2018-2020. My guess is that by 2025 they will start reducing accidents and congestion in all networks, tolled or otherwise. By 2030 self-driving cars will probably be 30-40% of the fleet in our roads, with lower proportions in emerging countries.

There is not much research yet on the effect SDVs will have on the road network, except that they will reduce accidents and incidents significantly. The work at Columbia University[56] suggest that non-communicating self-driving vehicles will increase main road capacity by some 75% when they become 80% of the fleet. The capacities will more than double at 80% of the fleet if the vehicles can communicate with each other. Local roads will benefit less because of the influence of junctions and traffic control.

---

[56] Tientrakool, P., Ho, Y., and Maxemchuk, N. (2011) Highway Capacity Benefits from Using Vehicle-to-Vehicle Communication and Sensors for Collision Avoidance. In Proceedings of Vehicular Technology Conference (VTC Fall), IEEE

Toll Roads

Other studies are less optimistic, for example Litman[57] believes that the process of adoption will be much slower, partly because of the additional cost of a self-driving vehicle and partly because of other barriers. He foresees some impact starting around 2030 and a longer ramp-up period into the 40s.

Fagnant and Kockleman[58] are more optimistic. They see prices falling very quickly and impacts on capacities and transport policy arising from 2020 onwards. They see very significant benefits to society with the adoption of SDVs, in particular a major reduction in accidents. This will speed up their policy acceptance and market share.

An interesting suggestion is that many (some say most) SDVs will be rented by the minute/hour rather than owned. This is likely to be particularly attractive in large cities like London, Paris, New York where parking is a problem. You will be able to summon a SDV to your door when needed and then abandon it at your destination to find the next customer or a place to wait for it. This changes the culture of mobility from ownership to a service or utility. The choice between renting an SDV or taking the bus/metro will be much more natural and less influenced by emotional attachment to something you own. If mobility truly becomes more like a utility it will change the transport landscape in ways that are difficult to fully envisage at present.

It is unwise to provide a definitive view on the future impacts of SDVs and their timing at this stage. However, no toll road or public transport concession study can ignore this risk.

Another source of uncertainty, relevant not only to toll roads but to all transport projects is the future of distant presence (via internet and video conferencing).

---

[57] Litman, T. (2013) Autonomous Vehicle Implementation Predictions: Implications for Transport Planning. Victoria Transport Policy Institute.

[58] Fagnant, D. and Kockelman, K. (2013) Preparing a Nation for Autonomous Vehicles: Opportunities, Barriers and Policy Recommendations for Capitalizing on Selfdriven Vehicles. Transportation

Managed Lanes

> *"Penny Lane the barber shaves another customer*
> *We see the banker sitting waiting for a trim*
> *Then the fireman rushes in*
> *From the pouring rain.*
> *Very strange."* **The Beatles**

15. MANAGED LANES

15.1 The concept

Managed Lanes include a number of related schemes usually associated with managing traffic on one or two additional lanes on an existing facility: High Occupancy and Toll (HOT) lanes, Dynamic Toll lanes (DTL), etc. More recent approaches seek to maintain a good level of service (LOS) on these lanes by allowing High Occupancy Vehicles (HOV) for free and Single Occupancy Vehicles (SOV)[59] paying a toll. The toll to retain this desired LOS must depend on traffic levels and congestion and therefore is variable during the day. Non-HOV drivers face the choice of using the DT or HOT lanes and paying a toll or staying on the General Purpose Lanes (GPL) for free but travel at a lower speed.

Sometimes Managed Lanes are combined with Park & Ride schemes (as in the FastLane in Tel Aviv and PR 22 in Puerto Rico) offering a good public transport service to a desirable destination.

The toll to be applied is generally variable and selected so as to retain free-flowing speeds on the HOT/DT lanes; this is why this approach is sometimes called "value pricing", the driver pays a toll and benefits from much better travel times. Drivers who value their travel time and reliability more can then pay and take advantage of a better service. This implies that for pricing one should not think in terms of $ per km but in $ per minute saved.

15.2 Dynamic tolling with Managed Lanes

There are two basic approaches to pricing DTLs, a time-of-day (TOD or semi-dynamic) and a full dynamic system, which in turn may come in different varieties.

---

[59] SOV may be a misnomer. If HOVs are defined, as usual in the case of Managed Lanes, as 3+ then SOV is any vehicle with less than 3 persons in it.

Better Traffic and Revenue Forecasting

Time of day approaches are used in the Stockholm and Singapore congestion charging schemes, in the Santiago ORTs, in SR91 HOT lanes in Orange County, I10 W in Houston, among others. The toll values are adjusted to expected congestion and therefore vary every few minutes (often 30); the speeds are measured regularly and toll are re-calculated and adjusted every three months having announced the changes in advance. This has the advantage of allowing drivers to plan ahead whether or not to use the lanes. It has the disadvantage that as volumes vary, day after day, the price is never optimal and in some cases the payer does not get the travel time saving she expected and valued.

For a dynamic system the general approach is to determine the optimal toll applicable every 5 to 10 minutes using real-time measurements on the conditions on the DT and GP lanes, as illustrated in the following figure:

FIGURE 38 DYNAMIC TOLLING OF A MANAGED LANE

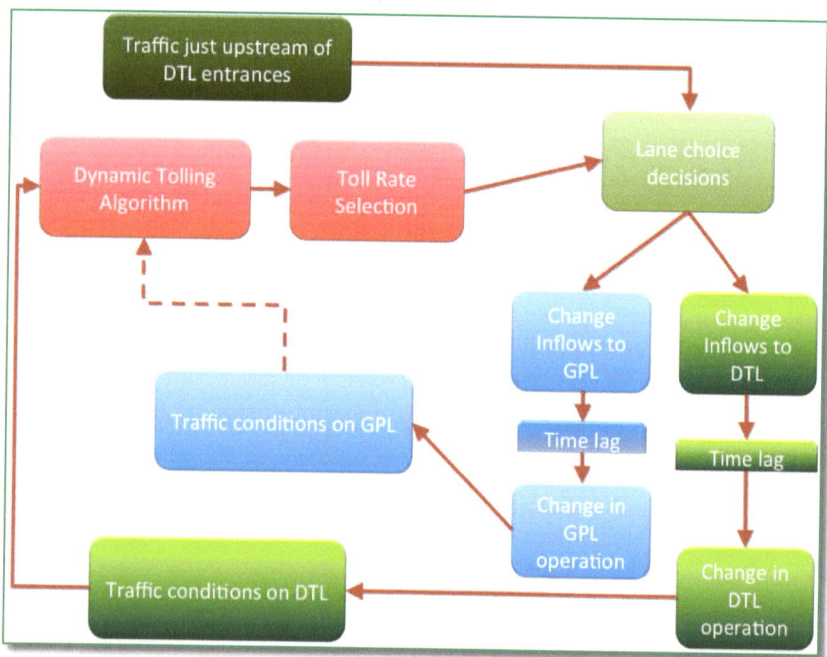

Note the recognition that there is a time lag between measurements, new tolls and changes in the flow conditions. The dotted line between GP conditions and the tolling algorithm reflects the fact that not all of them are directly concerned with time savings.

A dynamic tolling algorithm takes data from the existing operation of the GP and DTL traffic, selects a toll rate level that is then informed to drivers before they reach the DTL/GP decision point. The toll rate is

Managed Lanes

used to influence and achieve a desired level of inflow into the DTL and this, ideally, results in its optimal operation. In practice, no dynamic tolling algorithm is perfect and there is always the risk of over-reacting to changes in traffic levels thus generating oscillations (too low price leading to too much inflow followed by too high price leading to too little inflow) that reduce the efficiency of the strategy.

In most cases, the Level of Service (usually determined by the average speed) on the DTL traffic is considered to be the Measure of Efficiency (or MOE) or Key Performance Indicator (KPI). This may or may not be the optimal allocation of traffic seeking to minimise overall delay or the level of toll and traffic allocation that maximises revenue. However, speeds are easy to measure and keeping them above a minimum is a straightforward, easy to understand and communicate approach to setting toll levels.

Fully dynamic systems seek to optimise time savings or revenues. They are used in the Tel Aviv FastLane, SR 167 in Seattle 95, I 15 in North San Diego, I 95 in Miami and I 394 in Minneapolis. These systems rely on an algorithm that takes into account historical data, the current state of the GP and DT lanes as determined by sensors (usually speed and/or density) and an estimation of the time savings; a small number of parameters must be adjusted in situ from a starting point determined by a model.

For example, the pricing for the I 394 facility in Minneapolis is based on downstream densities and the use of a look-up table. In contrast, the SR 167 HOT facility in Seattle has a pricing algorithm based only on a closed-loop of information from the road system.

In all cases, there must be an element of short term forecasting of the future conditions, say 5-15 minutes ahead, in order to price the use of the facility. This forecasting element can be based on just short-term variations in flow and/or in historical profile data as implicit in the density look up tables of the I-395.

There are no, to our knowledge, universal algorithms that could be used in all circumstances. One must adapt them to the conditions, entries and exits, of each facility. It should also be noted that research has shown that whenever demand is stable, predictable TOD algorithms perform as well, or even better, than adaptive methods. The reason for this seems to be that all adaptive methods tend to oscillate around optimal pricing and optimal flow levels. If these oscillations are large there is a significant loss in the level of service and revenue collection. Predictable flows make TOD pricing more efficient provided it is well designed to cope with these flows. Of course, when conditions differ materially from the predicted levels then TOD becomes less efficient and adaptive algorithms cope much better.

15.3 The design and specification of Managed Lanes

Managed Lanes come in all shapes and sizes. Most of them add two tolled lanes to at least two GP lanes. If there is not enough space to provide the tolled lanes in both directions they can be established with tidal or reversible flow: usually towards a major city in the morning and the reverse direction in the afternoon peak. This requires a short period when the DT lanes are not operational as the direction is reversing. In some cases zipper barriers are used to modify access and exits to the tolled lanes when the directions change, for example I 15 HOT lane in San Diego.

There are a few cases where there is only one tolled lane, for example the FastLane in Tel Aviv. This is rare, as they work less well than dual lanes. It appears that no overtaking within the HOT lane and phantom friction from the nearby GP lanes significantly reduce the capacities of single lanes.

Before attempting any modelling of Managed Lanes it is important to understand the context and requirements that the dynamic tolling system must satisfy together with the physical design of the lanes, in particular the points of entry and exit to the DTL. Sometimes, DT lanes are provided in order to bypass a bottleneck; then, the GP traffic is often affected by delays that are not the result of a speed-flow relationship but simply a reduction in capacity.

DTLs allowing "queue jumping" can be very effective and in some cases quite short. Note that keeping traffic on the GPO lanes moving, albeit slowly, may be necessary to allow access and exit from the DT lanes. The design of entries and exits from the DT lanes is most important in estimating traffic and revenue. The direct access to the DT lanes is valuable but creates some very complex junctions. These issues call for closer interaction between road designers and T&R advisors than in other type of schemes.

Concessions to build and manage a DTL are usually set up with some specific requirements. For example:

- The minimum charge on the DTL should be $0.50 per section;
- To protect the Level of Service speed on the DTL should not be less than 20 km/hr below the posted speed on the GP lanes, and
- Flow on the DTL should not be less than 1300 vehicles an hour per lane to ensure a minimum use so that the GP lanes are less crowded.

These conditions determine the decision area for the algorithm that will define the toll at any one time. Care must be taken to ensure these conditions are feasible; for example the three requirements above may not be all feasible at night.

Managed Lanes

15.4 Projecting revenues on Managed Lanes

First, it is useful to distinguish two level of choices; (a) between alternative roads and the road with the DTL (this is common to toll road forecasting) and (b) between General Purpose (GP) lanes and Dynamic Tolled Lanes (DTL) within that road. Note that when facing the first choice (a) the driver will only have an approximate idea of the toll chargeable and the associated time delays. The second choice (b) is more sensitive to model for two reasons: (1) the travel distances are very similar and the main differences between routes arise from travel times and toll rates; and (2) the toll is adjusted dynamically every 5-10 minutes in response to variations in traffic that are not identified in a conventional network model.

It is therefore helpful to split the problem into two stages to estimate first the traffic that is likely to use the combined DTL and GP lanes, and then model in detail the dynamic nature of the toll system:

a. Develop a regional network assignment model to allocate a reasonable amount of traffic on the combination of DTL and GP lanes of interest. This would be a network model of the area surrounding the proposed DTL and will include all the zones relevant to define in-scope traffic. The model is then run with static assignment to represent each time period (say AM peak) and used to determine, through trial and error, an average toll that satisfies the requirements of the DTL. This would follow a process similar to that used to estimate tolls on urban toll roads. This identifies the *specific demand* for the combine Managed Lanes.

b. Develop an operational local model of the road (DTL and GP lanes) using the specific demand above but incorporating observed variations, say every 15 minutes, of traffic. In my experience focussing in variations in flow below 15 minutes is not worthwhile. This local model will treat in detail the pricing algorithm to satisfy the conditions of the concession and optimise the allocation of traffic to GP and DT lanes.

In both the network and the operational model HOVs (if exempted from payment) are pre-loaded onto the DTL; normally, lorries and other vehicles that are not permitted onto the DTL will be pre-loaded onto the GP lanes. Motorcycles will normally be pre-loaded where appropriate.

15.5 Pricing and revenue optimisation in Managed Lanes

There are two basic criteria for setting toll rates. The one stated above, to keep speeds above a minimum protects the level of service. A second possible objective for toll setting may be to maximise revenue; this requires estimating the time savings achievable using the DTLs and requires information of the performance of the GP lanes. In general terms, these two objectives do not result in the same toll rate. In my experience, revenue maximisation results in a slightly higher toll, and higher DTL speeds with somewhat lower flows.

Moreover, the dynamic tolling algorithms have some limitations in practice. Depending on their quality and that of the data collected to feed them, the algorithms usually underperform, in terms of revenue, compared to the ideal results from a modelled optimisation that usually assumes perfect information.

Consider first the drivers who have already chosen to join the combined Managed Lanes (GP and DT lanes), what we call the *specific demand*. They face a choice between Dynamic Tolled and GP lanes which can be stated in simple terms: "*Choose DT lanes if the generalised cost of using them is lower or equal to using the GP lanes*". Assuming that the DTL offers very reliable travel times the tolled facility will be chosen if:

$$DT_{time} + \frac{Toll}{VTTS_k} \leq GP_{time} + \beta \sigma_{tGP}$$

With *Toll* and $VTTS_i$ in consistent units and β is the coefficient to apply to VTTS to value travel time reliability (standard deviation of travel time σ_{tGP}).

As the sub-index k suggests, this choice will depend on the corresponding VTTS of a particular segment of the driving market.

When a DTL is in operation at a particular toll level those using it belong to two groups: HOVs, and those with a high enough willingness to pay for the time saved and the reliability gained; those on the GP lanes have a lower value of time.

There are two ways to handle this choice and both require assumptions about the distribution of VTTS. The first one is to segment demand into a few VTTS ranges and propose a Logit type choice between GP and DT lanes. This choice can be processed to generate an equivalent relationship between the proportion or fraction of the *specific demand* that will join the tolled lanes and the toll payable per minute saved. This can be translated into a diversion curve on the basis of one or more average VTTS.

A very similar curve can be produced with a more direct relationship with the distribution of values of time in the driving population. The number of drivers with a willingness to pay (VTTS) greater than a particular value will be willing to pay a particular toll to benefit from the time saving offered by the DT lanes. This provides a more direct approach to estimating the equivalent to the diversion curve above. Both curves are shown in Figure 39. Of course, depending on the scaling parameter the Logit formulation works well provided the VTTS distribution delivers a similar curve.

FIGURE 39 DTL DIVERSION CURVE

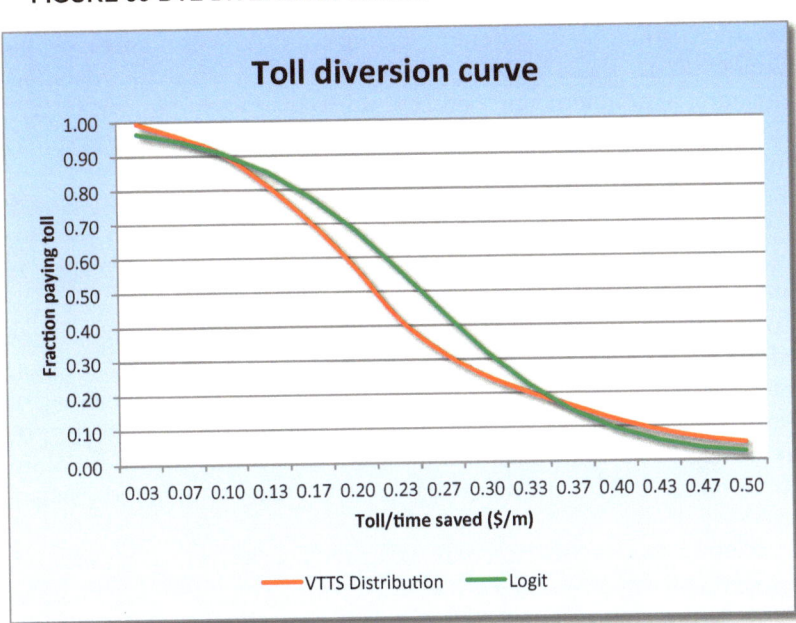

Once the road *specific demand* has been correctly identified using a conventional transport model it is possible to set up a spreadsheet model to represent these choices. Note that this assumes that the tolling of each section of the road can be handled independently, something I believe is generally the case. More complex pricing structures (capping of tolls, etc.) would need a more complex arrangement.

There are two possible approaches to handle the assignment of traffic to GP and DT lanes. The first one is to apply a choice (generally Logit) formulation with price and travel times on the two options as the key components of generalised costs. Before doing this one would select an appropriate level of segmentation so that the scaling parameter is not too critical for all the choices, say 6 segments with different VTTS.

Note that there is a possible limitation of this approach when applied to multi-section Managed Lanes. The model will probably compare the use of the full applicable DTL against GP lanes in terms of total toll and time savings. In practice, some users may select only those sections where the value of the time saving is greater than the toll, weaving in and out of the DT lanes as necessary.

The second approach, which I prefer, is to represent a very high level of segmentation for VTTS, at least 50 but more often 100 segments with VTTS associated to the observed income distribution in the area. If there are distinct and different incomes in different parts of the catchment areas these should also be identified and differentiated. Incremental assignment can then be used to load each segment to DTL or GP lanes, calculate travel times on each and adjust toll rate to satisfy the objectives.

Both models, the Logit choice and the incremental assignment with 100 classes, will finally have to be solved iteratively so that the best equilibrium between delays, tolls and allocation of traffic, for each 15 minutes time period, is found.

In simple cases, the operational models described above can be handled in a spreadsheet. In more complex situations it is better to use a mesoscopic (or meson-simulation) package like Avenue, Dynameq, or Dynasmart. At the time of writing micro-simulation models, despite their attractions, are not the tools of choice because of their limitations in route choice and the need to run them repeatedly to obtain consistent results.

It is often worthwhile to compare speeds (or travel times) and GP and tolled lanes and estimate when the limiting conditions are met and when revenue is maximised. For example the following figure shows speeds on GP and DT lanes and revenues collected for different levels of toll charge.

In this case the requirement for the DTL was to have speeds above 45 miles per hour. This is satisfied with tolls above $ 2.50. The toll that maximised revenue, however, is $ 4.00.

FIGURE 40 SPEEDS AND REVENUE IN MANAGED LANES

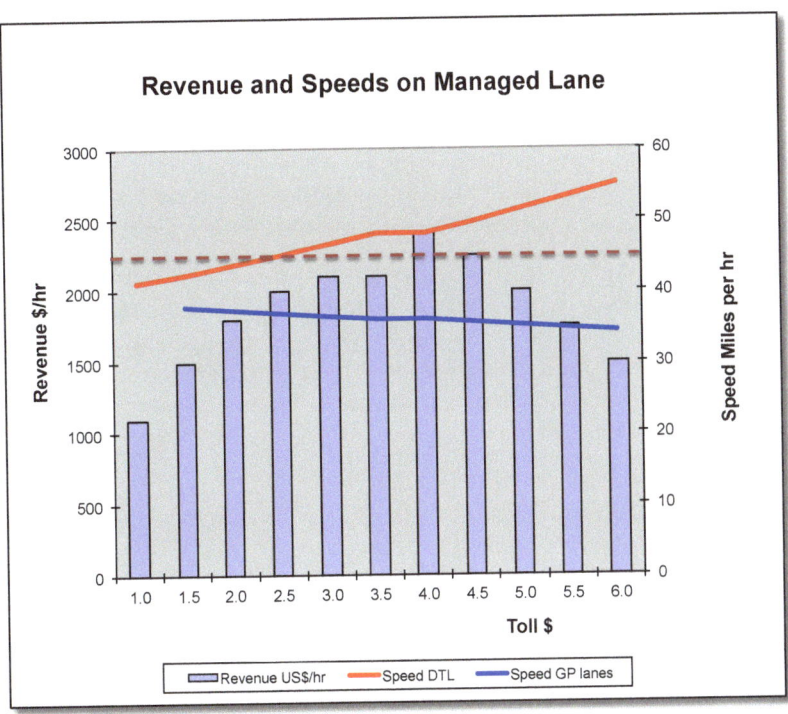

15.6 Imperfect information

The models described above assume drivers are perfectly aware of the travel times and driving conditions on both the general purpose and dynamic tolled lanes. This is never likely to be true, even with the best traveller information. Events may pan out that perturb the best estimates of future travel times; moreover, in most cases only very general information is available, the most notable of which is the current toll rate. In complex tolled lanes, even that information is only an approximation as different sections will implement different toll rates and drivers may come in and out of the DTL at will. There is some evidence that some drivers may even misinterpret a high price signal as indicating very poor conditions on the GP lanes: the higher the toll rate the more users will choose the DTL. The provision of good information is, therefore, critical to achieving welfare improvements using Managed Lanes.

One should also bear in mind that the data fed onto toll optimisation algorithms is unlikely to be perfect. Loop and other detectors fail and sometimes provide erroneous information. Good monitoring and maintenance of such sensors is essential for the successful operation of Managed Lanes. Ideally the toll optimisation software should also be able to cope with the failure of one or more sensors and default to TOD tolling in emergencies.

15.7 Sense checks

Sense checks will also be needed when projecting future traffic and revenue at Managed Lanes. These are analogous to those for toll roads with the added complexity that the tolls themselves are highly variable.

a. Check that practical capacities are not exceeded on the DTL. This is unlikely to happen in a good model, as the Level of Service retention is a critical element in the design of the Managed Lanes. However, it is useful to check manually the balance, under extreme conditions between time savings, flows and toll rates.

b. Congestion on the GP lanes. High congestion on the GP lanes is likely to be inconsistent with the assumptions in the regional network model used to estimate how many trips will be attracted to the combines DTL and GP lanes. It may be necessary to run this model again with different assumptions on peak-spreading, mode or destination choice to obtain more reasonable future total flows.

c. The average toll for a period, as estimated by the operational model, may turn out to be too different from that assumed in the regional network model; in that case it will be necessary to re-estimate the specific demand and repeat the process.

d. Confirm that traffic can actually perform the manoeuvres required with the flows levels estimated by the model, for example accessing the DT lanes. This may require the micro-simulation of critical interchanges but in most cases a good Traffic Engineer and Designer should be able to comment on this possibility.

Congestion Charges

"It is wrong to blame anyone for failing to forecast accurately in an unpredictable world. However, it seems fair to blame professionals for believing they can succeed in an impossible task".
Daniel Kahneman

16. CONGESTION CHARGES

16.1 Demand management

Nobody likes traffic congestion; it is indeed mentioned as one of the main factors that reduce the quality of urban life. Providing more road capacity solves part of the problem and only for a few years. Therefore city governments have developed a number of demand management techniques aiming to control, and if possible reduce, congestion. These techniques include the allocation of road space to different type of users (for example introducing bus and cycle lanes), parking restraint (controlling spaces and price), traffic management measures (one-way schemes, better signal coordination, traffic calming) and pricing schemes like congestion charges.

Some cities introduce tough measures to ration road space, for example restricting the use of cars certain days to those with number-plates ending in particular digits. For example, Bogotá's Pico & Placa system has permitted only cars ending in certain five digits one day and the other five the next day; this would ration usage to 50% of the fleet each day except for the exemptions awarded to some services; some wealthy families have acquired additional vehicles to get round this rationing system.

A significant component of the congestion problem is that drivers do not perceive all the cost society incurs when they join a traffic stream; they are aware of their own delays and in an imperfect fashion their own operating costs. They do not perceive additional delays induced on the rest of the traffic nor the impact of driving on accidents and the environment. In economic terms these are the externalities of driving and may be more significant than drivers' perceived own or private costs.

The case for congestion charging was first made some 50 years ago by the Smeed Report (1964) in the UK. Smeed observed that the general structure for motoring taxation dated from 1909 with a fixed element (unrelated to road use) the annual Road Tax, and a variable element related to car use through Fuel Tax. Smeed noted the ineffectiveness of this method to reflect the real costs of undertaking a particular journey, in particular costs incurred by others. Congestion generates significant

Better Traffic and Revenue Forecasting

externalities that waste energy and time unless internalised through a pricing mechanism.

Since Smeed's Report experts have advocated the adoption of road pricing mechanisms able to discriminate the location and time when congestion takes place. Two main considerations have delayed implementation of congestion charging. The first one is its possible regressive nature: the rich will pay and benefit from faster travel whilst the poor will have to use "inferior" modes of transport. The second objection, perhaps a more important one, is that voters will find congestion charging an unacceptable form of taxation. The London Congestion Charging (LCC) experience proved in 2003 that neither of these objections is sufficiently valid and opened up a new range of measures for demand management that could not only be self-funding but may even generate surplus revenues to invest in other schemes.

Although some of the elements of a congestion charge may be outsourced to the private sector the general rule is that such measures are planned, implemented and managed by city governments.

16.2 User charges and road pricing

The economic theory underpinning road-use pricing was first put forward by Pigou (the father of welfare economics) in 1920, with Walters (1961) relating it specifically to road traffic.

They basic issue is that road users do not perceive the true costs of their journeys, they only perceive direct costs (fuel) and charges (tolls, parking) and therefore the decisions they make are sub-optimal. In order to improve resource allocation (including route and mode choice) it is necessary to expose traveller to the true (social) marginal costs of every section of their journeys. It is argued that poor travel choices arise because the marginal private costs perceived by drivers are significantly less than the marginal social costs incurred by society.

This is illustrated in Figure 41. The green line represents the private perceived costs of a new driver on a link with capacity a bit over 2500 vehicles an hour. Demand is represented by a (yellow) down sloping curve and it is in private cost equilibrium with supply (in green) at 2000 vehicles an hour. The red curve shows the Marginal Social Costs incurred at different flow levels, that is the marginal additional delay experienced by the rest of the traffic. The difference between the two, indicated at a flow 2000, would represent the charge to be levied so that the private user perceives the social cost. However, at this price demand would decrease, for example to 1500 vehicles an hour and this reduces externalities and the necessary charge. The correct equilibrium is reached at an intermediate point (in the example around 1700 vehicles/hr) with an intermediate charge in red.

Congestion Charges

FIGURE 41 MARGINAL SOCIAL CONGESTION COSTS AND CHARGES

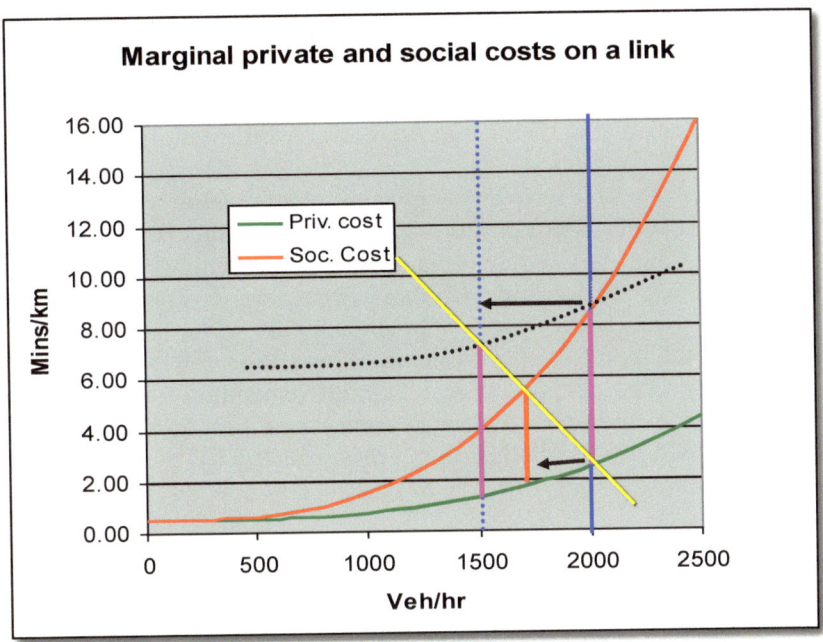

16.3 Congestion charging in practice

Singapore was the first country to adopt congestion charging in the form of a paper based Area Pricing in 1975. The immediate impact was a significant reduction in car traffic, congestion and increase in public transport patronage. In 1998 the paper-based system was replaced by better-targeted electronic charges with further reductions in congestion and traffic.

There were several studies in the UK and elsewhere and in 1986 the city of Bergen in Norway introduced a flat rate to enter the Central Business District from 6 AM to 10 PM Monday to Friday. Oslo, Stavanger, Trondheim and other cities introduced similar systems. The selling point of these Norwegian systems was the collection of revenue for investment in transport.

The introduction of the London scheme in 2003 represented a major breakthrough both technically and politically as it was been hailed as a success in a world city. Stockholm followed with a better system that took advantage of the geography of the city. Stockholm is particularly interesting as the scheme was introduced as an experiment, switched off after some months, and a referendum held to re-start it, in a slightly modified form. Milan has introduced an area charge scheme (Area C) replacing an earlier and less effective environmental measure. The most recent congestion-charging scheme has been introduced in Gothenburg in early 2013.

All the implementations so far have been of rather simple systems providing only a coarse approximation to optimal pricing. When a charging area is defined as in London, drivers pay a single fee to travel in it for the whole day. This discriminates very little in terms of location and time of congestion. Cordon systems, as the one in use in Stockholm, can charge every crossing of the boundary and can discriminate at different times of the day and therefore are able to price externalities more accurately. Singapore and Gothenburg have mixed systems with a cordon plus additional charging in other congestion "hot-spots" with charges varying during the day.

In general terms cordon systems, where the user pays for each crossing, perhaps capped to a maximum expenditure per day, are easier to set up and enforce. Area systems require charging all users in the designated zone, whether they cross a boundary or not. This, in practice, makes it very difficult to charge different rates at different times of the day.

So far, each practical congestion charging system has been different, trying to strike a balance between effectiveness, acceptability and ease of comprehension on the part of the user. Most systems have a range of exemptions and discounts to encourage public support and reduce any feeling of unfairness. In all cases the greatest beneficiaries of congestion charging have been bus users who gain in speed and frequency as the revenue from the scheme is normally spent improving public transport and other infrastructure.

16.4 Lessons learnt from existing systems

It is possible to summarise some of the lessons learnt so far as many affect modelling of such schemes:

a. Modelling has played a key role in assisting design, estimating revenues and costs and undertaking Cost Benefit Analysis; modelling has been useful in persuading key opinion leaders that the schemes have been properly designed.

b. All schemes have suffered from significant public opposition, including legal challenges that have delayed implementation. Lack of "fairness" has been the main stumbling block hence modelling should identify who benefits and who loses from any particular design.

c. Exemptions and discounts make a system more palatable but they are expensive to enforce; it is cheaper, and in economic terms fairer, to have no exemptions or discounts.

Congestion Charges

d. Most systems use only video with Automatic Number Plate Recognition as this is now reliable and low cost.
e. The cost of collecting the charge is high, higher than for toll roads. This is because there are many more detection points (some 200 in London alone but only 18 en Stockholm), many disputed charges, more uncollectables than on toll roads, enforcement is difficult and there are heavy requirements for customer support (Front Office) and low value transaction processing (Back Office). It has been difficult to reduce collection costs below 20% of the charges. Collection costs reduce the benefits of the scheme.
f. Socialisation, communication and consultation are essential elements to ensure acceptability of the scheme. Wherever congestion charging has failed to be introduced despite a solid case for it (New York, Edinburgh, Manchester) it has been because of a poor communication and consultation process.
g. Despite opposition, once established congestion charging becomes a normal part of urban life.
h. The main benefits accrue inside the charged areas with reductions in traffic of the order of 15%-20% and better gains in speeds. The most important impact seems to be change of mode[60] followed by change of route, time of travel and destination.
i. The location of charging points is far from trivial. It must be decided with frequent visits to potential sites to ensure good visibility of plates, no masking by other vehicles and space to locate the cameras without spoiling the urban realm.
j. In order to achieve acceptability it is important to give confidence to citizens that the revenues will be used to invest in local transport facilities, in particular improving public transport services.
k. All systems will change over time, requiring fine-tuning. The London system had to increase charges to keep pace with increasing willingness to pay; automatic electronic payment reduces collection costs but dulls behavioural response to the charge.
l. Some systems, like Milan, have a very high proportion of occasional users as most commuters already use public transport. This makes modelling more important but also more difficult.

---

[60] This assumes, as it has been the case so far, that public transport offers a suitable alternative to car travel to the charged zone.

m. Motorcycles are always exempt, as they do not have front number plate and the rear one is difficult to read. Taxis are exempt in London and Milan but charged in Singapore and Stockholm.
n. Despite early concerns the impact on local commerce and economic activity has been consistently small.
o. Congestion charging on its own will not solve many problems. It is necessary to make it a component of a more comprehensive set of interventions and be supported by significant improvements in public transport, ideally metro/LRT systems as in all cities where it has been implemented.

16.5 Modelling Congestion Charge Schemes

From the comments above it should be clear that a comprehensive multi-modal model would be required to represent and design a congestion charging system. The model should have significant disaggregation by willingness to pay to characterise travel choices. It is generally necessary to include in the model taxis, motorcycles and goods vehicles. One or two additional user classes will be required to represent users with exemptions or discounts as they would make different choices.

As most modern systems have time-dependent charges it will be necessary to model different times of the day to accommodate them. Variable charges imply cordon, corridor or screenline systems, as it is not easy to change charges over time with area systems.

Area systems are difficult to model as users pay even if they do not cross a boundary. It will often be necessary to model tours as the decision to pay involves the costs and benefits of all movements in the charged area during the day.

The introduction of congestion pricing implies a major emotional burden for citizens unaccustomed to pay for the use of roads. They will develop strong opinions about the fairness of the proposed system and this will affect willingness to pay and the ramp-up period. Attitudes developed during the design period, perhaps exacerbated by a poor communication and consultation strategy, will play a key role in determining usage and revenue, more so than in the case of a new urban toll road. This will mean that the model results will be more uncertain than usual despite the claimed accuracy of the modelling efforts in Stockholm and London.

Public Transport Concessions

> "*An advanced city is not a place where the poor move about in cars, rather it's where even the rich use public transportation*"
> Enrique Peñalosa

17. PUBLIC TRANSPORT CONCESSIONS

17.1 Rail and public transport concessions

Most of the original railway services were privately developed and owned; several of them failed spectacularly after implementation. During the first part of the 20th century most of these services were nationalised resulting in the strong, publicly owned, railways of Europe and elsewhere.

Then, the UK probably pioneered the idea of running rail services as franchises. After some faltering efforts the country now has a very good railway system run by Train Operating Companies (TOCs) that bid for the right to run a particular group of services. TOCs usually lease trains from leasing companies and the rail network, signalling and stations are mostly run by Network Rail, a state owned entity. In recent years Network Rail has entered into partnership with TOCs to operate stations and other elements of infrastructure. This is consistent with the European Rail Policy of separation of the management of the network from the operation of rail services.

Producing Patronage (Traffic) and Revenue projections for companies bidding for these concessions has become a very specialised undertaking. In Britain, these estimates are based on specialised models than include details of the timetables, historical demand by service class and type, competitors (rail and other modes) and very detailed socio-economic characteristics of potential catchment areas. The performance regimes demanded by the concession agreement require careful consideration and have a strong interaction with patronage and revenue projections. This very specialised approach is data and country specific and will not be discussed further here. However, the principles outlined in the rest of this chapter are, nevertheless, directly relevant.

I have been involved in producing T&R forecasts for completely new projects where no historical data exists for the mode in question. The techniques used in this case are more akin to conventional strategic transport models as discussed in Modelling Transport. These techniques have been adapted to the needs of preparing business cases and T&R projections for High Speed Rail and for Metro, LRT and BRT systems in different parts of the world.

17.2 Public transport modelling

Modelling public transport systems is fairly complex. An introduction is provided in Modelling Transport, Chapters 6 to 9 for mode choice and Section 10.6 for assignment.

Particular care is needed in building the zoning system and network. For a fixed track system one would like to have only one zone, representing the immediate[61] catchment area, associated with each station/stop. This may require splitting zones and may be too difficult for a system with frequent stops like a BRT/LRT, in particular if the stop locations are not fully decided in advance. Whatever the case, it will always be difficult to estimate accurately the number of passengers using each stop and the exact number travelling on each segment of the line. Competing modes should be equally detailed but the model granularity will decline away from the new facility.

The new system needs to be modelled in such a way that one can separate its demand and performance from that of other modes. This is achieved in slightly different ways in each software package.

It is important to represent walking and waiting time, as well as the time and transfer penalty as realistically as possible. Usually, the automatic estimation of walking time does not work well enough.

It is well known that all-or-nothing is not a realistic assignment technique for public transport. There are several assignment techniques that work better, in particular in the case of common lines or services on part of a route, see MT pages 373 -380. In these cases an assignment based on service frequencies or travel strategies would be appropriate depending on conditions. A couple of issues introduce additional subtleties in this type of assignment: congestion or crowding effects and whether timetable assignment would be more appropriate.

Waiting times may be modelled as a function of frequency; it is less usual for a new system to be modelled at this stage using timetable assignment. However, in some cases a new rail or tram service is tendered and required to be run on a timetable coordinated with other services to minimise the inconvenience of transfer and waiting times. In these case timetable assignment will be the most appropriate approach.

---

[61] Other trips may access the stations using feeder modes like bus, taxi or Kiss and Park & Ride (P&R).

Public Transport Concessions

In order to account for these influences the total generalised cost of travelling between an origin and a destination by public transport modes m for a person type k can be written as:

$$C_{ij}^k = \sum_m \{VTTS^k t_{ij}^m (1 + \alpha_{ij}^m + \beta\sigma_{tm}) + VTTwk^k Walk^m + VTTwt^k Wait^m\}$$
$$+ nTrans\rho^k + Fare_{ij}^k$$

$VTTS^k$ is the VTTS for person type k ($/minute)

t_{ij}^m is the travel time on mode m between i and j (minutes)

α_{ij}^m is now more complex. It reflects a combination of travelling under uncomfortable conditions (if this is the case) and the grater attractiveness of mode m. This will depend on how exactly crowding is modelled in the software package used; some do this through a penalty on frequency in which case this parameter reflects only mode quality.

β is a coefficient to apply to VTTS to value travel time reliability

σ_{tm} is the standard deviation of the travel time on mode m

$VTTwk^k Walk^m$ and $VTTwt^k Wait^m$ are the value of walking and waiting time multiplied by the time required to walk and wait for each mode m

$nTrans$ is the number of transfers required

ρ^k is the transfer penalty for person type k ($)

The transfer penalty is usually valued at between 3 to 8 minutes depending on the quality of the interchange; this is then converted into money using $VTTS^k$.

I find it helpful to use mode choice and assignment with at least six person types; these could be a combination of purposes and income but must differ in terms of willingness to pay. Additional person types may be needed to account for discounted travel and special tickets.

Sub-mode choice can be undertaken by assignment (multi-path, stochastic or not) or by nested choice modelling. I find it easier to understand and interpret when it is done by assignment, perhaps with additional VTTS values to improve the spreading of route choices.

17.3 Access

Feeder services and opportunities to reach stations by other modes are often a key to the success of public transport, especially Metro or Suburban Rail. Opportunities for Park and Ride (P&R) must be designed from the outset as well as a policy for charging for it or incorporating its value into the fare. Early planning for access by bicycle (with secure parking) and also for motorcycles/mopeds is essential, as these modes require much less space and, in the case of non-motorised modes, are also healthier.

These requirements will normally be part of the proposed concession contract but one must confirm that they are sufficiently provided for; otherwise capacity constraints will limit access by feeder modes.

17.4 Mode choice

Most of the demand for a new public transport system will be transferred from other existing modes. This transfer is the most solid basis for future patronage of the new facility. The promise by the Government authority that the incumbent bus routes will be re-organised to become feeders rather than competitors is very difficult to implement in practice; one must see this as an element of risk.

Attracting car users to transfer to Metro/LRT/BRT is less easy, with difficulty increasing from Metro to BRT. The proportion actually transferred from car to Public Transport will depend not only on the quality of the new mode but also on the time savings achievable (congestion effects) and government policies outside the control of the concessionaire: parking policy, fare policy, fuel costs and eventually a congestion charge.

If stochastic assignment is used (with several person types) it is useful to compare it with the results with different levels of "spread" to ensure this is not exaggerating patronage capture.

Beware of complex nested choice and Mixed Logit formulations. The theory is sound, see MT 227-266, but the practice is tricky and is bound to produce difficult to interpret results until you get the model to work properly. It is useful to check against simpler sub-mode choice by assignment. However, there are many cases where it is unavoidable, especially if modes like Taxi, Motorcycle and Park & Ride must be included. It will take twice as long as you expect to get these to work well enough.

17.5 Competing modes

Depending on the context the most significant competing modes could be:

a. Incumbent bus operators, even if informal; it will be difficult to get them to serve as feeder modes only.
b. Long distance coaches and low cost airlines competing with rail services.
c. Taxis; in some countries, for example Colombia, they are extremely cheap and a good alternative, especially for shorter trips.
d. Motorcycles. Also very cheap and in many countries, especially SE Asia and China, more numerous than cars. Their operating costs are similar to most fare levels and they offer a mostly door-to-door service slipping through queues and congestion. Adverse weather and accident risk are the main deterrents but these take time to bite if motorcycle use is already widespread.
e. Future self-driving cars that avoid parking restrictions and could be cheap to rent by the hour/minute; this is as yet an uncertain element but it is worth reminding ourselves of this possibility.
f. The non-availability of the promised feeder services, P&R facilities and easy and safe pedestrian and bicycle access; not really a competitor but many a project has failed because this feeder access was never implemented as it should have been. The urban realm in the neighbourhood of stations must be safe and high quality, something sometimes forgotten when planning a new system.

17.6 Fare systems

Fare structures can be very simple or very complex. From the point of view of revenue estimation independent flat fares are best; but bear in mind that sooner or later they will be integrated and normalised.

Modern software can model most feasible fare systems although care must be taken to ensure the model produces the data required to estimate revenues to the concessionaire. For example, it may not be enough to obtain global boardings and passenger kilometres; these will be needed for each line as well.

Integrated ticketing systems often include discounts for the young, students, senior citizens and other deserving groups. In most cases a compensation is paid by the procuring government but this may not cover the entire difference between full and discounted fare (on account of additional patronage generated by a lower fare). As in most cases, it will be necessary to estimate separately revenues generated by these groups, thus increasing the segmentation required to accurately model demand.

A revenue reconciliation spreadsheet model will be necessary to account for expansion factors and fare differentials that are not captured in the network model.

Period (season) tickets add complexity to the calculations. This element of revenue is often addressed as a post-modelling correction in the revenue reconciliation model. Ideally, experience on the use of period tickets would be available locally: how many commuter journeys are made, how many other "free rides" in a month, and so on. Failing that, assumptions will have to be made based on experience elsewhere.

The yield management techniques used in many passenger rail operations are very difficult to model. It is sometimes necessary to identify a few representative fares and markets and adjust results as a post modelling correction.

The use of electronic means of payment has similar effects to those discussed for toll roads: reducing the impact of fares and getting public transport closer to a utility like mobile phones. Smart cards can be introduced fairly quickly but a trial period is necessary as well as sufficient locations for topping them up.

Fare evasion is much more common in public transport than in toll roads. Extremely high rates of evasion (up to 30%) have been observed in many different countries. True evasion is difficult to measure accurately but can be done with sufficient personnel and good methodologies. It is possible to keep evasion below 5% in many cases, with good automatic barriers, enforcement and a good communication programme. But keeping it as low as we would like is a tough and expensive task so evasion is never completely eliminated.

17.7 Crowding

Some expensive and in principle attractive public transport systems have failed spectacularly because of poor consideration of crowding on the vehicles. Depending on configuration the number of passengers on a bus or carriage may become very uncomfortable and even prevent additional passengers from boarding.

Tram and railway carriages and bus capacity requirements vary widely according to the length of route and density of occupation. A first level of comfort, and maximum value to attract passengers from cars, is achieved when all passengers can find a seat. Standing is tolerated for shorter journeys. Generally, standing capacities are established as passengers per square metre. These range from 4 passenger per square metre, considered tolerable in the US and

Public Transport Concessions

Western Europe, to 8 pax/m² in some Asian cities. These variations are explained by both physical and cultural or historical differences.

Longer, commuter and outer suburban routes tend to limit standing to 20 minutes for any journey. Originally, 10% of standing passengers was considered to be a maximum but the UK Department for Transport raised this to 30% in 2008; passengers are certainly unhappy with this.

Public transport assignment models can cope with the two effects of crowding: uncomfortable ride and inability to board at a station or stop. However, each tends to follow their own approach so care must be taken to understand it and interpret results accordingly.

17.8   Sense checks

The T&R advisor will have to adopt some sense checks to ensure the results are reasonable and robust. Depending on the conditions of the proposed concession these may include:

a. Contrasting the modal shift suggested by model results with benchmarks from other similar schemes elsewhere. Any significant modal shift will require support from independent sources, as model results will not be enough to persuade investors.

b. Check that the number of passengers in each unit does not exceed capacities. If the model results require more than 4 passengers per square metre the results must be reviewed and its realism put in question; this level of crowding is already uncomfortable.

c. If the new service attracts additional passengers it is important to understand where they are abstracted from and check whether this is realistic compared to experience elsewhere.

d. For urban systems ensure that the walking times implied by the model results are reasonable and not a feature of how the centroid connectors were coded. Unreasonable walking distances/times may be the result of an overoptimistic "quality" assigned to the new mode.

The Future

> *"Prediction is difficult for us for the same reason that it is so important: it is where objective and subjective reality intersect. Distinguishing the signal from the noise requires both scientific knowledge and self-knowledge: the serenity to accept the things we cannot predict, the courage to predict the things we can and the wisdom to tell the difference."* **Nathan Silver**

18. THE FUTURE

18.1 Introduction

With the models now in place and some reliable data about future inputs the T&R team will be able to estimate future patronage and revenue projections. The models will be run for some key future time horizons. These will coincide with major events affecting the concession: the opening of the new facility and, if this is in stages, more than one period during ramp-up. Next, key time horizons will be selected when other expected changes will take place: introduction of a competitive service, opening of a major plant in the area, etc. For each of these horizons the model, fed with the appropriate inputs, will produce traffic and revenue figures. Intermediate years will be interpolated assuming constant growth rates.

Inevitably, these projections will be subject to future uncertainties; the best to account for them is the subject of this chapter.

18.2 Future uncertainties

Uncertainty is unavoidable in any forecast of future conditions. In this text, risk is a quantified uncertainty, at least in probabilistic terms and often with a subjective element. In risk analysis, the analyst seeks to quantify uncertainty and present this in a form that assist decision making.

Having identified risks and used them to focus data collation, collection and modelling, the T&R Advisor will be able to produce an initial set of projections. The other members of the consortium will be asking for these early projections claiming that no work can be progressed on estimating Operations & Maintenance (O&M) costs or building the Financial Model without them. This is more a posture than a reality but the T&R Advisor must play along and provide early figures with all the necessary caveats. Bear in mind that the transport concession field is now prone to litigation and every figure in an email or document can be retrieved and used in Court.

Once the model produces reliable results it is time to address the risk analysis stage. In this we look into some of the apparently solid inputs to any forecasts: population, GDP growth, competitive schemes that may feed or subtract demand. Any uncertain parameters in the model should also be included at least in sensitivity tests, for example VTTS and its likely evolution in the future. There is often more uncertainty in the base year in-scope demand that generally recognised, in particular if the trip matrices have been generated by a synthetic model.

In Figure 24 we identified four main sources of future revenue uncertainty:
- Accuracy in establishing the base year.
- Uncertainty due to the quality of the model.
- Uncertainty about future data inputs.
- Uncertainty about future scenarios.

It is useful to identify what we can do to reduce risks and where we can only prepare ourselves to face the future.

We can certainly reduce the uncertainty in establishing the base year. This requires good data collection. The Government would reap considerable benefits for its constituency from providing a good and extensive database that is quality assured and up to date. Consortia bidding for a concession would do well to collect complementary data to confirm the database and to provide them with more detail where it will reduce risk and perhaps offer a competitive advantage.

The most promising source of data is that resulting from GPS and mobile phone operations because of its sample size and the fact that it can cover any day one could possibly require. In the next few years we will gain experience in its use and how best to complement this source of data with other measurements.

Another good way of reducing uncertainty is building a better model. Again, the provision of a good Reference Model by the Procuring Authority would help in speeding up the process of building one tailored to the needs of a bidder. Most of this book deals with this task.

A danger lurking complex models is over-fitting. Apparently Von Newman said: "with four parameters I can fit an elephant, and with five I can make him wiggle his trunk." It took 57 years to prove this assertion correct[62]. Over-fitting makes our model look better on paper, may justify publications and even persuade others to adopt it; but when used to support forecasts will lead you astray.

---

[62] Mayer, J., Khairy, K. and Howard, J. (2010) "Drawing an elephant with four complex parameters". American Journal of Physics Vol 78 (6) pp 648-649.

The Future

To reduce this risk one should keep the model as simple as possible consistent with the requirements of the project. Focus on what matters most, perhaps greater geographic granularity, more realistic treatment of willingness to pay. One should be intelligently sceptical about claims about new and more accurate models. They are sometimes exaggerated and they are always tested against their ability to fit the base year. The more parameters the easier it is to get a good fit, remember the elephant in the model. For forecasting purposes the model should respect the amount and quality of the data and the inherent uncertainties about future inputs. Many models fail as future data requirements are impossible to satisfy with any degree of confidence, even with the best methodologies.

Uncertainty about future input data requires securing the services of the best local planners, the development of sensible growth models and sensitivity tests. We discuss this in this chapter and next.

Finally, we can only prepare for future scenario uncertainty and deal with it by understanding better the drivers to develop different, plausible and consistent scenarios.

18.3 Population and land uses

This is often critical. Many projects have failed because future developments (industrial, residential, commercial) did not materialise, or took place at completely different locations. The Regional and Urban Plans from the procuring Government are often perceived as overoptimistic in this respect.

Sadly, most land use transport interaction models are of little help in the short timescales of a tendering process; they take a year or so to be implemented and require many assumptions that are difficult to validate. Indeed, they have often been criticised as applying a lot of theory and speculation on very limited data.

The preferred approach is to involve independent and experienced local planners. They should be independent from Government but familiar with previous regional plans and how well they were attained. They should have a local understanding of the role of infrastructure on development (see the next point).

These local regional planners should be able to prepare a couple of development scenarios: one that follows Government plans moderated with reality checks and another one that follows current trends more than anything else. The scenarios will cover allocation of population, commercial and economic activity and leisure plans as well as potential changes to transport networks.

It is very important to ask not just for the corresponding tables but also for a narrative accompanying them. We need to attain a deeper understanding of what makes the region work as this is crucial in interpreting model results, sense checking them, and providing, in turn, an understandable story to those unfamiliar with the complexities of modelling and forecasting. Forecasting without a narrative is likely to be misinterpreted and generate mistrust in the results.

These scenarios will enable an allocation of differential growth in different parts of the area of interest and convey these into different components of the transport model system.

18.4 Changes in supply

It is often the case that Transport Plans exist covering the next 5 to 10 years but not beyond. Whatever the case, as with land use evolution, government plans may not be implemented in their original form. Local planners will also be able to provide an independent view on future changes in the network and their timing.

An important risk is that of competing services. Are there any non-compete agreements in place extending to prohibitions on competing routes? Most of the time these are unlikely and even if they are the track record of Governments enforcing their own promises is poor. Are there any guarantees that feeder routes will be effective and link roads will be maintained and signposted?

Present and future transport policies are also important in the success of a public transport or urban road concession. Parking restraint and pricing often features in the explicit transport policies but may be difficult to implement and often delayed by public pressure. The implementation of congestion pricing or the adoption of road rationing via number plate restrictions will affect congestion and the advantages offered by new public transport or urban toll roads. On rare occasions there may be a price competition among toll roads serving common catchment areas. More likely, this price competition will take place among public transport service suppliers, a risk difficult to manage in many cases.

One should not assume that no more investment in the network will take place after the 10 year Plan. The network capacity will continue to increase, at least for one of two reasons. First, governments will continue to respond to public demand for greater road capacity. Second, even if they do not, self-driving vehicles (SDV) will increase capacity by themselves, from 2025 onwards. One possible assumption, used by me even before SDVs were in the picture, is to increase capacity on each link in the network (except the toll road) by 0.5% per annum. The figure comes from an observation about average annual growth in capacity in a specific country. There is no reason to believe this trend is universal but failing local information it is a reasonable assumption to make

With the prospects of SDVs in the next decade, the increase in network capacity should speed up, probably to 1% - 3% per year until we know for sure what they will mean in practice. Of course, this could be part of one or more scenarios.

In the case of public transport projects, it will be necessary to form a view on the most likely actions of incumbent operators or some possible disruptive newcomers. For example, when discussing High Speed Rail in the 1990's and 2000's it was important to gather intelligence about future plans from low cost airlines, the likes of EasyJet and Ryanair. If they decided to set up a hub in a region this would affect the demand prospects of any fast rail service. Today, the market is a bit more settled, at least for the major low cost operators, but there is always the opportunity for a newcomer to shake this relative stability.

Incumbent operators may change their business model, as the ferries did after the opening of the Channel Tunnel. They adopted variable pricing and changed their offer from a reliable crossing to "a pleasant break in the journey" between two countries. Against expectations they survived and continue to serve channel crossings, albeit with some challenges.

18.5   Growth drivers

Almost any regional government will have its own perspectives on growth. However, it is always useful to develop an independent view of this.

Population growth is, of course, very important. Alas, the track record of population forecasts is not particularly good; see for example the work of Smith[63]. He has been following populations forecasts and their accuracy for years and finding that the more detailed (disaggregated) they are the less accurate they become. Hence the need for an independent view as stated above. This can be complemented by simpler models (again Smith found that more complex models did not perform better than simpler ones) to provide some complementary evidence on growth prospects.

---

[63] Rayer, S. and Smith, S. (2008) An Evaluation of Sub county Population Forecasts in Florida. Paper presented at the annual meeting of the Southern Demographic Association, October 2008. Bureau of Economic and Business Research. University of Florida

Car ownership forecasting is, of course, important for toll roads and public transport services. While most countries have decent population data the information on car ownership is more variable. In some cases, it deals with registrations but does not cope very well with the scrappage of vehicles. Some countries even have semi-legal vehicles with somewhat obscure record keeping.

One must consider with care vehicle ownership data in those countries. An understanding of how the market works helps considerably and it is important to have a clear view of what are the prospects for growth for both cars and motorcycles.

Information on present and future employment prospects is poorer than that on population, with a few exceptions. This will be difficult to forecast and this is one reason why some toll road models prefer to segment the market just on the basis of willingness to pay, not journey purpose.

Again, an independent view from local planners will help considerably in delivering reasonable forecasts to base our scenarios.

18.6 GDP and demand growth

GDP growth is critical to most concessions but in particular to sub-urban and interurban facilities: toll roads, Managed Lanes, rail projects. There are two elements to this: the adoption of GDP growth forecasts for the Base and Upside and Downside cases and what is the best link between GDP growth and demand growth.

GDP will normally be considered as a main driver to freight movements in the study area. GDP per capita will normally be seen as a key driver for car ownership and therefore congestion. In some cases, straight GDP will also be considered a combined (car ownership and travel growth) driver of personal travel.

First, we need to identify good forecasts for GDP growth. Ideally, estimates of future GDP growth will be agreed with lenders and financial institutions involved in the transaction. This, however, is no guarantee of accuracy. It is no longer desirable to accept just a single estimation of this growth either coming from official institutions or other reputable sources. There is strong evidence that pooled forecasts are more reliable, according to Silver[64], up to 20% more than individual ones. Publications like Consensus Forecasts[65] include 10 or more forecasts for the economy of a country and this enables you to obtain

---

[64] Silver, N. (2012) :"The Signal and the Noise". Penguin-Allen Lane, London.

[65] Consensus Forecasts is published by Consensus Economics Inc., 53 Upper Brook Street, London, W1K 2LT, United Kingdom; Web: www.consensuseconomics.com

The Future

averages (that are more reliable) and standard deviations that will help in defining stochastic risk analysis later on.

The second question relates to the link between GDP growth and demand growth, in other words the elasticity of demand to GDP. This relationship is strongly influenced by the locality, the level of development and economic activity in the region, its alignment with the rest of the country and the availability and use of transport infrastructure. In the case of toll roads, the usual approach is to collate a number of sites with traffic counts collected over a number of years. It is then possible to fit a model linking these flow changes to GDP growth:

$$\%TrafficGrowth = A + Beta * \%GDPGrowth$$

Beta here is the elasticity of demand growth to GDP growth.

A is the intercept.

Note that this model assumes symmetric elasticities for GDP growth and decline. This is a common assumption but not one that is often confirmed in practice. Recessions are often pre-announced by reductions in freight movements but personal travel behaviour may display a lag. Models can be developed to account for these effects but lack of sufficient data limits their usefulness.

It will be normal to develop different growth models for different types of traffic; at least one for passengers and one for freight as they are driven by different factors. Technology will also play a role. There has been a consistent tendency in most countries for lorries to become larger to increase efficiency and reduce costs. This trend tends to moderate growth in road haulage traffic; it is not uncommon to find negative or no growth for single trucks and positive growth for larger articulated vehicles and trailers. There is a similar trend for road haulage companies to become larger and more professional thus understanding their costs better; this would affect the proportion of trucks with a higher willingness to pay tolls to save VOCs and time.

Although most growth models are linear reality rarely fits that model. It is important to challenge long-term projections based on this linear assumption. For example, car ownership tends to accelerate when GDP per capita overtakes the US$ 10,000 mark. In the same way, car ownership tends to slow down as it nears saturation.

In my experience different countries and even different regions display different traffic growth elasticities to GDP per capita. This is illustrated in the table overleaf collated from different studies.

TABLE 17 DEMANDS TO GDP PER CAPITA ELASTICITIES

Country	Elasticity
USA	0.22
UK	0.55
Austria	0.60
France	0.67
Spain	0.82
Portugal	1.58
Greece	1.61
Argentina	1.64
Mexico	1.78
India	2.02
Taiwan	3.33
Thailand	4.30
Malaysia	4.98

Note that developed countries have elasticities well below 1 whilst emerging ones have elasticities above unity. It appears that as the country evolves the required intensity of transport diminishes as services become more important and logistics more efficient. It must be recognised that this data is quite noisy: the definition of demand growth varies across countries as do the quality of this information. The question remains: at what rate would this elasticity decline over time?

Again, from a number of studies and experiences I have collated a number of cases for the evolution of elasticities with different levels of GDP per capita. These are illustrated in the figure overleaf with elasticities on a log scale.

What this curve implies is that for each additional $1,000 per capita the elasticity (Beta) declines by 0.03. The deceleration is more marked at higher per capita income levels.

This result shows that it is not enough to find a good relationship between traffic growth and GDP per capita in the last few years. It is not appropriate to retain that elasticity and project it as a constant over the next 30 years of the concession. It is important to allow for its reduction in line with economic growth.

The Future

FIGURE 42 ELASTICITY OF DEMAND TO GDP/CAPITA GROWTH

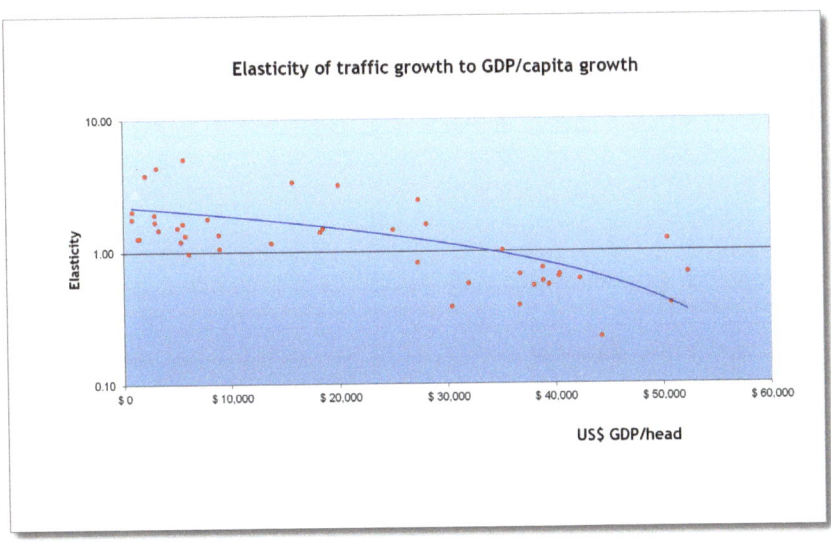

One should be aware that recent GDP growth is not always a good predictor of future economic growth in part because there is a significant amount of measurement error in the numbers that are reported during the first few months. The revised numbers that come out later are better at predicting future GDP, but by the time they are out, the near future has already passed in most cases.

More ambitious models for demand growth are possible, incorporating more variables and relationships; see for example the excellent classic work of Washington el al[66]. Their adoption depends crucially on the quality of the data available, a condition seldom found in our field.

Finally, it is highly desirable that the Traffic and Financial models adopt the same assumptions about GDP and income growth. This consistency is required for a fair interpretation of any sensitivity tests and risk analysis.

---

[66] Washington, S., Karlaftis, M. and Mannering, F (2011) Statistical and Econometric Methods for Transportation Data Analysis. Second Edition. Chapman and Hall/CRC Press

18.7 Sensitivity analysis

Sensitivity analysis is an essential component of a Traffic & Revenue Report. It is performed to find out how much model results depend on small changes in model parameters and inputs. It is used for two reasons: first, to ensure that the model responses are reasonable and explainable; second, to identify what are the key risks and drivers most likely to affect the financial strength of a project.

Sensitivity tests must be undertaken for at least the following dimensions:

- VTTS, this is so important that we need to understand how small errors in estimating them or their evolution can affect revenues. Variations of +/- 10 or 20% on VTTS are useful to assess how dependent are the estimated revenues on our evaluation of these parameters
- Growth rates usually linked to GDP; we will see in Risk Analysis a more systematic handling of this issue. Financial institutions linked to the project should be able to provide estimates of possible variations of future GDP growth. These will affect incomes and therefore car ownership, patronage, traffic and revenue.
- Timing of competing projects and toll or fare levels.
- Timing and extent of potential developments in the area that may bring additional demand.
- Toll and fare level sensitivity tests are also important as discussed before. We need to make sure the services will be operating at the left hand side of the maximum revenue point.

Sensitivity tests to journey purpose are less common. With the advent of new car technologies it will become necessary to study sensitivity to estimates of key future capacity and levels of service, as discussed above.

The results from these sensitivity test are valuable on their own, to provide comfort on the reliability of the model, and also to deliver elasticities and cross-elasticities (for example to fares/tolls and GDP). These elasticities will have, in turn, two uses. First, they will help benchmarking against intuition and other contexts; second, they will play a key role in Monte Carlo Risk Analysis.

A useful way to summarise the sensitivity tests is to combine them into a Tornado Chart (en.wikipedia.org/wiki/Tornado_diagram). This usually depicts the impact on the Net Present Value (NPV) of the revenue stream under different plausible future variations on the demand drivers. An example of this is shown in the next figure where

The Future

CEMEX stands for a possible change in the size of a major cement plant in the area of influence of the project.

FIGURE 43 A TORANDO CHART

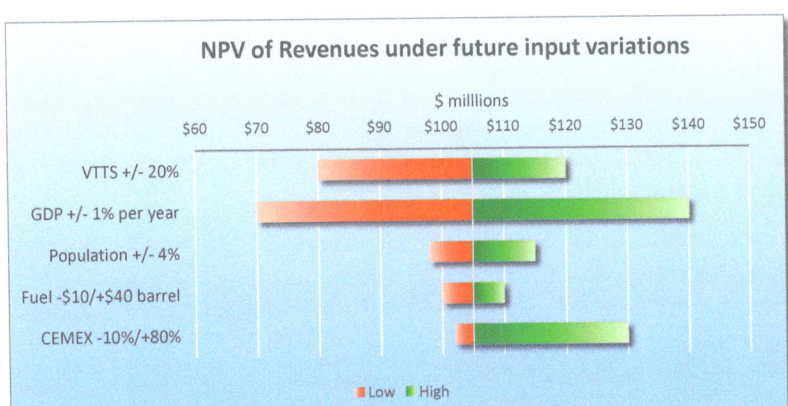

18.8 Future scenarios

Scenario Planning is a technique that has been extensively used in several areas, most famously developed and used by Shell in their strategic planning. The key elements of this approach can be summarised as follows:

1. Decide drivers for change/assumptions. Identify what are the main drivers affecting future traffic and revenue in a specific transport concession. For example, it could be GDP growth, population location, self-driving cars and what the competition will do.

2. Bring these drivers together into a viable framework. The longer list of drivers must be prioritised and, ideally, linked together: how may GDP growth affect future VTTS and the advent of self-driving cars.

3. Produce 7-9 initial mini-scenarios. These scenarios should be consistent, for example high economic growth linked to VTTS growth. These scenarios are described and its elements quantified in as much as possible in a "first cut" approach.

4. Reduce to 2 - 4 scenarios that can be described in detail, quantified and that are sufficiently different to teach us something. Identify mitigation measures that could be taken to make this future a bit malleable.

5. Draft the scenarios, in other words convert them into quantitative inputs to the model plus qualitative considerations for the interpretation of outputs.

6. Run the model under each scenario and produce the key outputs, in our case revenue profiles.

7. Identify the issues arising and how they affect decisions. This could help define whether the overall uncertainty makes it too risky to bid, or that the potential upsides are sufficiently attractive to be aggressive.

It is useful to bring different disciplines and backgrounds into this task to avoid the trap that considers the unfamiliar improbable. For sure, the scenarios should be agreed in advance by all stakeholders.

Time is short when preparing a bid. It is quite common to run at least three different "scenarios": Base, Upside and Downside cases. More often than not these are just related to a small number of assumptions like GDP growth and the timing of some key competitive projects. This is a shortcut and short changes the concept of scenario analysis. The Base Case is sometimes called Expected or Most Probable scenario. The Upside scenario is sometimes called an Equity Case and the Downside a Lenders Case. This helps to clarify the different perspectives although an effort should be made to be more explicit about the assumptions adopted and the reason behind them; naming them is not enough.

In my view, this default approach is likely to be a minimum and tends to reinforce linear thinking focussed on one scenario with some variance around it. The next 30 years are likely to be very different from the past 30 and this calls for the design of scenarios that do not reflect only the different perspectives of equity and lenders. It is desirable to identify consistent scenarios that reflect possible and realistic futures without brushing uncertainty under the carpet. It is later on that equity and lenders will decide which of these scenarios, or a combination of them, reflects better their own perspectives on risk.

18.9   Model review

An independent Peer Review of the model and revenue projections is one of the most reliable ways of reducing and potentially eliminating any optimism bias.

The involvement of a peer reviewer from early on in the project is strongly recommended and this type of work should not be done only from a distance and at arms-length.

Any model needs assumptions and reviewing them should confirm how reasonable they are. Moreover, the model and the interpretation of results rely on judgments. The greater the experience and skills of the reviewer the more solid these assumptions are likely to be.

These judgments should not be hidden in the documentation; they should be transparently in the open. After all, there is evidence that judgment improves the quality of forecasts, as shown by the work of Stephen K. McNess[67]. He found that judgemental adjustments to statistical forecasting methods resulted in forecasts that were about 15% more accurate.

Sometimes a Technical or Audit Review is organised. This usually happens towards the end of a forecasting effort and is requested by financial institutions or other partners. The Lending Traffic and Revenue Advisor, or LTRA, is one such a role. This is a difficult task, as most of the assumptions would have been agreed by this stage. It is also very difficult for an external technical auditor to be able to check the model thoroughly. Therefore, requests for additional tests in order to confirm the model are reasonable are often a key element of the audit.

18.10 An audit checklist

The following points are those I have found helpful in the past when reviewing a model and a set of Traffic and Revenue Projections. These are not meant to be exhaustive and must be adapted to the conditions in each case.

A General
- Visit the site if at all possible to get a feeling for the conditions and context
- Investigate the stated rationale for the project, what benefits it will bring to the community; do they make sense?
- Ascertain the general population and economic growth in the area.
- Historical experience with the payment of tolls, new modes and policies.
- What are the expected uncertainties and risk, the Risk Register; complete enough?
- Evidence of local support for the scheme, objectors, controversies.
- Competitive context, supply side risks; have they been fairly included in the analysis?

---

[67] McNees, S. (1990) "The role of judgment in macroeconomic forecasting accuracy" International Journal of Forecasting, Vol 6, 3 pp 287-299.

B **Methodology**
- General modelling approach; software(s) used; sensible?
- Identification of what matters most.
- Behavioural responses included (and excluded) in the model; are they sensible?
- Reasonable adaptation from an existing model; appropriate granularity (geographical and person type), times of the day/year; network detail?
- Enough data available and fresh data collected? Current, evidence of Quality Assurance?
- Sensible growth projections?
- Sensitivity tests, risk analysis?

C **Surveys**
- Origin Destination surveys? Appropriate corrections and expansion?
- Travel Time surveys; sufficient, well documented?
- Traffic/person counts; historical and current, on a common base?
- Stated Preference, apparent quality and processing; sensible results?
- Application to willingness to pay; sensible, comparable with experience and local evidence?
- Annualisation factors; based on one or more sets of counts; how chosen?

D **Base Year Model**
- Review zoning system; data to support that zoning today and tomorrow?
- Centroid connectors, software generated or by hand?
- Network, source, congestion, speed-flow curves; junction modelling? It is impossible to check all links and all centroid connectors, so ask for a session with the modeller to sample some and also to undertake some select link analysis for sensible routing.
- Person types, user classes (consistency in all sub-models) and their VTTS.
- Bonus and malus in the network; sensible enough?
- Trip generation – growth. Type of model, too complex? Is growth assumed forever?
- Destination choice model used? How are trip matrices generated? Synthetic, observed or hybrid? How current?
- Mode Choice; relevant? Type of model, sensible parameters, avoid over-complex models.

The Future

- Assignment; UE or SUE? How many user classes and their VTTS.
- Treatment of trucks and buses?
- Calibration; good evidence and documentation?
- Validation; using different data, well documented? Not just general but also local to the proposed scheme?

E **The project**
- Detailed description of the new facility. Toll/ticket values, discounts, exemptions. Indexing for inflation, price escalation, sensible, feasible?
- How is it modelled? Too many advantages given to it?
- Runs on the Base Year with and without the project; are the results sensible?
- Is in-scope traffic/demand identified; quantified (with nil toll, for example); capture rate.
- Where does the project demand come from (select link analysis and other); evidence of strange routeing?

F **The Future**
- Feeder modes and roads; already there? Promised? Any evidence they will happen?
- Development; read the independent report; sensible? Identified land use changes. Growth expected short and long term for passengers and freight.
- Modelled years, interpolation.
- Induced traffic? Why?
- Evolution of means of payment. Planned and realistic?
- Ramp-up; realistic and well supported by evidence?
- Capacity constraints, in the project and the rest of the network, respected?
- Competitors, modes and roads; network changes expected or unavoidable.
- Capture rates and their evolution; sensible, possible?
- Peak spreading considered? Why not?

G **Sensitivity tests**
- Enough sensitivity tests? Well summarised and interpreted?
- Scenario analysis undertaken? Simplified or realistic?
- Risk analysis done? Sensible distributions for variables (fat tails?); dependencies recognised or all assumed independent?
- Elasticity analysis sound?
- Benchmarking?
- Treatment of Self Driving Vehicles and peak car?
- Make up of future traffic and revenue well analysed?

H **Final**
- Reasonable demonstration that the project is well understood and sensible?
- Good combination of existing and new data?
- Data collected and mode developed according what matters most?
- Sensible model development and good parameters?
- Sensible growth projections.
- Good sensitivity and risk analysis.

18.11 Uncertainty envelope

The development and processing of 3-4 scenarios on the basis of the variables and analysis above should to the production of an uncertainty envelope: a range of possible future outcomes for the prospective concession. The interpretation and use of this envelope will require judgement and possibly a more systematic risk analysis.

This is discussed in the next chapter.

Risk Analysis

> *"It is far better to foresee even without certainty than not to foresee at all"* **Henri Poincaré**
>
> *"Doubt is uncomfortable but certainty is absurd"* **Voltaire**

19. RISK ANALYSIS

19.1 Handling Risk

As we have stated, we consider risk as a quantifiable uncertainty, unavoidable in our field. If it is possible to assign a monetary value to this uncertainty we have, in our case, the revenue *at risk* component in the projections. Scenario analysis deals with uncertainty about what the future, in particular the competition, will look like. Comparing results from different scenarios is possible to allocate a money dimension to this issue; however, it is much more difficult to assign a probability to each scenario, except using experience, judgment and a modicum of common sense.

In dealing with risk, the perspective adopted is critical. Risk is not an absolute concept. In fact, different actors in a transport concession quite correctly perceive and value risks in a different way. Timing is also important. Once the concession is in operation a number of the risks originally identified in the Risk Register would have practically disappeared.

We focus here on Traffic & Revenue risk. There are two main complementary ways of handling this: one is Stochastic or Monte Carlo Risk Analysis and the other is the De-construction of Revenue.

19.2 Stochastic Risk Analysis

Stochastic risk analysis involves the use of Monte Carlo simulations usually implemented as an add-on to a standard spreadsheet, for example Crystal Ball or @Risk. Although these are the most common there is a large number of such add-ons, for example:

http://en.wikipedia.org/wiki/Comparison_of_risk_analysis_Microsoft_Excel_add-ins (visited 1/7/14),

The first step is to agree with stakeholders those inputs or model variables that will be considered to be the most important stochastic drivers and relate the outputs from the model to them. As a T&R advisor you will have a view of what they are but these must be confirmed by the main stakeholders in the project preparation and tendering process.

The second step is to undertake conventional model runs to identify, for example, how variations in GDP growth affect revenues; in other words, the elasticities of changes in inputs to final revenues. Most of these would have been undertaken as part of the sensitivity tests mentioned previously.

The third next step is to agree the probability distributions that are most likely to represent the future variability of those input parameters. It is tempting to assign a Normal probability distribution to all of them. However, we should be warned that more realistic the probability distributions of some key variables (GDP is a good example) would have "fat tails"; that is, they will display extreme values more often than in a Normal distribution, see the extensive discussion on this issue by Taleb (2007). Some variables will not accept negative values that are always possible in a Normal distribution. A truncated or a lognormal distribution could be used in this case.

The next step is to construct a model where this handful of variables influences revenue outcomes and where their probabilistic distributions are sampled repeatedly in a Monte Carlo simulation. This model is usually constructed on the basis of elasticities applied to the Base Case Revenue growth for each year x. As an example, we take only two elements of variability: GDP and VTTS.

$$SRevGrowth(x) = BRevGrowth(x) * \left(\frac{SGDP(x)}{GDP(x)}\right)^{\beta} * \left(\frac{SVTTS}{VTTS}\right)^{\gamma} SRevenue(x)$$

$SRevenue(x) = SRevenue(x-1) + SRevGrowth(x)$ or

$SRevenue(x) = BaseRevenue(x) * SRevenueFactor(x)$

Where

SRevenue(x) is the stochastic revenue for year x

BaseRevenue(x) is the Base Case Revenue for year x

BRevGrowth(x) is the growth in revenue for year x in the Base Case

SGDP(x) is the stochastic GDP growth for x

SVTTS(x) is a stochastic value for VTTS

SRevenueFactor(x) is a value that summarises the effects of all stochastic variables on that year

β is the elasticity of revenue growth to GDP growth

γ is the elasticity of revenue growth to VTTS growth

Risk Analysis

These stochastic values are sampled from the agreed probability distributions using a Monte Carlo approach. Note that in most cases these distributions are assumed to be independent. This is convenient but may be more difficult to accept in the case of the recognised relationship between GDP and SVTTS. In fact, it has been argued that most Risk Analysis models failed to quantify the real exposure of the complex structured asset based securities (CDOs and others) pre-2007/8 crisis simply because of this independence assumption: failure to service mortgage payments forced repossessions that in turn reduced the value of properties triggering a vicious spiral not foreseen when these effects were considered independent.

Therefore, to make this analysis more realistic it is necessary to recognise the dependence of GDP to VTTS and perhaps also other variables, depending on those incorporated in the Monte Carlo simulation.

Each run of the Monte Carlo simulation reflects one possible revenue path diverging from the Base Case and generates a stream of SGDP and SVTTS for each year. These simulations are repeated 1000 or more times. This is illustrated in the next figure, where each path represents a sampled evolution of the *SRevenueFactor*. A revenue factor value of 0.95 in one year implies that collections in that case would be only 95% of the Base Case for that year.

FIGURE 44 STOCHASTIC PATHS OF THE REVENUE FACTOR

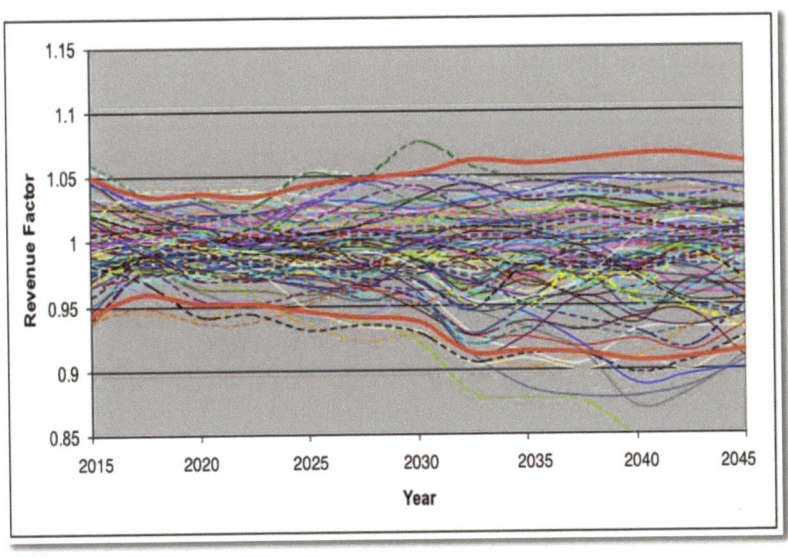

These can be converted easily into probability bands as shown in the next figure.

FIGURE 45 REVENUE BANDS IN STOCHASTIC RISK ANALYSIS

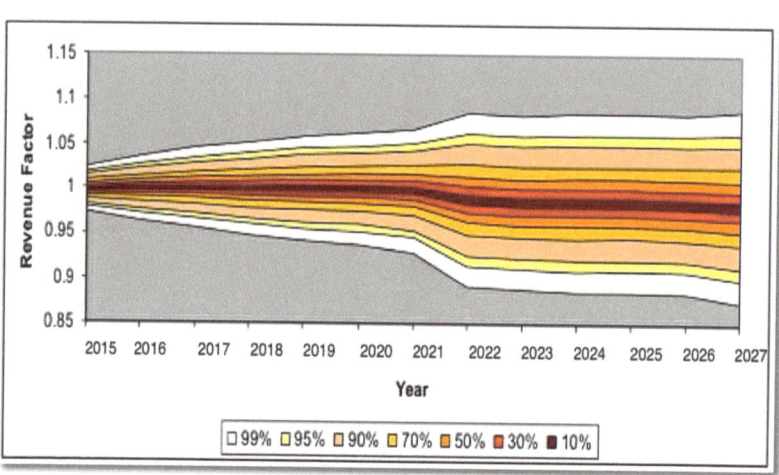

The end result is a distribution of revenue outcomes over the life of the project. Of these ranges, lenders would be more interested in the so called P90 or P95 revenue streams, which are the revenues that would be exceeded 90 or 95% of the time according to this analysis. P50 is approximately the expected or Base Case revenue stream. Equity investors might be interested in P40, i.e. revenues that have only a 40% probability to materialise but represent a significant upside of the project.

Stochastic Risk Analysis add-ons offer outputs in a number of different ways and these can often be edited within Excel itself. Figure 46 illustrate such an output when the two inputs that have been allowed to vary stochastically are GDP growth and VTTS.

The P95 and P90 are shown as well as the Base Case curve.

This type of analysis is useful and required by most financial institutions. However, it can be misleading. It reflects only variations around a base case and it does not provide deeper insights on what are the main drivers behind future revenue. It would be desirable to provide the same analysis for each valid scenario, not just the Base Case, but this is unrealistic in practice.

Risk Analysis

FIGURE 46 STOCHASTIC RISK ANALYSIS ON REVENUES

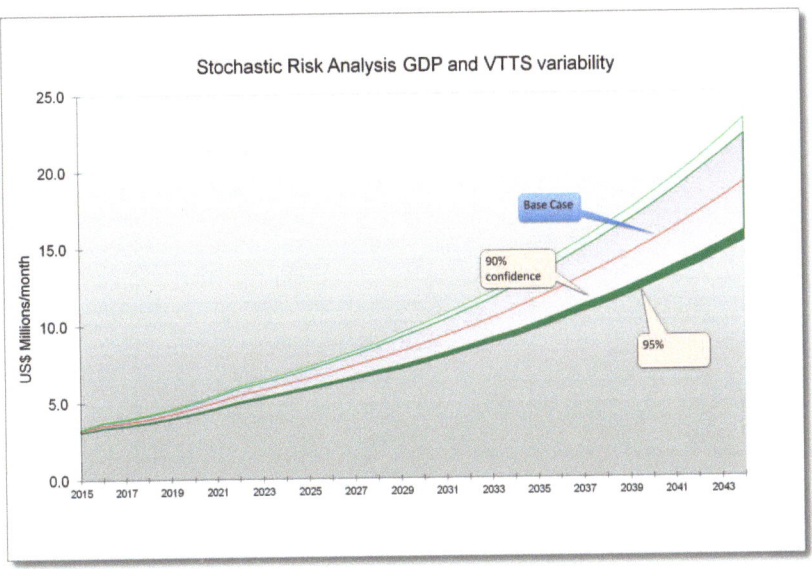

19.3 Forecast de-construction

Different components of our forecasts are associated to different levels of confidence in their values. We tend to believe more in the results of an assignment model because when it fails to fit the data on the base years this is very easy to diagnose. Our confidence on mode, destination and time of travel choices is less strong because of the complexities of the implied behavioural changes. Induced traffic is even more elusive.

Showing these components of future revenue (or demand) separately is a useful way of explaining what is behind the figures and helps to develop a narrative for the future of the facility.

Moreover, the drivers for some component of demand capture by the new service may be different from other contributors. For example, in analysing future patronage of a high speed rail concession, capture from air travel may depend on the pricing policies of low-cost airlines that are difficult to predict; capture from other rail services or car users may be more certain as their pricing policies are better understood and predictable.

A useful way of presenting these results is to de-construct the outputs of a traffic model in a manner that enables the interested party to assign their own risk assessments to different components of future demand. This is illustrated in Figure 47 for the demand a nominal Regional Metro:

FIGURE 47 CONTRIBUTORS TO FUTURE DEMAND OF REGIONAL METRO

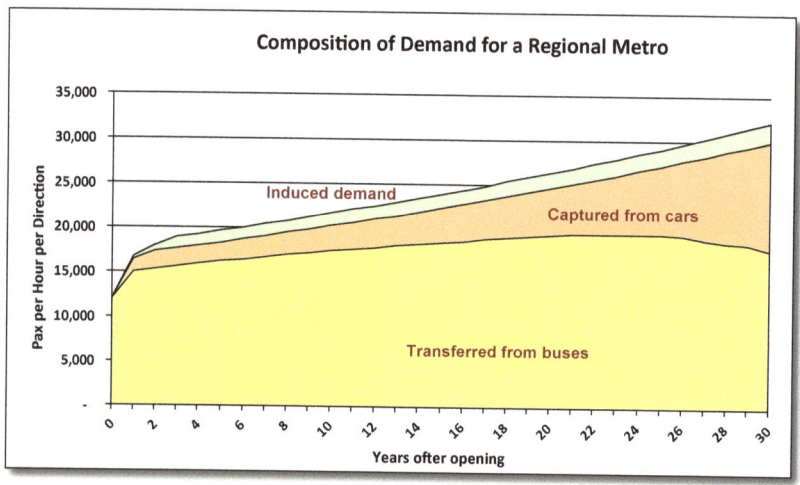

This can also be presented as contributions for total annual revenue as illustrated in the next figure for a different example, an urban LRT system in this case.

FIGURE 48 CONTRIBUTORS TO LRT REVENUE

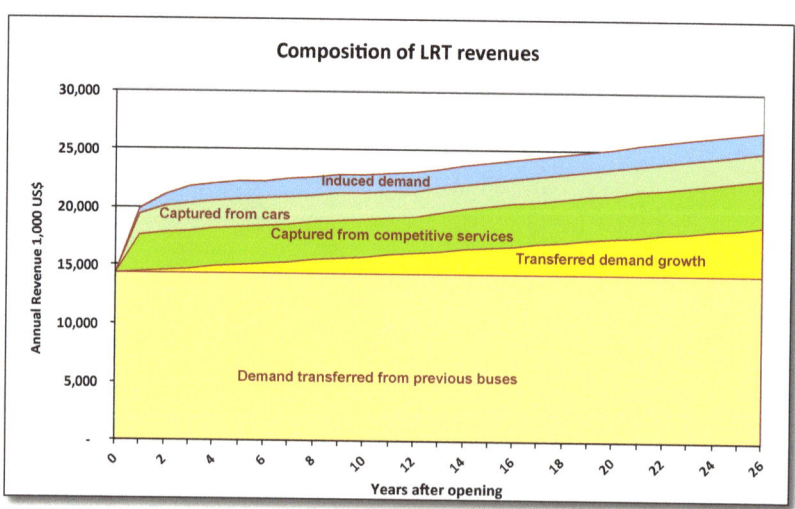

The figure shows the different contributions of Induced, Transferred from cars, Captured from other public transport services and Growth, in addition to that captured from buses removed from the corridor. A

Risk Analysis

bidder that knows the market well will be more confident of these particular components of future demand capture.

19.4 Mitigation

The future has not happened yet and therefore is not given; there may be ways in which a concessionaire can influence it. We look at toll roads first and then at public transport services.

It has to be recognised that for toll roads and managed lanes there is limited scope for influencing the future; nevertheless, some interventions can be successful. The first task is to eliminate or reduce elements that deter travellers from using the toll road. These may include:
- Lack of refuelling and rest stations.
- Lack of services (restaurants, shops, toilets).
- Poor signage; it is difficult to find the facility and once there difficult to use it.
- Problems in the accesses/feeders to the new service.

It is also worthwhile looking at the alternatives routes. In some places they may be attractive to overloaded lorries because there is no axle load control whereas the toll road has them.

If the facility is ORT then customer care becomes much more important. Drivers may complain if they do not understand the charges; it is important to maintain and enhance confidence in the system. The monthly billing, paper or electronic, create opportunities for contact and reassurance. Responding quickly and fairly to requests and inquires is a good way to improve relations with customers.

Maximising revenue and customer satisfaction is a continuous task, not a one off. In addition to a tolling structure it is necessary to have a Commercial Policy. This contains the detailed ways of progressing any special discount contracts, frequency and means of reporting transactions, interoperability issues, handling of disputed transactions, handling of equipment failures (on board or on-gantry), errors, incidents, problems elsewhere (if tunnels are closed, for example), approach to the first violation and how does it change for subsequent violations, and so on.

In some cases, it is possible to change a flat toll structure and offer a different one for different type of users, different prices at different times of the day. It is recommended that in planning these changes some controlled experiments be undertaken first. These are easier with ETC as there is an excellent database of how customers use the facility and they can be segmented into different potential markets. It is then possible to design different price experiments, collect data and interpret results.

Overall, delivering a good service, even beyond of what the contract requires, usually pays back in terms of customer loyalty and frequent use.

There are more opportunities to manage demand in the case of public transport and longer distance rail services. The same principles apply: provide good information, protect and encourage frequent users, and try differential pricing to enhance demand and revenue collections. Training drivers, conductors and other personnel to deliver an efficient and courteous service is very important in the medium and long run.

The provision of a reliable service is paramount. Every effort must be made to remove obstacles to this delivery. It is easier to engender brand loyalty when reliability is assured and the user feels respected and valued. The provision of good complementary services at stations is not just valued but often generates its own additional demand. Newsagents and snacks are commonplace but some enlightened rail and metro networks offer mini-libraries, information on events and more mundane services like opportunities to recharge and top up mobile phones.

Large railway stations look more like an airport with all kind of shops and services. Building on top of them has developed into an important source of additional revenue.

Finalising Demand and Revenue Forecasts

> "All progress, both theoretical and practical, has resulted from a single human activity: the quest for what I call good explanations. Though this quest is uniquely human, its effectiveness is also a fundamental fact about reality"
> **David Deutsch**

20. FINALISING DEMAND AND REVENUE FORECASTS

20.1 Introduction

All the work described so far is not enough to deliver a professional Traffic and Revenue Study. It is still necessary to write the Report and, given its importance, this task deserves enough time. This report is not written to impress (or to get paid) but to communicate the insights gained. A poorly written report devalues the effort and intelligence of the T&R Study.

The report must contain a summary of the work carried out but must also provide additional evidence that the results are credible, robust and make sense. So, there are some additional sense checks that must accompany the main effort.

The report should be written to communicate results and how they were arrived at accounting for uncertainty and risk. It is difficult to write in plain language explaining the intricacies of the models we use; however, we should not abuse technical jargon or assume modelling skills the reader is unlikely to have. Therefore, we should aim to deliver an easy-to-read document with good formatting (to assist comprehension) and consistent graphics and tables.

Readers dislike long paragraphs and in particular long and abundant tables with unnecessary entries; leave them for an appendix. Provide only the tables and graphs that are key to identify the strengths of the project, assist understanding and provide confidence in the results. Tables should be properly formatted and should not give a false sense of accuracy by providing more significant figures than is reasonable to expect. A table stating that peak flow on a link 20 years from now will be 3423.83 vehicles an hour clearly demonstrates sloppy thinking. Use the ROUND () function in Excel and make it at least 3420.

Finally, and this is most important, the report must deliver a narrative, a story, that demonstrates the deeper understanding of the conditions in the region and what the new facility will offer and achieve in that context. Storytelling comes to the fore and the narrative must be honest and persuasive.

20.2 Project rationale

Investors will usually seek to understand the main rationale of a project. This may be to provide a new service where none (or a very unsatisfactory one) is available at present, to reduce congestion, to permit exploitation of an isolated natural resource or another such objective. This main objective is sometimes described in the Terms of Reference of the concession but it is important that an independent assessment, by the T&R advisor, is given to the value of such statements.

This is a key element in developing a persuasive narrative. Analysts are sometimes reluctant to express this rationale as they may see a number of factors contributing to the success of the project. It is important to understand the investors perspective and identify no more than three main elements that support the rationale of the project. This must be fair and be supported by solid evidence and examples from successful projects in other locations.

Possible rationales include:

a. Congestion relief. This is easy to explain in the case of roads but may require a little more thought in the case of public transport, especially as financial professionals and investors are mostly car users. Issues of competitive versus feeder services and how will revenue be apportioned will figure as key concerns under this rationale.

b. To encourage modal shift. This is an unlikely rationale for roads, even when feeding onto park & ride facilities, but it is often present when dealing with public transport. If mode shift is a key aim then one would expect a raft of other initiatives: new services, subsidies, parking restraint and bus priority to be part of the plans. Implementation of these may be weakened by the electoral cycle when policies may change.

c. Social need. This is less ambitious than modal shift as an objective; it simply requires the provision of a useful and low cost public transport service or a road to enhance mobility. A key issue here is affordability and subsidies may be a way to solve this constraint. Some projects will combine social need, modal shift and congestion relief, for example the provision of Managed Lanes with a good BRT system as in PR 22 in Puerto Rico.

d. The enable property development. This was the main driver behind the private sector investment in extensions to the London Underground one hundred years ago. More recently, the investment and expansion of the London Docklands Light Rail service and Jubilee Line were instrumental in the success

Finalising Demand and Revenue Forecasts

of Canary Wharf and other developments in the area. The transport concession is dependent upon the successful development and monetisation of induced or derived demand. The financial viability of some public transport projects is enhanced by granting the concessionaire land near the stations to develop it and capture the added value of the new infrastructure; it must be recognised that this effect is stronger with rail projects.

20.3   Providing confidence in the results

It is important, of course, to provide evidence supporting the reasonableness of the results proposed by the T&R Advisor. One contribution to this is the quality of the calibration to the base year, something we have already discussed. But this is not enough; it is necessary to demonstrate that the model produces sensible results, consistent with previous experience. This is achieved by means of project reasonability tests. Several of these are used in practice. Some will be simply a more graphical way to demonstrate the sense checks undertaken during model development but applied to the final runs with the new service. Others will involve showing results in the context of similar projects elsewhere: benchmarking.

An important project reasonability test is the capture rate of the new service. There are two ways of defining "capture rates". The most common requires identification of a screenline across the facility, toll road or rail/LRT/metro service as illustrated in the next figure. If it is a toll road, then its expected traffic is compared with the total traffic across the screenline, as illustrated in Figure 49, and the ratio is considered the capture rate.

There is a problem with this definition. There will be trips across this screenline that are not real candidates for the new facility, short trips that would not be inclined to reach the interchanges to use the toll roads. Moreover, the wider the screenline is drawn the more these out-of-scope trips will be intercepted. All of this tends to deliver low "capture rates" that may generate a false confidence in the strength of the project.

An alternative definition is based on network model runs. The model is run assuming the toll road is free, uncharged. The resulting flow is the real candidate or in-scope demand. The model is then run with the toll prices included and the new flows estimated. The ratio between flows tolled over flows untolled is the effective capture rate. This approach produces a higher capture rate (there is no padding from shorter and irrelevant trips on the total) and reflects a more realistic estimate.

FIGURE 49 SCREENLINE ACROSS TWO PROPOSED URBAN TOLL ROADS

Stakeholders and modellers will also be interested in where the demand for the new service comes from. This can be presented in aggregate form using "select link analysis" and adopting a few large regions around the facility (otherwise too much information is lost). Alternatively, it is possible to show the differences in flow on the whole network with and without the new road/metro. This indicates where flows have been abstracted from to use the new facility and a few cases where changes in congestion or the need to access the toll road have resulted in higher flows on some untolled links. The following figure is an example of this.

There will be other request for displaying results in ways that provide comfort to stakeholders and the T&R Advisor will have to comply with these, provided they are reasonable and manageable

Finalising Demand and Revenue Forecasts

FIGURE 50 FLOWS WITH TOLL ROAD IN RED AND ABSTRACTED IN BLUE

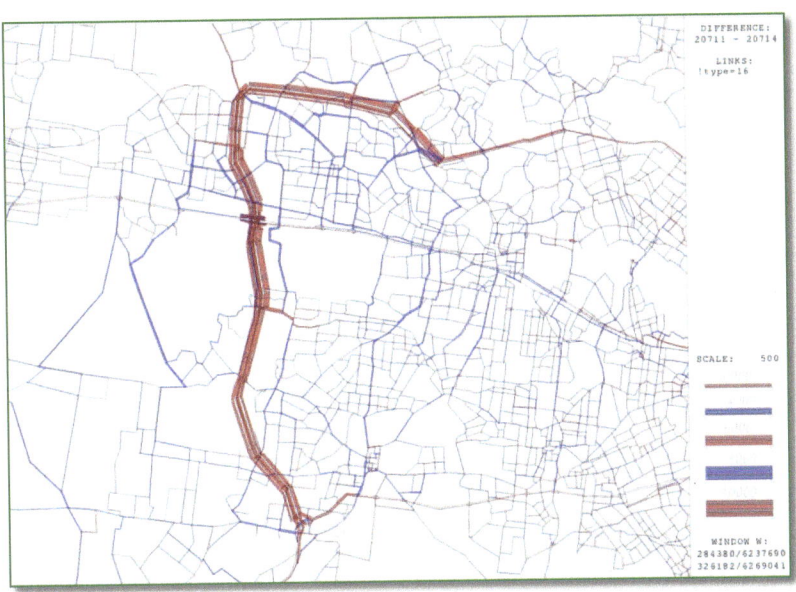

20.4 Unmodelled influences on traffic and revenue

It is also useful to look at those components of potential demand that have not been included in the model. These should be identified with comments added on their potential impact on Traffic and Revenue.

Examples of this include, depending on what was actually involved:
- Tolls have been modelled as cash when in fact will be collected electronically; this is an upside.
- Induced, redistributed or other traffic responses often not included in the model; also an upside.
- Motorcycles are seldom modelled but they are charged. Something similar happens with especially large vehicles, agricultural machinery and others not included in the model.
- Adjustments for leap years (they yield another day of flow and revenue); they should be included in the financial model.
- Fines and surcharges that may accrue to the concessionaire but were not explicitly included in traffic revenues.
- Revenues from advertising and rental from shops and other services in the area of the project; usually these will be estimated separately.

- Transport policies favourable to the public transport concession that have not been assumed in the model.
- Potential impact of changes in energy and other input prices that may have been assumed stable; upsides and downsides.

20.5 Interpretation of results

This text maintains that model results without interpretation and a narrative are not particularly useful. It is relevant, therefore, to provide some pointers on how our current understanding of the limitations of modelling may influence interpretation.

It must be acknowledged that readers of these reports are not really interested in these more esoteric issues. The comments below, therefore, are more useful internally to the T&R team to improve understanding and interpretation.

The first task is to list those aspects of travel behaviour that have been included in the model fully, those adjusted partially and those that are completely ignored in the analysis so far. It is then important to indicate what are the expected influences of these approximations and omissions; which ones reflect an underestimation of traffic and revenue, which are probably neutral and those that probably tend to be on the optimistic side, if any. The Traffic Advisor could provide a view on the likely impact of all these effects, potential upsides and downsides.

Internally, we could consider the aspects of travel behaviour that are not fully captured in the model as this is predicated on the *homo economicus* assumption. This post modelling analysis and comments may influence the traffic and revenue projections or provide themes for marketing strategies. Of course, the interpretations are project specific so we can only provide some examples:

a. The "experiencing self" and the "remembering self". Salient elements of the journey, and in particular the last one, are most important. Good wayfinding at the exits of stations, ease of payment, good and uncongested access and exits at urban toll roads; pleasant and friendly staff interacting with clients are particularly valued. There may be scope for improving design at these key points during the bidding process or negotiations.

b. We overvalue what we "own". Developing a sense of ownership of the project is usually an objective that provides good returns. This would have been initiated by the Procuring Authority but it is the SPV's responsibility to achieve it in practice, particularly in the face of disruptions during construction. Full information on what is planned, why and when will it happen, is valued by residents. Later own, it is

Finalising Demand and Revenue Forecasts

sometimes possible to use the sending of bills or statements to establish a regular contact with clients to keep them informed and encourage a sense of privileged membership.

c. Loss aversion. This is another version of the above. Planting 3 trees for each one removed will not go far; involve the community on the choice of location for these trees. Demonstration of how much fuel, and money, is saved may help to neutralise aversion to pay; so would residents or frequent user discounts. Commercial traffic would be sensitive to useful information on costs.

d. We care more about changes from the status quo than absolute values. If this is a brownfield tolled road that was previously free you may expect a longer ramp up as a result of initial resistance to pay; suspect a policy bias if SP data was collected on WTP. Bring examples from other areas or countries where toll roads have been successfully implemented in the marketing strategy; make registering for tags particularly easy and painless.

e. We may not react to small changes and we may only react to larger ones after some time. Prefer more frequent and smaller increases in tolls/fares with inflation. Monitoring travel times on HOT lanes and GP lanes and making this information available may help react to slow increases in congestion.

f. System 1 and System 2 thinking. A new LRT or a new toll road will create an opportunity for System 2 thinking that should not be wasted. This is particularly important just before opening and during the first few months of operation. Free use of the new facility for a couple of weeks will help discover the advantages it offers; however, charging information should be provided from the first day to reduce loss aversion effects later on. Communicating advantages like travel time savings and, in particular reliability improvements, will help in delivering more rational decision making on passengers and commercial managers alike.

20.6 Disclaimers and reliance letters

Given the current litigation climate there tends to be greater scrutiny on reliance letters, disclaimers and, to a lesser extent, success fees.

A Reliance Letter establishes who can use the Traffic and Revenue Report and any qualifiers to its value. It should be negotiated before any contract with the T&R Advisor is signed. In fact it should signed be before the budget is agreed, as there are important implications in respect of who can rely on the T&R study. Clients will normally like a wider reliance and consultants will prefer to restrict it, partly to reduce the opportunities for litigation against them and partly because the more people rely on the work the more additional explanations will need to be provided.

Disclaimers complement reliance letters. In the past these were fairly general, and some would say, generous: we have acted in good faith, used appropriate techniques, collected good data but we cannot guarantee results: you have to make your own mind up.

Today they are more restricted, something along the lines of:
"Professional practices and procedures have been used in the development of these analyses and findings. The projections of traffic and revenue contained within this document represent the Traffic and Revenue Advisor's estimates. While they are not precise forecasts, they do represent, in our view, a reasonable expectation for the future, based on the most credible information available as of the date of this report.

However, the estimates contained within this document rely on numerous assumptions and judgments and are influenced by external circumstances that can change quickly and can affect revenue.

There may sometimes be differences between forecast and actual results caused by events and circumstances beyond the control of the forecasters and not foreseen at the time the projections were produced. These differences could be material.

In addition, it has been necessary to base much of this analysis on data collected by third parties. This has been independently checked whenever possible. However, the Traffic and Revenue Advisor does not guarantee the accuracy of this third party data."

The Makings of a Good Forecast

"Why are human beings so stupid?" asked the disciple. "Because", said the Master, "people have learnt to read printed books and have forgotten the art of reading unprinted ones". **Anthony de Mello**

21. THE MAKINGS OF A GOOD FORECAST

This is a very personal section on my own ideas on how to deliver better traffic and revenue projections. They reflect my own experience and expectations so should be taken with a "pinch of salt". It is directed to the Traffic and Revenue professional, both the younger analyst and the more senior T&R Advisor responsible for the final figures.

One of the tenets of the approach in this book is that the analyst cannot hide behind the technical superiority of the model. Assumptions must be transparent, limitations recognised, outputs interpreted and a coherent narrative demonstrating a deeper understanding of demand has to be provided to support any traffic and revenue projections.

This is a tall order and no young professional would be able to accomplish this without experience. I have helped to recruit a large number of them and observed, in some lucky case, their development into fully-fledged T&R Advisors. So, what are the main characteristics of promising T&R professionals?

21.1 Desirable traits in the young analyst

A good level of **technical skills** is, of course, essential. No one should use a technically flawed model. There is enough good practice to avoid models that do not converge or that use inconsistent costs in different sub-models. This technical understanding can be acquired, in principle, at a University or a specialist course. However, it must be complemented by experience in dealing with the practical implementation of models with noisy data and using the best features of commercial software. The experience should extend to being exposed to the process of developing the Business Case for Procuring Authorities and/or preparing T&R projections for a team tendering for a concession and reaching financial close.

Curiosity is an essential element to develop a deeper understanding of demand and revenue drivers. This curiosity should be broad based, not restricted to the analytical side of the business. The young professional needs an inquisitive mind, to learn from his own experience. We make forecasts all the time: when we choose a University course, a partner for life or a simple place to visit during the weekend. Introspection will help in identifying flaws in our own decision making, in particular about travel related choices: new car, preferring a bicycle, choosing your place to live depending on how good the public transport services are.

A **wide range of interests** accompanies this curiosity. This assist in developing a deeper understanding of the limitations of modelling and how to complement it with judgement and the development of a story explaining the drivers of any project. Personally, I find reading The Economist particularly helpful because of its wide range of topics; it also facilitates understanding what the other stakeholders contribute and worry about in any tender.

Listening skills should come near the top, as without them there is little point in curiosity and wide range of interest. This skill should be developed as is particularly valuable when visiting a new site, perhaps in a new country that does things differently. Good listening requires avoiding prejudice at all costs. This may be difficult as we all have expectations and ideas about what is right and progressive. However, allowing time to learn the logic behind behaviour and plans helps to develop the necessary understanding.

A **questioning mind**. It is far too easy to become enamoured of the difficult and demanding model one has developed in sleepless nights and tough discussions. The good analyst is the first to question her own results before disclosing them to anybody. The professional that when looking at the results can immediately say "this cannot be right" is on her way to success. The first few results are always wrong. They are valuable to eliminate sources of error, not to be shown to other stakeholders. It may take very many failed runs to reach an acceptable model whose results can be shared.

Communication skills. A set of numbers is a poor outcome from a modelling effort. Interpretation and communication of the results in a manner that is understood by the listeners and stakeholders is paramount. If you can write as the Economist you are 90% there; have a look at their Style Guide[68]. Good presentations are essential and there will be many of them in any tender.

Determination and staying power; it is too easy to give up on a rigorous approach to model development, calibration and validation, especially under pressure from other professionals in the bidding team. A sometimes unpopular **ethical** stance is required to avoid compromising the whole exercise; in the end, the main capital of the T&R advisor is her experience and reputation.

---

[68] The Economist (2012) Style Guide. Also on
http://www.economist.com/styleguide/introduction

The Makings of a Good Forecast

Finally, the T&R advisor must be skilful at **prioritising** issues and adapting the methodology to the specific project and context in hand.

Modellers tend to have a poor reputation sticking to timescales. One must develop a realistic view of how long it takes to deliver reasonable results. It is often twice as long as the original estimate of an inexperienced analyst. Few things are more damaging to a reputation tan not delivering good results on time.

21.2 The T&R Advisor

The more senior T&R Advisor will need the characteristics above but will have added experience and judgment. She well be under pressure to deliver revenue figures and must have developed skills to cope with these. Some decision makers seek certainty when this is not possible. In the past, travel demand modellers have fallen into the trap of providing false certainty, pretending to know and predict things with an accuracy that cannot be delivered.

Realism is essential. Developing and using a good model to support T&R projections usually requires more time than originally assumed. Promising early results may not help anybody in the consortium and reduces the reputation of the analytical team. If the time made available to develop the model is too short, one should have that noted and adopt an approach that sits comfortably within those parameters, even if it is likely that timescales will stretch later on.

A cool head. During the preparation of a tender there will be numerous pressures including a couple of apparent crisis. The advisor is likely to develop an attachment to the project and a desire for success given the amount of resources and energy devoted to it. Sometimes she will receive aggressive criticism, sometimes adulation and encouragement. Keeping a cool head is difficult but necessary.

This cool head should help avoiding optimism bias. The involvement of a peer reviewer, especially an experienced one, is certainly a sobering influence. Ultimately, there is nothing wrong with optimism provided one is aware and transparent about its influence on any figures used to make decisions. For me, the question in my mind is: "How much of my pension fund I am willing to risk on this project and figures". It is a hypothetical question, of course; and you will be ill advised to put a large proportion of your pension fund on any single pot. But in essence, your figures will be used, at least in part, to answer that question for other people's pension funds. Infrastructure projects are quite attractive as they have long revenue streams with generally low O&M costs.

The Advisor should also have, for the same reason, high ethical standards. This is not just for the large critical questions: are these figures believable? It requires continuous honesty in acknowledging doubtful results, likely overruns and any judgemental parameters.

21.3 The process

There is no recognised best practice on how to develop Traffic and Revenue Projections. Perhaps this is not even possible given the fluid state of data collection and modelling analytics. It would be desirable however, to develop non-prescriptive guidelines that allow flexibility and rigour at the same time. It is possible to model toll road route choice in a number of ways and that none is actually the single "best practice". What one analyst can achieve with one approach can be as good as what another will deliver with a different one.

There is also a good case for developing benchmarking databases for different elements of the analytical processes: WTP, Generalised Cost parameters, Annualisation and Ramp-up factors.

The provision of a well-documented Reference Study and Model by the Procuring Authority should go a long way to reduce bidding costs, improve the reliability of forecasts and avoid costly failures later on.

I believe the involvement of the T&R specialist early in the project is important. There are useful inputs she can provide to the Risk Register and the understanding gained in the process will help focus the modelling effort.

Success fees should be avoided at all times for T&R work. They tend to distort judgement and create unwelcomed pressures.

The financial team will be eager to get the first impressions of the "top line" of their models: revenue projections. This first set is likely to be produced with a much simpler model than later figures. They may be based on judgement applied to the Reference Model results, or on a simpler spreadsheet model developed specifically for this purpose and to contrast, later on, with results from a more elaborate network model.

Understanding the local economy should be high in the list of priorities.

The T&R specialist must remember, above all, that the success of her work is not judged by financial close alone, despite its obvious value. The traffic and revenue projections must have served to support good decisions that result in a successful project for many years after opening date.

The Makings of a Good Forecast

21.4 Coda

a. Transport concessions and the involvement of the private sector will continue to play a central role in delivering better mobility.

b. The character of these concessions will evolve over time to cope with a changing world, improved understanding of risk and new technologies for movement and data collection.

c. The Traffic and Revenue Analyst will play a key role in delivering successful projects; this is an attractive area for professional development as good work is more clearly valued and respected than is often the case in planning.

d. However, forecasting is a risky undertaking in any profession; this must be recognised at all times and we must on no account oversell the accuracy of our projections.

e. Risk and uncertainty are unavoidable and forecasts must be delivered in that context and be explicitly nuanced.

f. Experience and good analytical skills are necessary to deliver and interpret sensible results.

g. Sound modelling techniques and communication skills should be deployed to convey this understanding of risk and support better decision making.

h. Ethical integrity is essential to protect discernment and reputation when the adrenaline of a tender may cloud judgement.

REFERENCES

Akçelik, R. (1991). Travel time functions for transport planning purposes: Davidson's function, its time-dependent form and an alternative travel time function. *Australian Road Research* **21**, 49–59

Ariely, D. (2009) "Predictably Irrational". Harper Collins, London

Bain, R. (2009) "Toll Road Traffic & Revenue Forecasts: an interpreter's guide". ISBN 978-0-9561527-1-8

Bain, R. and Plantagie, J. (2003) "Fair's Fair? Why tram projects are on a bumpy road". SStandard and Poor's Report July 2003.

Bain, R., Polakovic, L. (2005) "Traffic Forecasting Risk Study Update 2005: Through Ramp-up and Beyond". Standard & Poor's Report, August 2005.

Balcombe, R; Mackett, R; Paulley, N; Preston, J; Shires, J; Titheridge, H; Wardman, M; White, P.(2004) The demand for public transport: a practical guide. Transportation Research Laboratory Report TRL593. Transportation Research Laboratory: London, UK.

Barrios, S. Pycroft, J and Saveyn, B. (2013) The marginal cost of public funds in the EU: the case of labour versus green taxes. European Union Taxation Papers. Working Paper N.35.

Bates, J., Polak, J., Jones P. and Cook, A. (2001) The valuation of reliability for personal travel. Transportation Research Part E 37, pp 191-222

Bates, J., Gunn, H.F. and Roberts, M. (1978) A model of household car ownership. Traffic Engineering and Control **19**, 486–491, 562–566.

Boyce, D. and Xie, J. (2013) Assigning user class link flows uniquely. Transportation Research Part A 53 (2013), 22-35.

Carrion, C. and Levinson, D. (2012) Value of travel time reliability: A review of current evidence. Transportation Research Part A 46 (2012) 720–741.

Cherrett, T. and McDonald, M. (2002) Traffic Composition during the Morning Peak Period. European Journal of Transport and Infrastructure Research **2**, no. 1, pp. 41 – 55

Concas, S. and Kolpakov, A. (2009) Synthesis of Research on Value of Time and Value of Reliability. Report BD 549-37. Center for Urban Transportation Research. University of South Florida.

Douglas, Neil (2003) Patronage Ramp-Up Factors for New Rail Services. Douglas Economics unpublished report.
http://www.douglaseconomics.co.nz/reports.htm

Del Mistro, R. and Behrens, R. (2008) How variable is variability in traffic? How can TDM succeed? Proceedings of the 27th South African Transport Conference (SATC 2008) 7-11 July 2008 Pretoria.

Dutzik, T. and Baxandal, P. (2013) "A New Direction. Our Changing Relationship with Driving and the Implications for America's Future". U.S. PIRG Education Fund and Frontier Group.

Eisenhardt, K. (1989). "Agency theory: An assessment and review". Academy of Management Review 14 (1): 57–74.

Fagnant, D. and Kockelman, K. (2013) Preparing a Nation for Autonomous Vehicles: Opportunities, Barriers and Policy Recommendations for Capitalizing on Selfdriven Vehicles. Transportation Research Part A, forthcoming.

Felipe Ochoa Asociados (2010) Estudio de Demanda para la nueva infraestructura denominada Atizapán – Atlacomulco. Report to Secretaria de Comunicaciones y Transportes de Mexico.

Flyvbjerg, B., Skamris-Holm, M.K. and Buhl, S.L. (2005) "How (in)accurate are demand forecasts in public works projects? "Journal of the American Planning Association **71**, 131-146.

Flyvbjerg, B., M. Skarmis-Holm and S. Buhl (2006) "Inaccuracy in Traffic Forecasts". Transport Reviews, Vol. 26, No. 1, 1–24, January 2006

Gilbert, Daniel (2007) Stumbling on happiness. Harper Perennial. London.

Goodwin, Phil B., (1996) "Empirical Evidence on Induced Traffic," *Transportation*, 23, 1, pp. 35-54.

Hartgen, D. (2013) "Hubris or humility? Accuracy issues for the next 50 years of travel demand forecasting. Transportation 10.1007/s11116-013-9497-y.

Hensher, D.A. and Rose, J. (2009) Toll product preference and implications for alternative payment options and going cashless, Transportation, 36 (2), 131- 145.

References

Kahneman, D. (2013) "Thinking Fast and Slow". Farrar, Straus and Giroux. New York.

Knight, F.H. (1921) "Risk, uncertainty and profit". In Hart, Schaffner, and Marx Prize Essays, no. 31. Boston and New York: Houghton Mifflin.

Li, Z., Hensher, D. and Rose, J. (2010) "Willingness to pay for travel time reliability in passenger transport: A review and some new empirical evidence". Transportation Research Part E 46 pp 384–403.

Litman, T. (2009) Transportation Elasticities How Prices and Other Factors Affect Travel Behavior. Victoria Transport Policy Institute.

Litman, T. (2013) Autonomous Vehicle Implementation Predictions: Implications for Transport Planning. Victoria Transport Policy Institute.

Mayer, J., Khairy, K. and Howard, J. (2010) "Drawing and elephant with four complex parameters". American Journal of Physics Vol 78 (6) pp 648-649.

McFadden, D. (2013) "The New Science of Pleasure". National Bureau of Economic Research Working Paper No. 18687

Makridakis, S., Wheelwright, S. and Hyndman, R. (1998) Forecasting Methods and Applications, Third Edition. John Wiley & Sons.

McNees, S. (1990) "The role of judgment in macroeconomic forecasting accuracy" International Journal of Forecasting, Vol 6, 3 pp 287-299.

Ortúzar, J. de D. and L. Willumsen (2011) "Modelling Transport". Fourth Edition. John Wiley & Sons, Chichester, UK.

Pigou, A C (1920): *Wealth and Welfare*, London, Macmillan.

Rayer, S. and Smith, S. (2008) An Evaluation of Subcounty Population Forecasts in Florida. Paper presented at the annual meeting of the Southern Demographic Association, October 2008. Bureau of Economic and Business Research. University of Florida

Silver, N. (2012) :"The Signal and the Noise". Penguin-Allen Lane, London

Secretaría de Comunicaciones y Transportes, Mexico (2006) "Modelación de demanda para carreteras de cuota". Access at: http://uac.sct.gob.mx/index.php?id=526.

Smeed Report (1964): *Road pricing: The Economic and Technical Possibilities*. UK Ministry of Transport, HMSO, London.

Taleb, Nissim (2007) "The Black Swan". Random House, New York.

Tientrakool, P., Ho, Y., and. Maxemchuk, N. (2011) Highway Capacity Benefits from Using Vehicle-to-Vehicle Communication and Sensors for Collision Avoidance. In Proceedings of Vehicular Technology Conference (VTC Fall), IEEE

UK Department of Transport (2007) Forecasting Travel Time Variability in Urban Areas Deliverable D1: Data Analysis and Model Development. UK Department of Transport

UK Department for Transport (2008) "Design Manual for Roads and Bridges", Volume 6, Section 3 Highway Features.

US Federal Highway Administration. "Quality Control Procedures for Archived Operations Traffic Data: Synthesis of Practice and Recommendations".

US Federal Highway Administration (2005). " Highway Economic Requirements System-State Version" U.S. Department of Transportation Federal Highway Administration.

Walters, A A (1961) *The Theory and Measurement of Private and Social Cost of Highway. Congestion.* Econometrica 29(4), pp 676-697.

Wardman, M. (2001) Inter-temporal variations in the value of time. *ITS Working Paper 566*, Institute for Transport Studies, University of Leeds.

Wardman, M. Chintakayala, P. de Jong, G. and Ferrer, D. (2013) European-wide Meta-Analysis of Values of Travel time. Final Report to the European Investment Bank. University of Leeds. Institute for Transport Studies.

Welde, M. (2011) "Demand and operating cost forecasting accuracy for toll road projects". Transport Policy 18 pp 765–771

Washington, S., Karlaftis, M. and Mannering, F. (2011) Statistical and Econometric Methods for Transportation Data Analysis. Second Edition. Chapman and Hall/CRC Press

Willumsen, L.G. (1978) "O-D matrix from network data: a comparison of alternative methods for their estimation". Proc. of PTRC 6th Summer Annual Meeting, Vol P168, pp 294-304, Warwick. PTRC Education and Research Services, London

Willumsen, L.G. and Russell, C. (1998) "Reducing Revenue Risk". Proc. PTRC 25th European Transport Conference, PTRC Education and Research Services, London.

www.ingramcontent.com/pod-product-compliance
Lightning Source LLC
Chambersburg PA
CBHW042056290426

44111CB00005B/71